STILL ANGRY

By; The Last Angry Man

JACK WALTERS

Order this book online at www.trafford.com
or email orders@trafford.com

Most Trafford titles are also available at major online book retailers.

Printed in Victoria, BC, Canada.

ISBN: 978-1-4269-3246-5 (soft)
ISBN: 978-1-4269-3247-2 (ebook)

*Our mission is to efficiently provide the world's finest, most comprehensive book publishing
service, enabling every author to experience success. To find out how to publish your book, your
way, and have it available worldwide, visit us online at www.trafford.com*

Trafford rev. 5/13/2010

 www.trafford.com

North America & international
toll-free: 1 888 232 4444 (USA & Canada)
phone: 250 383 6864 ♦ fax: 812 355 4082

About the Author

I graduated from the University of Buffalo in 1954. I joined The Firestone Tire & Rubber Co. and worked for Firestone for the next 28 years. I was promoted to the position of Plant Manager for three ever larger plants ending my career at the Des Moines, Iowa plant in 1982.

A few months later, I was invited to be a member of newly elected Governor Terry Branstad's staff as the Director of General Services. I served in that position for 8 years. When my wife died suddenly in Feb., 1991, I resigned and have been retired since that time. Two projects stand out as my favorites. The first was the design and construction of a new $25 million dollar Historical and Library Building. The second was starting and completing 35% of the exterior restoration of the State Capitol Building.

I retired to Tucson 17 years ago. I am an outdoor enthusiast. I belong to the Southern Arizona Hiking Club and just before my 70th birthday I completed the 315 peaks award which at that time was the highest award given. These peaks were within 75 miles of Tucson. Later a new club goal was established at 400 peaks. The distance from Tucson was increased to 100 miles. This added several new mountain ranges. I accomplished this goal just before my 80th birthday in April 2008. I continue to hike but due to a blood clot that developed in my right calf in November 2009, my hiking has been limited. It is getting better and I should be back in another couple of months. In the interim I walk the dogs or walk Sabino Canyon. I also quit golfing but as of February 2010 I have started back. I'm hoping the layoff will improve my game which has never been anything to brag about.

I started writing in March, 2003 when I purchased my first computer.

My first book, "The Life and Times of Jack B. Walters" was essentially my recollection of important events in my lifetime.

After finishing the story portion, I decided to add letters I had written during those years, to explain as best I could what I believed, so that the reader would know not just the events but my beliefs as well.

While I was concentrating on my biography I was also composing articles of general interest relative to our country. Some were published as editorials in the Arizona Daily Star. I decided to collect them and put them in my second book.

I entitled it "The Last Angry Man" because most are very negative as I railed at the lack of leadership from the major parties. These were written between 2003 and 2006. As discouraged as I was, I believed I would just stop there but I didn't? I continued to write and just now have decided to put them in what will be my third book. Its title is " Still Angry" It contains articles from 2006 to the present. It begins during the end years of President Bush's Administration. The ending is the start of President Obama's second year in office. My son Andy compiled my writing for publishing, and his daughter Jada created the cover art and graphics.

Read, analyze, discuss and do something for your country.

Preface

I just don't know how to stop writing. I thought after publishing "The Last Angry Man", I would turn to other things to keep me occupied. The continuing farce our leaders are committing won't allow me to quit. At this point I have no respect for anyone serving in Congress or the Administration. I am convinced that they are in the service of the mega corporations. Whatever they want they get. It doesn't matter which party is in power.

The nation in a rebuke to the Bush Administration voted overwhelmingly for Barack Obama and the Democratic candidates. I believe they felt as I did that we would see FDR type policies instantly put into place to put Americans back to work. We expected an orderly withdrawal of our troops from Iraq and Afghanistan. We expected a rapid program to provide health care for all Americans. We expected curbs to be placed on the huge corporations which recklessly brought our economy to a halt. None of this has occurred to my satisfaction in the first year of Obama's Administration. I see little hope that anything will happen. The Republicans do not care for us; their only goal is to see that Obama fails. Please explain to me why this is a good reason for allowing our country to sink into what will be anarchy if they don't start taking positive action.

The articles and letters in this booklet were all written in the hope that someone in a position to do something might read and then put these thoughts into positive action. I do not realistically think this will happen. Perhaps all it will be is part of a legacy of this generation and may be of historical significance.

At my age and physical limitation I cannot do more. I hope you may agree with some of the ideas and perhaps be in a position to put the ideas to work.

2007

2007

Articles listed by date written

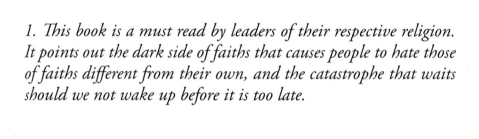

1. This book is a must read by leaders of their respective religion. It points out the dark side of faiths that causes people to hate those of faiths different from their own, and the catastrophe that waits should we not wake up before it is too late.

The End of Faith by Sam Harris

I purchased this book one week ago after learning about it from one of my thinking friends. He is concerned as I am with world affairs as they are today.

This has been on the New York Times Best Seller list since 2004. It is the boldest, most controversial book probably ever written on the subject of religion. Most of you, who this note will be sent to, should you read it, will be highly offended by its contents. He traces the history of the various religions while emphasizing on Christianity, Islam and the Jewish religion. It is not a pretty picture. The evil deeds, done over the centuries, are appalling to me.

In my own book several of my articles touched on this but not to the researched detail done by Mr. Harris. In a nutshell he concludes that if we cannot as a civilization back off from our superiority in our beliefs as compared to other faiths or non-faiths, then we are going to witness the destruction of life on an unimaginable scale in the not to distant future.

Of particular concern of course are the radical Muslims who carry out their evil deeds on a daily basis. They even torture and kill other Muslims who are of a different sect. It is total madness to kill men, women and children who live in the same country, who look and dress alike and speak the same language. How can they let centuries old doctrine determine who should live or die.

Once they obtain the weapons they seek they will bring their hatred to our shores and all other countries of the world. This will happen unless we fight back in a coordinated fashion and defeat them before they can destroy us. If it were possible to re-educate them away from the Koran by teaching general subjects needed by most people to function as producing citizens, then perhaps over time this blind hatred would diminish. I have little hope that this will occur.

Christians and Jews could do their part by accepting all human beings as equals regardless of the church or synagogue they attend. Stop using faith as a means of dividing people into the saved and damned. None of us have the absolute knowledge of whether there is life after death. Many have faith that this is true. My continuing point on this thought is that we should all strive to live the best we can because it is the best way to live not just to receive eternal life.

I highly recommend reading this amazing book. It just might start a trend towards accepting all we meet as equals instead of the feeling of superiority that does prevail in the world today.

February 15, 2007

2. Mr. Tinsley, who is black, wrote a guest article in response to Don Imus's misuse of "black" slang. Imus on his radio program had referred to a girl's basketball team as "nappy headed hoes". This of course we would all agree was totally wrong. Mr. Tinsley however inferred that black people could use the term but white people couldn't. He separated all of us into groups based on race. I strongly disagreed.

Ernest D. Tinsley Guest Opinion — 4/16/07

Mr. Tinsley has let his color overpower his avowed Christian beliefs. He advocates that persons of color may use the ugly jargon of the Rapper set as they see fit but white people say these things at their peril. This type of thinking keeps us separated into groups instead of being united as American citizens regardless of color. This is the same as Muslim governments and their citizens being outraged at cartoons in a Danish newspaper while at the same time continuing to kill others of the Muslim faith because of some ancient writings.

April 16, 2007

3. I wrote asking her to support the ban on assault weapons. I and America lost in my opinion. The NRA won as they usually do.

Representative Gabrielle Giffords
502 Cannon House Office Building
Washington, DC 20515

Dear Representative Giffords,

When the assault weapon ban was allowed to lapse I wrote the following letter and mailed to my Congress persons, the Arizona Daily Star and as many of my friends that I could reach. I stand by those comments. The tragedy at Virginia Tech might still have occurred but the numbers would surely not have been as great had he not been able to purchase those automatic weapons.

On Jay Leno's Tonight Show last night, he was talking with Tim Russert. Mr. Russert stated that the Democratic Party did not have the will to take on the gun lobby. I am writing to you in the hope that you will take a leadership role and prove him wrong. Assault weapons of the type now so easy to purchase have only one purpose and that is to kill people. This is not about hunting. Take a stand now while this incident is fresh and perhaps you will prevent the next kook to come along from repeating what this young man did.

Sincerely yours,

April 18, 2007

4. An article I wrote for general distribution about the intent of our founding fathers when they wrote the Second Amendment to the Bill of Rights. It made sense to me but to few others.

THE RIGHT TO BEAR ARMS

The issue is whether or not the Second Amendment to the Bill of Rights should apply to present day assault weapons. Clearly it can be reasoned both in favor and against.

To start this discourse let's begin by re-stating the exact language of the amendment. It is," A well regulated Militia, being necessary to the security of a free State, the right of the people to keep and bear Arms, shall not be infringed."

The Bill of Rights was adopted in 1789. It was written by intelligent patriots who desired to produce a Constitution that would last a long time. We can all agree that they did a magnificent job. We are still functioning today.

Many learned scholars have interpreted this amendment over the years. This will be my attempt to understand and state my own conclusions.

At the start of the conflict with England, America did not have an Army nor did it have State National Guard units or for that matter State Troopers or even police except in the larger cities. All it had were its citizens. Most if not all families had long rifles for hunting and to defend themselves from the native Indians and wild animals. They would band together in time of trouble. These were the men called to arms to fight for our independence. I therefore conclude that the amendment was written to have arms available to fight for their country as required and secondarily provide them the right of self defense.

In the 218 years since written there has been a huge difference between then and now. Today we have huge Military establishments directed by the Pentagon as well as State National Guard units, State Patrol, County Sheriffs, police departments and of course the F.B.I. At the present time these are all voluntary services. In time of war the government might be compelled to initiate a draft for personnel but whether volunteer or drafted the people called are not asked to bring their hunting rifles with them. It is possible therefore to conclude that arms possessed by the people are not required for the defense of the nation. They could of course be used by those citizens who desire to overthrow the government. I cannot believe that was the intention of the drafters of this amendment. A secondary use might be for citizens to fight against a foreign invader like the partisans did in Europe during the Second World War. This latter then would support the need to keep and bear arms.

As a nation more of our citizens own weapons than any other "civilized" country. We see every day on TV the carnage being inflicted on people in what

I will refer to as un-civilized countries. These are the ones who parade around with their AK 47's and wearing face masks.

One of the differences is that until recent times the weapons owned in America were hunting rifles, shotguns and pistols all of which were limited in fire power. I am not sure when assault weapons became available for purchase but I do know that an assault weapons law was in effect during the Clinton administration and allowed to lapse in 2004 during the administration of George Bush.

It is even possible today to purchase high powered sniper rifles capable of shooting down domestic aircraft. All of these new weapons are designed to kill people, lots of people, such as we have just witnessed at Virginia Tech. This will not be the last, in fact I believe other copy cat types will be inspired by this and try to set higher goals of mayhem. The members of the NRA and all everyday citizens should be assured gun ownership but not these new killer weapons. Surely we can agree on this, can't we?

April 19, 2007

5. Bill Bradley wrote an outstanding book about what was needed to restore our nation to its former greatness. It was encouraging as he held out hope his dream could become reality. I wish I could be as positive but I cannot. Things in Washington continue to deteriorate with the two parties more interested in power than in solving America's problems.

The New American Story
By Bill Bradley

This is a New York Times best seller book written by a former Senator and Presidential candidate. It is extremely well done in my opinion probably because many of the issues discussed were enumerated in my own book, "The Last Angry Man". The difference is that he was involved while I was a distant observer and he has name recognition while I am a no body as far as the reading public is concerned. I can't even get the Arizona Star to review it. They were given two copies in early February and to date it has not been reviewed.

I highly recommend reading by those who still care and believe that we can once again be a great country. He doesn't pull any punches. He and I want our country to pull back from using our military as the first attempt to resolve the earth's problems. He believes that universal health care for our citizens is absolutely necessary and doable. He wants us to be energy independent. He wants decisions made for the good of all not just the current party in power regardless of which party. He, as a Democrat, wants the party to return to being the party of the people not big business.

You will be interested in the two chapters entitled," Why Republicans Can't" and "Why Democrats Don't". They contain a history of both parties from the beginning and the forces that shape their decisions.

I have loaned out my copy. I am sure it is available at your public library.

April 26, 2007

6. President Bush announced his decision to install interceptor missiles and radar sites in the Czech Republic and Poland. I see this as the Russian leadership does that it poses a threat to them. If we could not accept Russian missiles in Cuba, under what rational should they? As far as their intended use against Iran, again in my opinion they will be useless, as our enemies are Islamic terrorists not countries. Who would we fire on?

Another useless project from the current leadership in America

We learn this week that the United States is deploying interceptor missiles and radar systems in the Czech Republic and Poland. We are told this is necessary because of threats of nuclear missiles from Iran and North Korea. Russia reacted negatively as they perceive this as a threat to their own country and may suspend the arms control treaty.

As we continue expanding our world wide military bases in these former satellite countries next to Russia I believe that eventually there will be serious backlash and that these countries will suffer severe consequences such as occurred this past winter with the cutoff of natural gas. Russia is certainly capable of retaliating in other ways as well including the use of their military.

We already possess enormous nuclear weapons which would be unleashed against any nation foolish enough to use them against us. The most serious threat is from the Islamic extremists. Once they obtain these weapons they will use them against us. When they do there will not be a nation for us to hit back.

What we should have learned by now in Iraq and Afghanistan is that our conflict is not against a country but rather against radical Islamists. All the missile and radar sites in the world will not deter them. We, together with the rest of the nations who are threatened should devote our collective resources to wipe out these mad men. We must strike them wherever they are in the world without mercy or the civilized world as we know it will cease to exist. In the meantime we continue to bleed our country financially, building systems here and there that would have been helpful in the past but no longer.

April 27, 2007

7. The Senate under the leadership of our own John McCain tries to ram an illegal immigrant bill down our thoughts before we know what is happening. This time many people like me let them know our disagreement. It failed but don't hold your breath, the present administration has the same intention and will push a bill through rapidly as soon as the health care issue is resolved.

A Call to Action

The U.S. Senate is trying to force a vote quickly on their secret immigration bill, (reported at 1,000 pages) which up to now has not been seen, much less understood, by anyone including the Senators themselves. It is strongly endorsed by the President, most Democratic and some Republican Senators. It is reported that there are enough vote's already to pass regardless of the content. They are eager to push thru before any serious discussion can take place. They know that those of us who care will be outraged. They want to silence us before we have the chance to show our disagreement.

They present this as an either or situation. We have heard Senator McCain many times asking the question of what to do with over 12 million illegal immigrants already in this country. His answer is to give one and all a path to citizenship. He challenges us to find an alternative. Here is mine. Accept their presence and give them temporary work visas which need to be reviewed on a yearly basis. As long as they remain gainfully employed allow a one year extension. If they are on welfare send them packing to the country they came from. Only grant citizenship to those who follow our immigration laws and have applied and followed all the rules. To do otherwise is to state that we are no longer a nation of laws. If this law is ignored, how about ignoring all other laws. Can I ignore traffic signals if I don't wish to wait for a light to change?

The bill grants in-state tuition for children of illegal immigrants but not to the children of citizens who might wish to send their children to college in another state. This is particularly repugnant to me and makes no sense whatsoever.

It allows them credit for wages paid using forged Social Security documents and puts them in the system while citizens are required to pay for a number of years before becoming eligible. Where is the logic for this?

As far as I can tell it does nothing to punish employers for hiring them in the first place some of whom place orders for "coyotes" to smuggle them into the country for jobs in their factories.

Of course, they just don't care about American workers who see their earnings decrease year by year as the illegal worker will work for lesser wages. Just as with NAFTA, CASPA and all of our other trade agreements the American workers welfare continues to be ignored.

I am sending this out prematurely. As more information comes to light I hope, you as a knowledgeable citizen, will review and get involved. I am sending this to Senator's Kyl and McCain and also Representative Gabrielle Giffords. It will not influence the Senators but might my representative in the House. Please do likewise.

May 21, 2007

8. Those of you who know me well will understand why Mr. Iacocca's book was so meaningful to me. I have always admired him as a strong leader who could solve complex problems. His assessment is right on target. Our so called leaders are not leaders at all but just trained seals mouthing platitudes they are instructed to say.

Where Have All The Leaders Gone?
Lee Iacocca

As soon as I learned about this new book I sent out an e-mail which contained copy from his first chapter entitled, "Had Enough"? After reading it myself I was hooked and the next day went out to purchase a copy. I still really believe that my book," The Last Angry Man", covers more topics and if anything is more forceful. As I said when I sent the e-mail, the difference is that millions will read his book while mine has only reached a little over 150 and then only because I gave away all but a handful.

Every time a person of influence like this puts out a new book another nail is driven into the black heart of the current administration. I cheered as I turned each page. He exposes the sinister practices that drive their ideologies be it the economy or the Middle East.

Whenever I take the time to promote a book I take pains not to repeat what is written, preferring that you buy one for yourself and add the content to your brain cells. This time I am making an exemption on one part that confirmed for me how distorted our election process has become. It starts on page 239 ("In 1991, Pennsylvania Senator John Heinz died in a plane crash. My friend John Murtha came to me with a proposition: Robert Casey, the Democratic governor of Pennsylvania, wanted to appoint me to complete Heinz's term, and then I'd have run on my own in the fall. Murtha would see that I got some juicy committee assignments, and he thought it would be a stepping stone to the presidency for me.

They sent in a brash young man named James Carville to explain things to me. Carville was blunt and fast talking. Didn't even stop to ask me what I thought about the issues. He shoved some papers at me. "Here is your position on abortion," he said. "Here is your position on jobs". "Here is your position on…"

Finally, I interrupted. "Wait just a minute," I said. "Don't I get to…?"

"No, no," he dismissed me; "we've already done all the studies and focus groups."

"So, you want me in office, but you'll tell me what to believe?" I asked.

Carville shrugged, and started to continue his lecture. At which point I told him where he could shove it. That was my short- lived flirtation with the U.S. Senate.)

Take this experience of Mr. Iacocca and multiply it thousands of times by aspiring candidates for office without regard to party. These studies and focus groups identify what the prospective voter wants to hear and then they are told what to say on the stump. Is it any wonder things are so out of kilter today and why the leaders Mr. Iacocca is looking for are continually muffled and turned into robots?

If you don't want to buy it go to your local library. Even those who still believe President Bush is doing a great job need to get the perspective this giant of industry has to share.

May 2, 2007

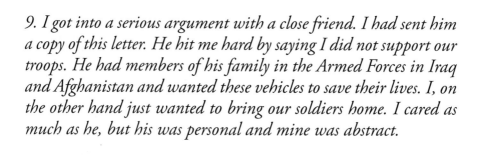

9. I got into a serious argument with a close friend. I had sent him a copy of this letter. He hit me hard by saying I did not support our troops. He had members of his family in the Armed Forces in Iraq and Afghanistan and wanted these vehicles to save their lives. I, on the other hand just wanted to bring our soldiers home. I cared as much as he, but his was personal and mine was abstract.

Radical Suggestion

The headline article in USA Today for May 10, 2007 told about the new transport vehicle designed to protect our troops in Iraq. It has a vee shaped bottom which deflects a planted explosive device outwards keeping the soldiers safe. It costs in excess of $1,000,000 each. The Army and the Marine Corps have ordered $8,000,000,000 worth with the promise of buying many more. I can only assume that funding for this has been included in the appropriation bill being debated in Congress as they consider a three months appropriation while the President continues to rant about their micro managing his private war.

I am writing this as I am sure that it will not occur to the news media types who tell us what we should think on a daily basis. How about this for an alternate suggestion to keep our troops safe, as a first step place them in their fortified bases and then start rotating them home to the good old U.S.A. Find something else to spend $ 8 billion on.

May 10, 2007

10. I show my disillusion with Congress including members of the Democratic Party for approving Billions to continue the wars in Iraq and Afghanistan.

War Funding for Iraq and Afghanistan

Last week the House of Representatives voted 397 for and 27 against on a $645.6 Billion military budget which included $141.8 Billion for 12 months war in Iraq and Afghanistan. In addition it includes $4.1 Billion for developing blast-resistant combat vehicles.

We have been listening to the speeches from the Democrats on stopping the war for weeks now. In the end, as we all knew they would, they caved in and gave the President all he asked for and probably more.

Another fortune is to be squandered in this useless conflict that continues to produce American casualties every day as well as countless Iraqi citizens.

Those of us who voted last November for Democrats with the hope they would stop this bloodletting have been let down. It seems that no politician other than Dennis Kucinich and 26 others have the guts to stand up to Bush. None of them want to be considered weak on defense. What is left for us to do? Must we take to the streets?

May 21, 2007

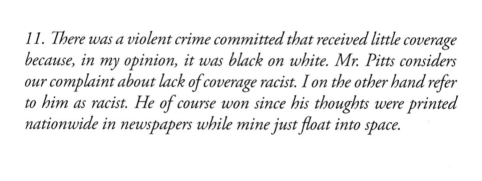

11. There was a violent crime committed that received little coverage because, in my opinion, it was black on white. Mr. Pitts considers our complaint about lack of coverage racist. I on the other hand refer to him as racist. He of course won since his thoughts were printed nationwide in newspapers while mine just float into space.

Leonard J. Pitts Jr. article entitled "Lunatic fringe focuses on "oppressed" white people" dated June 4, 2007

He misses the entire point of the issue. I have received the same e-mail he did and I took the trouble to confirm that it was true. One of the most brutal crimes in our history whether the victims were white or black.

The fact of the matter is that the news media in general did not report it. In contrast the Duke alleged rape and Don Imus's blunder with language was reported hour after hour on all TV Networks and radio for weeks and months. Jackson and Sharpton had a field day accusing rich white boys of wanting a black girl and depicting Imus as a vulgar aging white man. We all know that the Rap community use the same words over and over, but that is OK because they are black. Also the black youth of America are exhorted to never snitch on a brother and further if placed on a jury to never convict a brother.

If Mr. Pitts thinks this is OK he is dead wrong. All he and the others are doing is increasing the divide between Americans of different pigmentation.

June 5, 2007

12. *I wrote this complimentary letter mainly because of reading his books which I felt included sensible ideas for our country.*

Al Gore
c/o (Imprint) Publicity
375 Hudson Street
New York, N.Y. 10014

Dear Mr. Gore,

I have purchased your books, "An Inconvenient Truth" and "The Assault on Reason". They are both powerful writings that will reach millions of readers and hopefully will have the positive results you hope for.

I have also written a powerful book entitled, "The Last Angry Man" which includes letters and articles written by me over the past four years with my own admonition of the danger to our democratic system. I truly believe that what I have written should be read by as many people as possible. The difference between you and me is that you are invited to book signings and are interviewed on TV and the print media while as a non entity I have given away 150 copies and have sold a few at Borders and Amazon but have neither the recognition nor resources to promote and so my message that I felt was so important is not being read.

That is my problem not yours. I have written to the above address as consulted by Penguin as the way to reach you. My purpose is to ask if I could send you a free copy in the hope that it might be of benefit to you.

Finally, there are no candidates running for office worthy of my vote. At the right time I as well as many others hope you will sacrifice and get in the race for President. We need you to lead us back to sanity.

Sincerely yours,

June 27, 2007

13. Vice President Gore compares FDR's admonition to not be afraid with President Bush's trying to make us afraid.

The Assault on Reason
Al Gore

I have just finished reading Al Gore's new book entitled, "The Assault on Reason". It is a forceful attempt by him to point out the danger to our way of life by the chipping away of the original documents that laid the foundation of our American democratic republic. It is not an easy book to read. He includes deep thinking theories about how fear and falsehoods are swaying the voting patterns of most Americans.

He compares the Bush, Cheney scare speeches with Roosevelt's admonishment that all we need to fear is fear itself. At appropriate times the danger color is put out to alert us that we are in imminent danger and therefore should place our complete faith in Mr. Bush to protect us.

He itemizes all of the drastic policies of Bush, Cheney; such as eavesdropping on our conversations over the telephone, e-mails, and books we read. Bush declares his right to hold persons without the benefit of our legal system, actively promotes torture as a national right ignoring all aspects of the Geneva Convention, deceived Americans that Saddam Hussein was responsible for Sept. 11. Fifty percent still believe this. The powerful onslaught of he and his administration that the mushroom cloud was imminent persuaded Congress and the public that he should attack Iraq before it was too late.

He points out how big money interests have taken control over the election process and how much time our elected officials spend pursuing contributions instead of debating the issues or even reading bills before voting on them. On C Span we see orators emoting without anyone there to hear or debate.

He is frustrated that Bush stands behind big oil to the detriment of our fragile earth and refuses to exert leadership on the global warming issue nor will he take any steps to break our dependence on OPEC.

As I stated at the beginning, this is not any easy book to read but if you care as I do you will take the time. My copy is available. Just let me know.

June 27, 2007

14. In this one I try to alert my readers of the growth in the numbers of highly paid mercenaries and the potential for disaster implied.

Soldiers of Fortune
An article published in a Los Angeles newspaper June 21, 2007
Written by Sandra Svoboba

The article was mailed to me by my niece who lives in California and knows of my continuing concern about serious national issues.

The reality that mercenaries are operating in Iraq and elsewhere is well known to those of us who pay attention to these things. What I did not realize is the extent it has grown in size during the Bush Administration. The numbers have swelled by 88% between 2000 and 2006 according to a Congressional Research Service report. We have been told repeatedly about the "surge", which brought in 30,000 additional combat troops which brought the total to 145,000 troops. What we weren't told was that at the same time there are about 130,000 private contractor mercenaries in Iraq. For the most part these mercenaries are outside of U.S. law. Those working for the Coalition Provisional Authority are exempted from Iraqi law. In addition since they are not military they are not subject to court-martial. Deaths and wounded are not reported. Most are no bid contracts. Surprisingly only 21,500 are Americans. The industry has grown to $100 billion in annual revenue.

There are many reasons to be concerned. Since these people are paid from $350 to $1,000 per day, I can only imagine the morale problem of our military that do most of the fighting and dying for considerably less. If I were to put my life on the line I think I would think seriously about re-enlisting with this much at stake.

What incentive does a contractor have to see peace achieved when that would end the financial rewards? The article concludes with the following thought, "We're likening corporate profits to the business of war---You build in an incentive to keep the conflict going".

Now I want to share my thoughts on this subject. I don't remember the name of the General who was sacked after stating at the beginning of the war that 300,000 troops would be needed to keep the peace. If you add 130,000 to 145,000 you get 275,000. I would guess that the General was pretty accurate in his analysis. Since the cost is six to seven times higher than our military that means to me we are paying considerably more in the administrations attempt to hide the fact that these many troops are needed. Of course we all know that this is still not enough as our progress has not been acceptable to date.

What worries me even more is that the president has control over his own private Army who it appears will do his bidding without question as long as the price is right. In the aftermath of Katrina he tried to get the Congress to give him authority to move troops into a State without the agreement of the Governor. This was not granted but could he not accomplish the same end with mercenaries. They actually were brought to Louisiana to protect private interests for wealthy customers so it is conceivable a President might take this course of action if a Governor balked.

Every day it seems that Bush and Cheney keep pushing for more and more power resisting all attempts by the Congress on oversight. I call this the imperial executive branch which disdains legislative procedures.

The purpose of this paper is to get the reader concerned and forewarned.

June 28, 2007

15. The Senate under the leadership of Senator John McCain failed in their attempt to pass an amnesty bill to grant citizenship to millions in this country illegally. The American people spoke up and stopped it.

Illegal Immigration

As happy as I was to see a majority of our U.S. Senators vote down the unbelievably bad amnesty bill, I am equally unhappy that they are now content to recess for their 4th of July vacation and wipe their hands of this serious issue.

As I listen to commentators on TV and radio they talk about how sad it will be if families are broken up with breadwinners deported. I have a better idea. As I understand it the 1986 amnesty law that was passed contained language on penalizing employers which was only briefly attempted and has been spotty at best. My idea is to concentrate on the larger employers many of whom it is well known actually put in orders for illegals. Gather evidence then take severe action including prison time and fines for the President of that company and others in the chain of command who have knowingly hired illegals. Skip for the time being the small mom and pop businesses. As soon as it appears that our government is serious others will get the message and take illegals off of their workforce. As this gathers momentum the illegals will find it harder to find jobs and many will return to their country. In this way the problem will decrease in seriousness.

We cannot continue with business as usual. The overwhelming cost to our country is not sustainable. There are many other ways to deal with this issue but the more complicated it is made the less likely anything can ever be accomplished.

June 29, 2007

16. I enthusiastically endorse this documentary and try as best I can to alert others to how we can join the rest of the civilized world in caring for all of our people. I also show where the funds can be found to accomplish this most worthy goal.

Sicko
A documentary film written, directed and produced by Michael Moore

I went to the first showing today (6/30/07) at 11:00 A.M. at El Con movie house in Tucson. I was pleased to see that the theater was nearly full. I went alone as no one else seemed interested. The audience thoroughly enjoyed the experience. There was laughter, sighs, groans and even applause. Compliments are in order.

He trashes the health care industry in the U.S. as well as shows the hypocrisy of politicians from both parties. During Hillary Clinton's attempt to create a universal health care system she was attacked as a Socialist promoter and yet today she is the second leading benefactor of campaign contributions from the health care and the pharmaceutical industry. He spares no one including Ronald Reagan, Bob Dole and both George Bush's.

He travels to Canada, England, France and Cuba. Each of these countries provides complete health care for all of their citizens with low or nearly no cost. They consider it the right of all regardless of stature in life. None of them are the same but all have the right to health care essential for their people. The question is raised how they can do it with the cost so high. He doesn't really answer this question but I will.

None of these countries bleed themselves in the attempt to shape other countries into doing their bidding. Only the United States spends over a trillion dollars every year on military and space war technology. Only the United States maintains military bases in over 7,000 places around the world including occupation forces in Germany, Japan and Korea 60 years after those conflicts ended. We don't call it occupation but that is what it is. Only the United States declares it has the right to declare war on any nation even when not threatened by that country. We are the largest producer of military hardware and believe we are helping others by giving them arms instead of real assistance. We currently are creating conflict with Russia over installing missile bases in the Czech Republic and Poland. Can you not remember our own missile crisis when Russia was installing bases in Cuba? Why should they trust us? We didn't trust them. We are developing bunker busting nuclear weapons and as I understand it from e-mails received we want to replace our aging nuclear weapons with newer ones while at the same time demanding other countries to cease and desist.

He does point out in a conversation with a British citizen what a true democracy can accomplish if the citizens are not beaten down with propaganda and depression as we are. All we have to do is insist and they will have to respond. We proved it this week when the outrageous amnesty bill went down in defeat when the Senators were bombarded with e-mails, calls and letters. I am pessimistic that this will happen for the health care issue but perhaps this movie will generate the spark necessary to get real change. There is so much at stake for these large corporations that they will fight to the death any candidate brave enough to attempt a change of this magnitude. Only an aware electorate can resist the propaganda.

The least you can do is see this movie, discuss it with family and friends and the regardless of political affiliation start your own grass roots attempt to get meaningful change. It can be done. These other nations have proved it.

June 30, 2007

17. This book is a must read for anyone interested in understanding the "war" our soldiers are forced to fight under unfavorable conditions. The restrictions placed in their way makes it nearly impossible to win without taking excessive casualties.

The Long Road Home
By Martha Raddatz

This book was suggested to me by a friend who has two son-in-laws in Iraq at this time and whose daughter is scheduled to go in November. One of the sons-in-law was wounded in the battle and has returned to Iraq. None of us who read the papers and watch TV News can have any understanding of the emotions of family whose sons and daughters are in harms way on a daily basis. He, of course is a strong advocate of the war while I remain equally as adamant that we are fighting the wrong war in the wrong place. There can be no disagreement that radical Islam is on a worldwide effort to take over civilization as we have known and enjoyed for many years. We must be actively engaged wherever they appear and wipe them out one by one. There is no reasoning with them. You convert, live as a slave or die. Those are their only options. My disagreement is in how we are fighting this enemy of civilization.

Ms. Raddatz has written an outstanding first hand account of the events that took place on April 4, 2004 in Sadr City, Iraq. By piecing together the memories of those survivors the book reads like a novel it is so complete and relentless. It all starts with what is considered a peacekeeping mission. A patrol on a routine visit to the city with "honey" wagons is attacked by hundreds if not thousands of Mahdi militia under the leadership of Moqtada al-Sadr, a Muslim Cleric opposed to Americans being in his country. The "honey" wagon patrol consisted of trucks which sucked up raw human waste from the streets. This was not an accident. It was a near total collaboration by most of the citizens. Children were actively engaged including throwing lighted torches and firing weapons.

While the patrol was quietly doing their job the people barricaded all of the major streets leading to the area where they were working. They piled refrigerators, cars, carts, dead animals and everything else they could find. The patrol trying to extricate found it impossible and made their stand in a tall building and fought awaiting rescue. The rescuers had the same problem trying to reach them driving in through the debris while being under constant attack from rooftops, windows and alleyways. The greatest numbers of casualties were the rescuers. It took three attempts before the patrol was extricated. The third and successful try consisted of seven tanks. Eight of our men died that day and over sixty were wounded.

A soldier back at base camp sitting in a stupor asked his officer why they left their tanks at Fort Hood, Texas. The reply was that we didn't want to look like an Army of Occupation and therefore left the heavy military vehicles at home.

I cannot lay blame for what happened. Up until this day resistance had been light and scattered. The emphasis was as peacekeepers with our troops doing things to improve their lives. After this occurred however I do blame those in authority as they were slow to realize the new situation and found the only way to respond was to send in the troops on foot or in open trucks where they have been sitting ducks for snipers and the ever increasing deadly roadside bombs.

My thought would be that the next time a similar happening occurred we should have sent in tanks and other heavy military vehicles with orders to shoot at any target without regard to civilian casualties. Further we would immediately call in air strikes on buildings in near proximity to the action. In today's Daily Star I read that air strikes are now at the highest level they have been up to now in support of the Army and Marines. This is good to know but why were they so reluctant to use air power before this year?

This book is a must read by all Americans who care. The courage and devotion of these men is inspiring to read. We must always show our respect and gratitude for these young men, women and their families back home.

July 15, 2007

18. *The article speaks for itself. Radicals in the name of religion threaten the peaceful co-existence of people everywhere.*

Is Religion Dangerous?
By Keith Ward

I found this book at the public library. I brought it home and read it, looking as I continuously seem to be these days, trying to make sense out of the crazy world we live in. It was interesting in that he wrote it as a devout Christian. Much of the book is devoted to his attempt to prove there is a God and there has been since the creation of the Universe. His arguments are well articulated.

As to the title of the book, his conclusion is that religion is not dangerous and that whatever evil has been committed in the name of religion was done by radicals who have used it to further their purpose.

Following the 9/11 disaster I got and read three books about Islam trying to understand how and why we were attacked. They all confirmed as does this author that it is a peaceful religion. He states that "The God of Judaism, Christianity and Islam is a being of justice, mercy and loving-kindness, who commands humans to be just, merciful and kind, and who promises those who are just, a life beyond death in unison with absolute goodness".

He mentions Sayyid Qutb of the Muslim Brotherhood who wrote in his 1965 book, Milestones on the Road. He stated, "One should accept the Shari'a without question and reject all other laws in any shape or form. This is Islam. Every society is either Muslim or jahiliyyah. Muslim societies are those that live in complete obedience to Shari's." He states that all of the societies existing in the world today are jahila and that they are all illegal. He concludes that all political systems that legislate laws- including, apparently all existing so-called Muslim societies are illegal. By contrast, in a truly Muslim society only God legislates laws. There can be no compromise or even co-existence. There is no Islam in a land where Islam is not dominant and where it's Shari's is not established. He continues that they must take the initiative in abolishing jahiliyyah. It is not just a defensive war; it is the use of force to establish properly Muslim societies everywhere in the world, so that ultimately there will remain only Muslims, enemies of Islam to be fought, and Dhimmies, those who pay tribute-money to their dominant Islamic society.

It is thus not religion that causes Islamic terrorism. It is a version of Islam that has been corrupted by the most successful anti-religious movement in the twentieth century. They are not motivated by the love of God. It is hatred of almost everyone in the world, belief in very simple political solutions to intractable social problems, belief that resorting to extreme violence is a reliable means to future freedom and peace, and an intense certainty that one's own beliefs are uniquely correct and morally pure, whereas everyone else's are irrational and corrupt. I believe his conclusions are valid. We are not in a religious war but nonetheless we are in a world wide war with radicals who want to conquer all nations and convert them to their belief system. Knowing this, the countries of the world need to unite and fight this evil wherever it surfaces without mercy. They cannot be reasoned with so they must be eliminated wherever they are found. Therefore the battle is not against Muslims, it is against those who have perverted Islam to suit their goals.

August 7, 2007

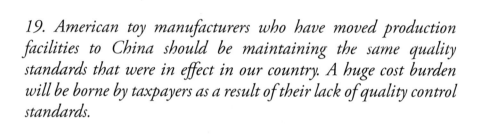

19. American toy manufacturers who have moved production facilities to China should be maintaining the same quality standards that were in effect in our country. A huge cost burden will be borne by taxpayers as a result of their lack of quality control standards.

Toy Recall from China

Mattel and Fisher Price have announced huge recalls of contaminated toys manufactured in China. It seems that these companies knew there was a problem but did not react until outside groups exposed the problems. That in itself calls for condemnation, but the thought I want to put forth in this note is the lack of quality control in those factories. I spent most of my adult working life in factories at a number of different locations in America and Canada. The common denominator was that wherever the factory was located, that factory was duty bound to follow the specifications that originated at the main office. There were large numbers of staff assigned to assure that the product was produced according to the specifications laid down by Corporate.

It is inconceivable to me that these American Corporations who moved their production lines to China, did not insist on the same quality standards that applied to American factories. I can only assume that in their zeal to produce at the lowest cost that they did not insist on these Chinese factories employing the same number of quality control employees to assure adherence to specifications. If this is so, the leaders of these companies should face severe punishment, as the cost of adding thousands of Federal inspectors at the ports will be borne by all of us as taxpayers, a cost that would not be imposed if the products were made in American factories under normal quality control surveillance.

August 18, 2007

20. This book reaffirmed my great respect for John and Bobby Kennedy. I am saddened when I consider how different it might be today had they lived to carry out their dreams for a peaceful world.

Brothers
The Hidden History of the Kennedy Years
By David Talbot

Mr. Talbot did an excellent job in writing this book. He did extensive research and had countless interviews with those who were a part of these critical years. It is a glowing tribute to Jack and Robert as they tried their best to change from the madness of nuclear destruction to peace. They fought a battle with their military advisors, the FBI and the CIA throughout their administration. It proved to me once again that we are a militaristic country. How else to explain why we pour billions each year into the military including the maintenance of our vast nuclear arsenal, space war technology, development of newer, deadlier weapons, paying outlandish bribes to get new recruits and keep those in the services from retiring, and fighting at the present time two wars with other countries on the hit list.

The Bay of Pigs invasion of Cuba had been supported by President Eisenhower. Kennedy agreed to allow it to proceed but insisted that the US military would not be used. Those supporting the invasion knew that our military would be required and just assumed when things went bad that Kennedy would acquiesce but he didn't. Even yours truly was angry about this, but in retrospect it was the right thing to do. I only wish he had not allowed them to invade.

Robert Kennedy as Attorney General aggressively prosecuted members of the Mafia and Jimmy Hoffa of the Teamsters. He did it without support from J. Edgar Hoover.

The CIA was constantly plotting to kill Castro against the President's orders to stop. They poisoned crops and did other things to disrupt the Cuban economy. The Kennedy's were trying to find the way to normalize relations while this was going on.

They stood up to racism culminating in the confrontation at the University of Mississippi with their successful effort to allow James Meredith, a Negro, to attend the all white college. The Army and the FBI did not support the President forcing him to push them harder than he should have had to do. This took a great deal of political courage as the Democratic Party lost the South as a result.

The author convinced me that Jack Kennedy was only waiting until after the election to start pulling advisors out of Vietnam. He did not believe Vietnam was that important. Berlin, the Soviets and Cuba were enough for him.

After the assassination of the President, Robert left the government and ran for and was elected Senator for the State of New York. His ultimate goal was to be elected President to carry on the work started by Jack. In his campaigning he was ecstatically supported by the workers of America. He also visited other countries and received tumultuous responses everywhere he went.

Both Jack and Robert were hated by many groups including the Mafia, Cuban exiles, white supremacists and those in the military industrial complex which former President Eisenhower had warned against. I never bought that either assassination was the work of one man. With so many vicious enemies they were both doomed. Today it is even worse. A man or woman elected as a peace President will be stalked and killed. The money involved dictates that this is so.

For those of you who lived through these years as I did, I highly recommend reading this book. For those born after the 60's reading it would give you an understanding on how through these two courageous men hatred for America around the world could have been lessened. The world we live in could be so much better had they finished their mission.

August 29, 2007

21. This is my attempt at satire to show my contempt for the current administration and the enormous power of the mega corporations.

Of the Corporations, by the Corporations and for the Corporations

I don't think this was what President Lincoln meant when he coined his precious words 140 years ago. The Corporations get bigger and more powerful every day. There doesn't seem to be anything they won't do to extend their power world wide. I am not only referring to American Corporations. There are huge mega firms in other countries as well as our own.

The money they are willing to spend to buy the legislation they need and want is readily available. This money has so corrupted our voting system, I despair that it can ever be made right again. With such resources available they can affect the defeat of any candidate who refuses to do their bidding.

I firmly believe that our military is sent into harms way repeatedly to protect corporate assets. There are many examples to prove this point.

1 – Iraq - For all the fancy talk and spin emanating from the white house, you will never convince me that the unprovoked attack had any other purpose than to establish a military presence in the Middle East to control the vast petroleum resources there.

2 – Columbia - Occidental Petroleum has a pipe line that needs to be protected from rebels. Who are these rebels: are they led by drug lords or are they the disenfranchised people who are denied the benefits of the nation's resources? I have been to lectures where the sins of the Coca Cola Corporation were exposed. They had threatened or murdered union leaders who were attempting to organize in the effort to give the workers a voice. In India they dammed a major river for their use depriving villages in the area water for their own use.

3 – Afghanistan – I wonder if the time is ripe now to start building the pipeline to the sea that Russia wanted to do and the reason they invaded some years ago? I always like to rub it in that this was the time Osama bin Laden was our good buddy. We made him what he is today with our Stinger missiles and support of every kind.

September 11, 2007

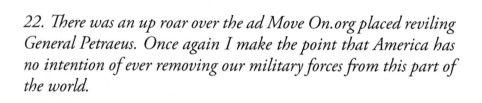

22. There was an up roar over the ad Move On.org placed reviling General Petraeus. Once again I make the point that America has no intention of ever removing our military forces from this part of the world.

Iraq Deception

Move On .org has caused quite a controversy with their advertisement in the NY Times newspaper about General Petraeus. In my opinion it distracted from the real issue of President Bush's long term intention to occupy Iraq as we continue to occupy Korea, Germany and Japan 50 years after the end of WWII. We do that to have forces readily available should they be required. As far as Iraq is concerned, the purpose is to ensure oil supplies are always available for our use.

When Pres. Bush talks about a gradual reduction he hopes to appease his allies and foes in Congress so that funding will allow him to continue through the end of his second term and force the next occupant to continue to pay for occupying forces decades into the future.

With over 180,000 contractors in IRAQ, many of whom are Para military he doesn't need 160,000 troops to accomplish his goal. These contractors are building permanent bases throughout IRAQ for occupancy by US forces. Pres. Bush does not intend to leave. The 750 million dollar, self sufficient, US Embassy in Baghdad also proves the long term intention.

After all of the speeches are made, the Congress will give him the funds he needs. It is sad that members of Congress cannot or will not address the issue I put forth in this letter. We as voters need to evict these weaklings from their vaulted positions, Democrats as well as Republicans and elect outsiders who will do what is right and end the carnage at least as far as our involvement feeds the fire.

September 16, 2007

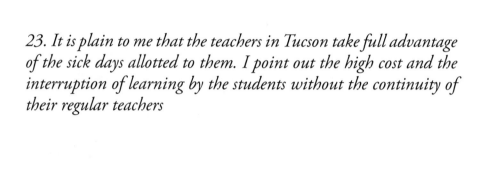

23. It is plain to me that the teachers in Tucson take full advantage of the sick days allotted to them. I point out the high cost and the interruption of learning by the students without the continuity of their regular teachers

TUSD Sickout

I read the 9/15/07 article in the Arizona Daily Star with interest. I took particular notice that out of 3,500 teachers, over 500 are out sick on most Fridays. It doesn't compute that this many could actually be sick enough to miss work to that high a percentage. To me, it shows a disregard to the learning experience of students and a misuse of the benefit provided. Since the policy is generous enough to allow them to carry over days to the following year it fosters the premise that the days are theirs to take without regard to sickness.

Perhaps, if they are so interested in higher paychecks, they might be willing to trade some of this and other benefits for higher wages. The cost of hiring replacements must be huge but more importantly, the loss of continuity by having the same teacher must detract seriously from the learning experience.

One more thought. I remember the high number of teachers who were absent during the "amnesty" sick out day earlier this year. It would be interesting to see if these were the same teachers who took part in this recent sick out.

September 16, 2007

24. The story of Lou Gehrig's life was inspiring to me. He was a man who devoted himself to becoming a better player at a time when sports were fun not big business as they are today.

Iron Horse
Lou Gehrig in his time
By Ray Robinson

My reading in recent years usually pertains to heavy issues. I took a breather when I spotted this book at the Public Library. Lou died in 1941. I would have been 13 at the time so I can't really claim to have known all about him but I was a baseball enthusiast and knew about the Yankees, the Dodgers and Giants. Regardless of my knowledge, this book brought back memories and filled in the many blank spaces with the full story of this man's life. His life and others like him in those years are completely different from the prima donnas of today. Their pay was miniscule in comparison. They truly played for the love of the game.

Lou didn't smoke, drink or play around. He spent all of his energy trying to become a better player. His work ethic was outstanding during his never to be bested playing streak of 2,130 games. During that streak he often played with broken fingers and other serious injuries that would keep average players on the bench.

I have nearly given up interest in professional sports today. Hardly a day goes by without some new revelation of a player or manager committing some offense. The brutality also lessons for me the fine points of sports.

I hope that someone of you will try to get a copy to read for yourself. It is not only a well written sports story but even if you have never been a sports fan you can enjoy reading about a person who strove to succeed and excelled at his chosen profession.

September 19, 2007

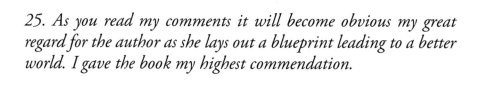

25. As you read my comments it will become obvious my great regard for the author as she lays out a blueprint leading to a better world. I gave the book my highest commendation.

The Idea That Is America
Keeping faith with our values
In a dangerous world
By: Anne-Marie Slaughter

As my readers understand, I have been on a multi-year struggle to understand the world we live in and to try to think of ways to preserve and enhance all life forms and the world itself. To that end I read vociferously books from all points of view. I usually fall back in confusion as ideas tend to cancel out other ideas I felt pertinent. This book is so coherent, reasonable and simple to understand that I must give it my highest recommendation as a must read book by those who care as I do. I will go so far as to believe it should be a required course of study at the High School level. The premise is such that it would promote quiet debate rather than the strident discourse we live with on a daily basis.

She devotes specific chapters to; Liberty, Democracy, Equality, Justice, Tolerance, Humility, Faith.

It might seem as if these would all blend in without being entities unto themselves but she proves capable, and after each chapter a better understanding of each emerges after which in her conclusion she ties them all together.

She may offend readers as she is very critical of the current administration and its arrogant attitude towards the world community with the assertion, "You are either with us or against us", and the other "We are on a Crusade" which implies a holy war. She warns that forsaking basic values in our Constitution and Bill of Rights in order to confront terrorists only assures that the bad guys win as even Benjamin Franklin stated that if we are willing to give up rights out of fear then we have lost our rights.

She doesn't confide her criticism to one administration; she traces problems throughout our history, issues such as denying women and minorities or groups of immigrants or religions other than Protestant, from enjoying the blessings of Life, Liberty and the Pursuit of Happiness.

We desperately need to search for leaders who will reassure our citizens and the citizens of the world that we still believe in our core values and demonstrate leadership towards improving life for all. What a great world we could have if we could be the "Beacon on the Hill" we once stood for. READ AND BE INSPIRED.

September 20, 2007

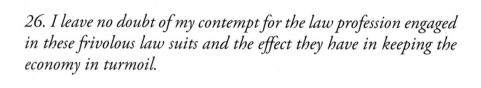

26. I leave no doubt of my contempt for the law profession engaged in these frivolous law suits and the effect they have in keeping the economy in turmoil.

Outrageous Law Suits

I am using the "lost pants" $54 million law suit against the South Korean Dry Cleaner family to make my point. The Chung family ultimately was successful in fighting this two year suit but it was a hollow victory as their expenses exceeded $100,000 and the litigant; Mr. Pearson, believe it or not, is appealing the District of Columbia Court's opinion.

According to an article in today's edition of the Arizona Daily Star the Chungs have had to sell two of their three establishments as a result of lost business and the trial expense.

Justice, according to me, would require that the Pearson's of this country, who file these outrageous law suits should be required to pay all costs incurred by the defendants as well as compensate them for the harm done to them emotionally and monetarily.

Frivolous suits are being filed on a continuous basis, and why not. The litigants have nothing to lose and gain a small percentage of any money available after the law firm takes its cut. Until the system is changed to hold the law firms and litigants responsible for costs incurred in these ridiculous suits, the game will continue. These games take an inordinate amount of the legal systems time, keeping it occupied and unable to address more important issues before the courts.

September 20, 2007

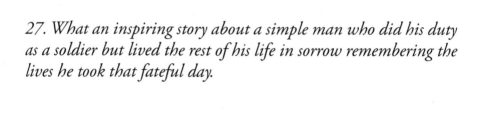

27. What an inspiring story about a simple man who did his duty as a soldier but lived the rest of his life in sorrow remembering the lives he took that fateful day.

Phantom Warrior
The Heroic True Story of Pvt. John Mc Kinney's One-Man Stand against the Japanese in World War II
By: Forrest Bryant Johnson

My favorite books are biographies about people who make a difference with their lives. I lucked onto this book at the Public Library. Everyone has heard about Sergeant York and his exploits in World War I. Gary Cooper played the role in a movie about him. The similarity between these two men is striking. They were both simple, hard working, quiet types who were poor farmers eking out a living in the South. Their pastimes were hunting and fishing. Actually pastime is a misnomer as the food from animals and fish caught provided needed food for their families. The skills developed hunting made them both dead shots.

Pvt. McKinney won the Congressional Medal of Honor for his exploits during a battle at a place called Dingaling Bay on the East coast of Luzon May 11, 1945. He and about 70 other soldiers were attacked before sunrise from two sides. About 148 attacked the main group from the North and an equal number from a sand bar to the South. The account pieced together from eye witnesses and a count of dead after the battle confirmed that those attacking from the South were all killed by this one soldier with the exception of 6 shot by a soldier that came to his aid as the battle was winding down. The total battle lasted about 36 minutes. You have to read it to comprehend how it was possible. It took a long time to get the approval for the Medal of Honor because it was so unbelievable. In the citation it mentions 40 as the number of Japanese dead.

The book is 304 pages long. It details his early life and events leading up to this battle. The war began for him in New Guinea and ended with this battle. He was removed from the fighting so that he would survive the war and be a symbol for Americans of the heroic exploits of our fighting men.

He returned home and returned to the life he had lived before joining the Army. He is described as a man of sorrow. From time to time he would say to a relative or close friend, "Why did they have to die." Find it and read it. You will inspired by this unbelievable story.

September 28, 2007

28. This is a hard book that does not pull punches. It was demoralizing as the conclusion is that our country is in peril with little hope it will recover.

Failed States
By Noam Chomsky
The Abuse of Power and the Assault on Democracy

Of all of the heavy intellectual books I have read recently, this one stands alone in its complexity and overall content. As a life long patriot I found much in this book disagreeable and not at all in tune with the beliefs I have nurtured over my lifetime. I cannot say I recommend you to read it but perhaps it should be read by those who hope as I do for a better world for all mankind and nature.

Actually what he writes is not much different from other authors but he does it in a harsher manner that made me cringe. It is hard to be told of the actions taken by our government over the decades since WWII including fostering violent overthrows of democratically elected governments such as Iran, Chili, Nicaragua, Guatemala and our ever increasing dependency on military force to get other nations to comply with our dictates. The current administration only differs from previous ones in the audacity with which it projects its power. Previous administrations were more subtle but nonetheless effective in achieving their purposes.

He takes us around the world but in the last chapter concentrates on what is happening in our own country. He points out, as most of us who pay attention already know, that the electorate is manipulated into voting based on sound bites which are intended to persuade voters to reject candidates' based on emotion and not on fact. The other proven technique is to scare the voter with threats from evil groups around the world. The two party systems that used to be are no longer discernable. The main reason of course is the amount of money needed to win office. He states that there are now 34,750 registered lobbyists living and working in Washington. Can you imagine what a day in the life of a politician is like with an army this size descending on them and their staffs as they try to get legislation to aid their respective causes none of which are for our benefit?

He discusses poll after poll which confirms the issues most important to the majority of thinking voters. They want to vote for someone who supports these ideas, but in the end confused and persuaded, they vote hoping for change but it never happens and in my opinion will never happen until or unless we as citizens force it by whatever means is possible to us.

October 15, 2007

29. I was angered that the Governor of New York would order public officials to grant divers licenses to illegal immigrants.

Drivers Licenses

N.Y. Governor Eliot Spitzer has ordered public officials to grant drivers licenses to illegal immigrants. Many have refused stating their responsibility to only issue to citizens with social security cards and addresses. Some State Legislatures are promising a law suit effective Nov. 1, 2007 if he does not rescind his order.

A driver's license allows you to board an airplane or enter a public building. It may not be much but it has some meaning and is universally used to keep others from entering. It is estimated that there are over 500,000 illegal immigrants in N.Y. California will no doubt be the next State to duplicate N.Y.

Where is the Federal Government on this issue? I haven't heard from the Administration, Homeland Security or any member of Congress. Are they all so wrapped up in their concern to not offend that they do not have the intestinal fortitude to take a stand and uphold their #1 priority which is to defend the citizens of this country.

October 16, 2007

30. I first wrote about this subject July 1, 2004. It was part of my "Last Angry Man" book. I have added it to the bottom of this new letter. This letter was my second attempt to try to get someone to perhaps review it and hopefully accept my request. If this is of interest, check in the 2009 listing. It got quite interesting as I discovered more about why they did it as they did.

What I am writing is probably not new to you. Veterans of this war are dying off by over 1,000 each day, not only the veterans but also those other citizens such as me who lived through those trying times. In a few short years we will all be gone. Younger Americans visiting this memorial will think it is a fine tribute to the Americans who did what had to be done and will never get the full significance of President Roosevelt's Declaration of War speech he gave to Congress after the attack on Pearl Harbor. The words he spoke inspired the nation. Whoever edited his speech to its essentials in order to carve it into the monument left out the most important part of that speech?

If you search the web go to WWII Washington Memorial then click on fact sheet and then inscriptions. The Pearl Harbor Speech is condensed as follows;

DECEMBER 7, 1941, A DATE WHICH WILL LIVE IN INFAMY... NO MATTER HOW LONG IT MAY TAKE US TO OVERCOME THIS PREMEDITATED INVASION, THE AMERICAN PEOPLE, IN THEIR RIGHTEOUS MIGHT, WILL WIN THROUGH TO ABSOLUTE VICTORY.

That is all that is inscribed. There was a lot of detail in the speech that did not need to be inscribed but his final words were the words that inspired the nation. They were;

WITH CONFIDENCE IN OUR ARMED FORCES-WITH THE UNBOUNDED DETERMINATION OF OUR PEOPLE-WE WILL GAIN THE INEVITABLE TRIUMPH-SO HELP US GOD.

You can find this by searching FDR Library then click on selected public papers and speeches.

I have written previously to Senators Kyl and McCain. Neither has felt it important enough to do anything about it, so I am now asking you. Those words must be made a part of the memorial or it will be meaningless in years to come.

October 18, 2007

WORLD WAR II Monument in Washington, DC

I have confirmed that it is true that the speech inscribed on the memorial by President Roosevelt has been altered, presumably so that it would be politically correct, as experts see things today. Only those of us alive and old enough to understand can remember what he said and how he inspired a nation to come together in a common cause to defeat the Axis Powers who had declared war on America. A decade from now there will be few of us left and people visiting the memorial will believe that the words inscribed are what he said to us. I am referring to his address to Congress asking for a declaration of war. He ended his speech, "with confidence in our armed forces, with the unbounding determination of our people, we will gain the inevitable triumph, so help us God'. The inscription on the memorial leaves out "so help us God".

For comparison purposes read the following words near the close of President Lincoln's address that he delivered at Gettysburg. --- That we here highly resolve that these dead shall not have died in vain – that this nation, under God, shall have a new rebirth of freedom ---

If it is the right thing to remove Roosevelt's reference to God, then I sarcastically suggest that the reference to God be removed from the Lincoln Memorial as well.

Hundreds of thousands of Americans died in WWII defending freedom. The days after his speech, millions of young men enlisted in the armed forces. Sixty years later when most have already died, an incorrect inscription is foisted on Americans. We believed then that we were doing God's work. How dare the commission do sacrilege to this memorial? This is not even about separation of state and religion, it is about rewriting history. George Orwell's prediction has come true.

I demand that this be corrected immediately and that those responsible be required to apologize to those few veterans still alive today. Further I request all who receive this letter partition their members of Congress to correct this distortion of history.

July 1, 2004

31. I did not recommend reading this book as it was demoralizing to me with her insatiable striving for the highest office.

Her Way
THE HOPES and AMBITIONS of HILLARY RODMAN CLINTON
By Jeff Gerth and Don Van Natta Jr.

Once again I found a book I felt I should read, after all Hillary may become the next President of the U.S. This is not her biography, in fact neither she nor her staff would co-operate with the writers. In spite of this handicap, it appeared to me that they tried to be factual and shared the good with the bad. It follows her from a young girl to 2007. She has the ability to attract supporters for her staff and other groups who are intensely loyal and dedicated to her.

Her first challenge as first lady was to get a bill passed to provide medical care for all Americans. She strove hard but in the end accomplished nothing. The lobbying power of the industry prevailed.

The one common denominator is her driving ambition to reach the highest possible level of achievement which for her will be to become President of the U.S. The writers make a strong case that there was a pact or plan that Bill and Hillary worked toward and that was for both of them to be two term presidents. Bill got his and now she is close to realizing her dream as well. When the Monica Lewinski affair could no longer be denied she stood by him when it was expected that a divorce was a natural consequence of his marital infidelity. To leave at that time would have ended any hope of achieving this lofty goal so she stuck it out.

The book recalls all of the turmoil that they went through as Kenneth Starr the independent council and his group pursued the Clintons on various and sundry issues including their Whitewater investment, Madison Guaranty Bank and her Rose law firm. Other issues were the death of Vince Foster, the women who claimed Bill had made advances to them including Paula Jones and Kathleen Fisher. Starr's final report included 110,000 words. After spending millions they were never found guilty of any impropriety except for lying about his relationship with Monica. The report stated that there was a record of the president's "abundant and calculating lies" under oath, obstruction of justice, and an abuse of power that "may constitute grounds for impeachment." The Republican controlled Congress did all they could to accomplish this but in the end failed.

I detected a pattern in her voting record as U.S. Senator of N.Y. In my opinion after reading I believe she votes more to protect her image than concern for whatever issue is being addressed. A case in point was her vote to give President Bush the authority to invade Iraq. She felt that a no vote would be interpreted as being soft on military matters.

I searched carefully to find some information about the role Bill and Hillary played during John Kerry's bid for the White House. There was nothing. I remember during that year that Bill was recovering from some illness and she naturally would take the time to be with him. Whenever they did make a speech I noted that they seldom mentioned Kerry by name, instead they would talk about democratic values. I was upset with them as I was actively involved with the Democratic Party as we worked to remove President Bush from office. Their personal ambition contributed to Kerry's defeat to the detriment of us all. Where might we be now if Kerry had won? I was not a big fan of him but as I jokingly said at the time, I would vote for Mickey Mouse if he was on the ticket. We felt that we could persuade him to move in what we considered to be the right direction.

Today as we all know she is receiving record contributions from citizens and also from Corporate America, the same corporations that destroyed her first efforts to provide health care for all of our citizens.

I don't really recommend reading this book. If you are an active thinker and have followed Washington issues for a long time, then you will find very little that you don't already know. It was good as a refresher but reliving some of the past was tedious. It was hard for me to concentrate.

November 2, 2007

32. The interesting thing about this letter that I sent to the editor of the Arizona Daily Star is that Mr. Portillo only wrote one more strident letter dated Dec 21. After that he has concentrated on human interest articles that are enjoyable to read. I would like to think that mine and others who complained got their attention.

Ernesto Portillo Jr., Arizona Daily Star Columnist

When are you going to stop supporting his continuing haranguing against any and all who disagree with his philosophy which supports open borders. He is a broken record who takes every opportunity to push his position.

Mexico has a deliberate and successful program to relieve their overpopulation and lack of good jobs by shipping surplus citizens to our country. The money sent back to Mexico is that countries largest source of income.

He uses the term immigrant in his articles as if we are against immigration of Hispanics or others from around the world. Nothing could be further from the truth. What we are against is illegal immigration, those who slip over the border or who overstay their visa limits. We cannot continue to be flooded in the current fashion. There must be order to the process or else the standard of living for those who do physical labor will continue to decline. What does he care? I assume you pay him well for his writings.

In his way of thinking, if someone has eluded authorities for a period of time, then if found out, should be allowed to stay no matter what. He was outraged that the student and his family were deported over the drug incident recently. He was elated when the Police Department officials stated they would never again inform Homeland Security. I on the other hand, deplore weak leadership that turns that agency from enforcing all laws on the books.

His latest article was an attack against Mr. Tom Horne, the state superintendent of public instruction. Mr. Horne does not support ethnic studies programs. In my opinion schools should teach reading, writing and arithmetic as they used to do. There is a need for history, geography and world events but special programs to emphasize our differences that foster adversarial feelings between different racial, gender and place of origin are not beneficial and a waste of time and resources. He concludes outrageously by printing Mr. Horne's office address and requesting readers to deluge his office with outrage.

November 19, 2007

33. I did not try to minimize the great respect I still hold for this great man. Oh how we need someone like him today to get us inspired once again.

FDR
JEAN EDWARD SMITH

Mr. Smith published his biography this year (2007). I found it at the Public Library in the new book review section. It is astounding in the detail contained that could only be accomplished after exhaustive research. It took me several weeks to read. I confess I read slowly and deliberately whenever a book of this importance is in my hands. The text is 636 pages long and written in small type. The notes and bibliography uses another 224 pages.

This is not the first time I have read a biography about Franklin Delano Roosevelt. I had my own copy of a previous biography which I gave to my son Andy for his library. I was born in 1928; President Roosevelt was the only President I can remember from my youth. I don't profess knowledge of his first two terms as President but I was 13 years old when Pearl Harbor was attacked, December 7, 1941. From that point on I knew who he was and followed as best a young boy can the war and his leadership of the country and the allies. As a family we would sit in front of the radio to hear his "fireside chats" Sunday evenings as he addressed the American people. There were a minority of citizens who despised him but the vast majority loved him and followed his directives as we all pulled together to save the world. We truly believed we were fighting a just and noble war and to this day I have never deviated from that premise.

The book starts by informing the lineage leading to his birth in 1882. It describes his boyhood, college years and his forays into politics. He was the Governor of N.Y. for two terms before becoming President. At that time the depression was devastating. President Hoover took a hand off attitude assuming that in time the economy would correct itself. Roosevelt couldn't wait to assume control as he was determined to take whatever steps were necessary to get the recovery under way. His programs were referred to as "The New Deal".

On page 601 at a press conference on 12/28/1943 he was asked by a young reporter about the new deal and whether it was still in effect. He answered no and then went on to state why it was necessary at the time. He followed with a partial list of things entailed in his program including; saving the banks by setting up a sound banking system, the Federal Deposit Insurance program to guarantee bank deposits.

(As an aside my father refused to put funds into any bank during his entire lifetime. At his death we finally convinced our mother to have her social security check deposited in a bank checking account. I remember her asking, "How will

I know it is there".)

Other programs mentioned were H.O.L.C. (Home Owners Loan Corporation) which helped save homes from foreclosure. F.C.A. (Farm Credit Administration) saved farms from foreclosure. Triple A (Agricultural Adjustment Administration) rescued agriculture from disasters, Soil Conservation; protecting investors through the (Securities and Exchange Commission) also Social Security, unemployment insurance, aid to handicapped and infirm, minimum wage and maximum hours legislation, abolition of child labor, rural electrification, flood control, the public works program, the TVA, the Civilian Conservation Corps, the WPA, National Youth Foundation and many others. Some of the above are still in effect to this day. His exhortation to staff was to try something. If it didn't work then try something else. Doing nothing was not acceptable.

Two major mistakes during his presidency were trying to pack the Supreme Court in 1937 and placing American citizens of Japanese descent in camps in 1942. The first was because the court had ruled against a number of his new deal programs and the second because of the concern in California where a number of defense plants were located that Japanese citizens might commit sabotage. Pearl Harbor created this hatred and concern.

He was a remarkable man, very intelligent and energetic. He contracted Polio when he was 39. With ample recourses available to him he could have retired and devoted his years to improving his health and enjoying life as best he could without the use of his legs, but he choose to fight it and remain active in whatever government service availed itself to him. It is incredible to me that he had the ability to campaign and to assume ever increasing responsibilities and perform with skill and effectiveness. Once he became President he had twice per week press conferences in the Oval Office and often on Sunday evenings he would talk to the people over the radio. He called them fireside chats. These would give the people confidence that someone cared about their condition and was working hard on their behalf to improve their lives. One early speech concluded with the famous line, "All we have to fear is fear itself".

During the late 30's it became increasingly clear that Adolph Hitler posed a threat to civilization as the world knew it at the time. Americans were united in their desire to not be drawn into another European War. Our armed forces had dwindled to where we were one of the weakest nations. Once war commenced between the Axis Powers and the Allies he lead us in small steps towards preparing for war. He proposed a lend lease program to provide materials to England after the fall of France. Should England fall then the world was likely to become victims as well. This was expanded to include Russia once they were attacked. He tried to persuade the Japanese to curb their territorial ambitions through diplomacy to no avail and in the end after Pearl Harbor we were in it fully with no turning back until absolute victory was achieved. The first few years were negative but gradually as our troops were trained and supplied with material of all kinds we gradually started to turn the tide. His leadership was absolutely necessary to keep up the morale of our people. He was elected to a third term in 1940 as America wanted his leadership as the threat of war increased and then a fourth term in 1944. We could not conceive of losing him as our President, upon his sudden death on 4/12/1945 we wondered if we could conclude the war without him.

Only Lincoln in my opinion was as great as FDR. They both faced incredible problems to solve. Both were the right men at the right time in history. Without their leadership and charisma who knows what the world would be like today had they not been there when the crisis needed to be dealt with.

If you take the time to read, I can assure you, that you will be enthralled to follow this great man's life as he fought for us and eventually died for us.

One last request, check out the FDR Library on the internet. You can hear portions of some of his most important speeches. You may be as enthralled as I was when I heard him as a young man.

November 23, 2007

34. Again my attempt to use satire to make a point. President Bush was eager to start another war, this time with Iran. The intelligence report put a stop to it.

Poor Bush, Cheney and McCain

I wonder what has happened to the people in the intelligence section that released the data showing that Iran ceased their work on developing nuclear weapons in 2003. I'll bet they have been reassigned to a much lower position.

Bush was so eager to attack Iran before his term ends and now his bubble has burst. He has lost any international support for military action or increasing boycotts. He will be forced to talk instead.

Let's not forget our own Senator; you know the one that sang his little ditty, "Bomb, Bomb, and Bomb Iran. He had such a cute smile while doing it. Should he win the nomination and become President, you can be sure he would find a way to attack Iran.

December 5, 2007

35. There had been numerous articles written about the absence of our basketball coach. I point out that of more importance to Arizonans and our country is the continuing absence of our Senator who would rather campaign than attend to the responsibility he owed to us since we had elected him to represent us in Washington.

Olson-McCain

Letter to the editor of the Arizona Daily Star-it was published

The Star continues on a regular basis to print on the front page data about the earnings of Lute Olson while he is on a leave. As far as I am concerned that issue is between Lute and the Athletic Dept. which is functioning in the black due directly to the success of Lute Olson's basketball program.

This letter is a request to place a front page article about the salary and perks being paid by taxpayers to our absentee Senator McCain. Every week for some time now when I look at bills voted on in the Senate he is listed as not voting. You can check it out easier than I but if researched I am sure what you will find is that he has been absent for the past six months or longer. While he is out campaigning he is not tending to the business of Arizonans who put him in office. There are many issues in Congress that are of concern to me and I trust others. He should be admonished for his lack of attention.

December 16, 2007

36. I was angry with the editorial staff and Mr. Portillo Jr. It was implied that there would not be a problem accepting illegal immigration if it weren't for transplants to Arizona from other States.

Response to Editorial and Ernesto Portillo's Column
12/21/2007

I can't let the Star off the hook for today's editorial content. You take aim at relocated Americans who have moved to Arizona either in pursuit of employment or to retire. I retired here 14 years ago. My first home was in Villa Sin Vacas. I kind of liked the sound of my new area. I had no hard feelings for Latinos or the Spanish culture. Illegal immigration may have been in full force but I was not aware of it.

As the years past by and particularly since I became a hiker I began to be aware on an increasing basis the garbage that was being strewn in the pristine wilderness areas through which I was hiking. Because I am an avid reader and keep myself informed I have come to deeply resent the invasion of my country by millions of illegal immigrants who are predominantly Mexicans.

I resent Mexican Presidents Fox and Calderone for interfering in our countries business by insisting that we accept all who wish to come here outside of our immigration guidelines. I also resent the fact that these so-called leaders do so little to provide employment opportunities for their people. Check out the Mexican government's immigration policies to see how they treat immigrants.

I also resent the fact that thousands of Mexican jobs that had been created by NAFTA have gone instead to China. This is a country that violates every facet of international trade by pegging their currency to the dollar, by pirating trademarked goods, by employing children working long hours for little pay, by exporting contaminated food products for people and pets and toys containing excessive amounts of lead and other poisons, by selling human organs removed from prisoners in their custody.

I deeply resent our current weak leadership in Washington for allowing them to do all this without sanctions. I also resent these same leaders for allowing illegal immigration to get so far out of control. As Mr. Portillo so eloquently stated there have been severe actions taken by our country to return Mexicans to their country. The first was by President Hoover. This was during the depression and millions of Americans were without work. The second was by President Eisenhower when the millions of returning veterans were in need of employment. The amusing thing to me is that our government had no problem finding and evicting on a fast track basis. They could do the same today but have no desire to do so.

My personal position is that temporary work visas should be increased if a labor shortage exists that is not being filled by citizens. People like you are fond of saying illegal immigrants are doing jobs Americans won't do. This may be partially true but equally true is the depressed wages being paid because of them which discourage Americans from taking these jobs. You in your arrogance like the fact that this keeps construction and manufacturing costs low so you can live in a bigger house and purchase goods for less. You care not one little bit that working Americans would also like bigger homes and to be better able to provide for their families.

Since you seem to resent other Americans from settling in Arizona, I have a question for you. Were you born in Arizona and were all other members of your editorial staff born here? If not, then you have no more right than I do to express your thoughts as you feel you have the right to do. I would also like to know if any of you have ever been employed in a labor intensive job. I doubt it very much or you wouldn't be so happy to see our industrial base collapse with jobs heading by the millions to communist China all for the sake of you being able to have all the goodies you want at low cost.

I took the time this morning to respond as I deeply resented both editorial columns. I made it longer than normal since I realize it wouldn't be published anyway. You can call us bigots if you want. We just want order to our immigration process not the chaos we are presently witnessing.

December 21, 2007

2008

2008

Listing in order by date

---

1. I tried as best I could to place the "recession" of 2008 in perspective to the real depression that started in 1928.

Recession 1928 vs. 2008

In 1928 the country was in desperate shape. Social Security did not exist, there were few programs in effect to alleviate real hunger, and unemployment was rampant. Farmers lost their farms; most city dwellers lived in apartments and could not afford the rent. By today's standards most Americans would be classified as poor. The banks quit issuing loans. Factories were shut down. Even if they could operate there were no customers for their products. For several years people lived in desperation just to exist. There were few who could afford to improve their standard of living. This existed until FDR became President in 1932 and immediately enacted the New Deal. One of his first actions was to close the banks and reopen them one at a time when they could assure their viability. Depositor's savings and checking accounts were federally insured to protect the average citizen. Jobs were created in construction and in the CCC which took men into the wilderness areas to build trails and huts among other things. Welfare was made available but the key to FDR's programs was that he wanted American men to go to work doing anything. He did not want to grant handouts while those receiving them stayed idle.

Now let's compare that era to the present "crisis" in 2008. The average home sells for over $230,000. Credit card debt is at an all time high, the restrictions that were supposed to be in place somehow were ignored allowing people to purchase larger homes than they could reasonably be able to afford. Personal assets and job security were not a requirement to purchase. Houses were sold with interest payments only on the mistaken belief that they would increase in value over time without ever dropping in value. Equity was taken out of home assets and used to fulfill other perceived needs or wants. Millions of manufacturing jobs were relocated to China and other nations which could provide cheap labor. Millions of service jobs have also left the country. Our government provides substantial income to those who lose their jobs allowing them to look for work but not be required to take a job below their perceived worth. It also provides retraining programs in the mistaken belief that there will be jobs in the computer field and others areas all the while jobs are being exported at an ever accelerating rate.

The federal government and all of the so-called presidential candidates are calling for a massive hand out program estimated to cost $150 billion dollars to "stimulate" the economy. A prudent person in debt would take the handout graciously and use it to pay down his debt but the government is wise enough to realize that they will instead do exactly as asked and go out and spend it quickly and wait for the next handout which will surely come as soon as it is apparent that $150 billion dollars is not enough. The money for the most part will certainly stimulate the economy of China and the other cheap labor countries but will do little to restore our own.

Our national debt exceeds $9 trillion dollars. In Arizona the State is facing a shortfall of $1 billion dollars. Most other States are in the same situation. In the meantime we continue to throw funds approaching $1 trillion dollars to support wars in Afghanistan and Iraq while at the same time threatening Iran and other Middle Eastern nations. Our military has been depleted to where drastic rebuilding of all types of weaponry is required. Over 1/3 of all the Air Forces planes are out of service.

We continue our reckless squandering of our grandchildren's future while determined to live beyond our means. When I was starting out as a young married man there was no such thing as credit cards. We waited until we had accumulated funds and then paid cash for every stick of furniture we wanted.

The Piper will be paid, if not today then tomorrow. With trillions of U.S. bonds in the hands of foreigners we are approaching catastrophe. They are buying up American assets and are beginning to purchase Euros instead of Dollars. They may pull the plug altogether and refuse to support our lavish life style. When that happens no stimulus package will have a positive effect.

So what do I propose? Let the chips fall where they may. Let the housing market seek its true value not the outlandish values in place today. Stop frivolous household purchases of Flat screen TVs, cell phones that take pictures and devices that hold thousands of musical songs. Each and all are deemed necessary. I am one of the holdouts. I have none nor do I intend to purchase any. I didn't "need" them before and I don't need them now. Take the hit and live frugally. The government should do likewise. They could start by banning earmarks added to every piece of legislation passed. Stop the wars, bring the troops and what's left of their hardware home and rebuild for when they are truly needed. Make balancing the budget and then reducing the national debt the number one priority. The list is endless on what should be done but won't because of opposition and the feeling that we are special and are ordained by God to live as if we were God's chosen people. How sad.

January 22, 2008

2. This movie was outstanding in pointing out that every life should be lived to the full. There were many jewels of advice sprinkled throughout. I tried to encourage others to see it and perhaps make adjustments to their outlook on living.

The Bucket List

I went to see this movie last night. Let me suggest that any of you who have passed the threshold of 70 must go to see it. The writers must have written the dialogue before the strike as it was superbly written. The messages keep coming out all thru the movie.

If you are not familiar with the story, it concerns two dying men placed together in a hospital room. One is a tycoon, the other a car mechanic. They both receive death notices about the same time and decide to use the list as a basis on how to spend the few months left to them. I will stop right here as I don't want to take away from the experience except to say, if you come away feeling as I did you might wish to make changes in your routine with the years remaining to you. I may not do spectacular exploits as they did but I will keep the thought in mind as I plan my life.

February 13, 2008

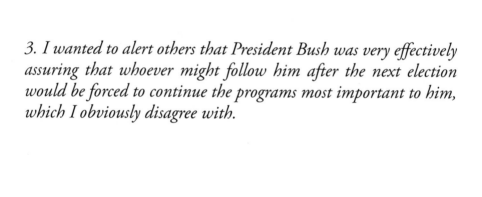

3. I wanted to alert others that President Bush was very effectively assuring that whoever might follow him after the next election would be forced to continue the programs most important to him, which I obviously disagree with.

Not a Lame Duck

When the voters put in a Democratic majority in the House and Senate they hoped to rein in President Bush. It didn't happen. He soon found that they would cave under pressure to where he essentially ignores them altogether. He is pushing forward as fast and as hard as he can to assure that his programs will continue no matter who is the next President. He is negotiating many treaties and trade agreements which will continue on long after his term is finished, such as:

1- He is negotiating a secret agreement with the President of Mexico to give $1.7 billion in military hardware, ostensibly to fight the drug trade, the funds to be taken from Iraq appropriations. Remember the Iran Contra deal. The beat goes on.

2-He is negotiating a missile base agreement with Poland. They are asking us to modernize their armed forces as compensation. Placing this base this close to Russia is not acceptable to Mr. Putin. He will take steps to keep it from becoming operational.

3-He is pushing for free trade agreements with S. Korea, Columbia and Chili, all of which in my opinion will continue to accelerate unemployment for American workers as the other agreements have done.

4-He is pushing the Iraq government to sign a long term agreement which will condone the permanent bases we have already built in their country. He will assure that we stay in perpetuity as we have in Japan, Korea and Germany.

5-He has just vetoed legislation to stop the CIA from using water boarding as an interview procedure. What must the rest of civilized states think about this? He is pushing hard to return to eavesdropping on all conversations without restrictions.

The above are only the ones I have made note of from the media. I am sure there are many more. His legacy will be long lived for sure.

March 13, 2008

4. This was just a short personal item relating to my hiking endeavors. I wanted the reader to know I had other interests other than changing the course of history.

Saddleback for Jack
Saturday, March 22, 2008

On a beautiful day for hiking, 54 enthusiastic friends joined together to celebrate Jack's accomplishment of completing the SAHC 400-Peak Award. The group included hiking friends from the past 15 years who turned out in force for this special occasion. We had a short break on the top of Blackett's Ridge for pictures and stories before starting towards Saddleback Peak. The cheering group lined the Saddleback route and formed a canopy arch with their hiking sticks to honor Jack as he strode past us and led us to the peak. We returned to the visitor center for a celebration party in a unique picnic area where Mike presented Jack with the 400-peak plaque. Thanks to everyone who helped with the party, and to all who brought the delicious food items. Special thanks to Sally's daughter for making the cake and decorating it with the 400-peak patch.

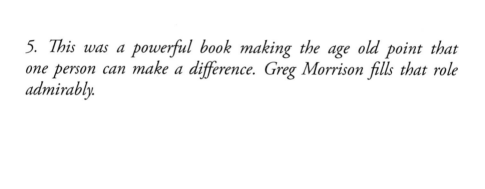

5. This was a powerful book making the age old point that one person can make a difference. Greg Morrison fills that role admirably.

Three Cups of Tea
By; Greg Morrison and David Oliver Relin

This book chronicles the life's work of Greg Morrison as he strove to provide educational opportunities for Muslim boys and girls in Pakistan and later Afghanistan. He mentions paying respects to Mother Teresa as she lay in state. His life parallels hers, in that he sacrificed all thought of personal gain for his family or himself on his striving to achieve bringing opportunities to children in remote mountain communities that had been ignored by their government. To this day he is continuing his work which has resulted in the building of 55 schools complete with books, supplies and teachers. The curriculum takes special care to not offend conservative religious leaders. All funds from donations by people he has convinced to support this effort. There is a website www. threecupsoftea.com. Check it out for more detailed information or make a tax deductible contribution to;

Central Asia Institute
P.O. Box 7209
Bozeman, Mt. 59771
406-585-7841
www.ikat.org

It is an inspiring book to read. I wish now to share several important thoughts as expressed in the book.

1-"Slowly and painfully, we are seeing worldwide acceptance of the fact that the wealthier and more technologically advanced countries have a responsibility to help the undeveloped ones, not only through a sense of charity, but also because only in this way can we ever hope to see any permanent peace and security for ourselves".

2-" I wish Westerners who misunderstand Muslims could have seen Syed Abbas in action that day," Mortenson says, "They would see that most people who practice the true teachings of Islam, even conservative mullahs like Syed Abbas, believe in peace and justice, not terror. Just as the Torah and Bible teach concern for those in distress, the Koran instructs all Muslims to make caring for widows, orphans, and refugees a priority".

3-While his efforts achieved positive results; we learn that our "friends" in the region, Saudi Arabia and Kuwait have spent millions constructing mosques in Pakistan and Afghanistan to provide impoverished children an Islamic education. They are referred to as Wahhabi madrassa. It is a conservative, fundamentalist offshoot of Sunni Islam and the official state religion of Saudi Arabia's rulers. Little in the way of education is provided in subjects such as math, science, history or geography. Many become recruits for the Taliban. The goal, it seems is to churn out generation after generation looking ahead to when armies of extremism will have the numbers to swarm over Pakistan and the rest of the Islamic world.

Why do our government leaders not recognize that Saudi Arabia is responsible for much of the continuing hatred of America? If a single individual like Greg Mortenson can make a positive contribution why doesn't our government offer assistance in countering this onslaught by our enemies? While our troops are fighting to restore order, the Saudis continue to stir the pot increasing the difficulty of our mission.

The above comments represent the most important issues that I gleaned from reading the book. I did not write in detail the story of his accomplishments. I leave that to you if interested. Purchase or go to your local library. Reading it is worth your time.

April 5, 2008

6. I wanted to point out the enormous waste of funds in both countries. I suggest a better way.

Wasteful Spending in Iraq and Afghanistan

Two recent news accounts have confirmed for me again that the wars being fought in Iraq and Afghanistan are for profit and greed, nothing else.

The first was in the Charlotte, N.C. paper the last week of March. It was an article by Jason Straziuso of the Associated Press that pointed out the absurdity of how funds are being spent. The main beneficiaries are five companies; KBR, the Louis Berber Group, Chemonics International, Bearing Point and Dynacorp International. The entire article was worthy of copying but the main point which stood out for me was the cost in high salaries, security and living arrangements. The average total is $250,000 each. The cost of an Afghan civil servant is $1,000. Wouldn't it make sense to employ 250 Afghans instead of one foreign national? At least then money would be flowing into the local economy instead of lining the pockets of corporate chiefs here at home.

The second was in the 4/5/08 edition of the Arizona Daily Star. The Pentagon has just renewed the contract with Blackwater. They have received $1.25 billion in federal business since 2000. Their employees also receive very high salaries. Their cost is probably the same as reported above. With more security agents in Iraq than our armed forces, we are paying far in excess of what our troops receive. It has been reported that many troops when their enlistment ends hire on with this company. Who could blame them? They would still be in harms way but at least they could better provide for their families.

In my opinion we have squandered billions in the last six years. When we overthrew Saddam, the Iraqi military and government employees were dumped. Without jobs or purpose many resorted to terrorism as their response. Had they been kept on they might have been eager to restore their country to normalcy. We will never know. In the meantime we continue to pour our treasury in wasteful endeavors as mentioned above without a chance of resolving the conflicts that continue on between warlords, different Muslim sects and terrorists who have infiltrated into the country.

April 5, 2008

7. *I list a number of instances where our government throws money to rescue organizations and people when the tide turns against them for whatever reason. I believe that if we want the freedom to pursue our dreams we must also accept failure should it occur. That is the essence of free enterprise and capitalism.*

THE RIGHT TO FAIL

A basic tenant of Capitalism is the right to fail. If each of us is to be allowed to pursue our ambitions without interference then we should accept the consequences if we are not successful. This has been blurred over the 200 years of existence of our country. We have come to expect sympathy and handouts instead. Should we become rich then in our greed we demand lower taxes on income whether it be in wages or profits from capital gains or dividends. Should we fail we demand to be rewarded for our failure. There are many examples of this. To name a few of recent times;

1- Just this week the U.S. Senate approved an addition $1 billion to cover losses from hurricanes Rita and Katrina. Included in this are grants of up to $150,000 per homeowner and accelerated depreciation for businesses. Sure the hurricanes were tragic, but I ask was there insurance available which was not purchased because it cost too much? Were the homes destroyed worth as much as $150,000? From the ones I have seen on television, I would conclude that they weren't. The billions that have been poured into this area for the most part were wasted. This is usually the case. The treasury is opened, vultures dive in to get as much as they can. Few dollars actually reach those most in need.

2- West coast salmon fishing industries. The salmon have been fished to near extinction. The government is considering a complete shut down this year in a desperate attempt to allow the species to rejuvenate itself. Those affected are fishermen, the tourist industry including accommodations, restaurants, supply stores and others. When business was booming they were happy to take their profits but now they are demanding handouts to cover their losses.

3- After the 9/11 tragedy, everyone it seems, living and working in the N.Y.C. area, requested and received generous handouts for lost income. I doubt if anything like proof was required.

4- One of my favorites I became aware of in 1987, when we went to Chapel Hill, N.C. to visit my daughter Amy on her spring break. We spent it on the outer banks. While driving along the narrow sand strips that are the outer banks we saw homes built on stilts, obviously very vulnerable. Hurricanes routinely strike this area with houses demolished. The homeowners could not buy insurance from private carriers but guess what our government does, which means that you and I on foot the bill.

5- The current implosion in the value of residences is another example. During recent years the value of homes escalated at an accelerated rate, far above realistic expectations. I remember an article about a doublewide manufactured home in California that sold for $1 million.

Families all across the country went on a binge buying and selling, making tremendous gains. Home ownership has always been considered a wise investment. Down payments of 20% were required. Proof of ability to pay the mortgage was essential. With that 20% cushion, a mild recession would still leave the mortgage less than the reduced value. When and how this reasonable standard was discarded I do not know nor am I willing to research, but it was. Millions purchased homes without any down payment at all under the stupid assumption that values would always increase. Sitting on a park bench watching my granddaughter play on a swing set I overheard a conversation between several young mothers about this person or another who had sold homes making hundreds of thousands in profit. People with mortgages took funds out to spend on other of life's enjoyments still with the same premise that their homes would continue to rise in value. Now that housing is losing value, they are demanding that the government bail them out. Congress, together with presidential candidates, is falling in line to do just that.

Bear Sterns is bailed out by the Federal Reserve to the tune of $28 billion in guarantees all the while the corporate chiefs continue to receive outlandish financial compensation. This was a first. They also pumped $20 billion into the banks to keep them solvent. In addition they have dramatically lowered interest rates. This has a very adverse result for people like me who withdrew from the stock market and put into fixed investments like money market. The interest is not enough to balance inflation. Do they care, of course not? Their only concern is for the huge corporations who created this mess in the first place.

As usual when I find an issue outrages me, I start pecking on my computer knowing full well that what I write or say will have no impact on the course of history. The books are stacked against the little guys of this world. Nonetheless I still insist that freedom to do as we wish includes the right to fail.

April 6, 2008

8. This article had to do with the upcoming Olympic Games scheduled to be held in China. There was an attempt to disrupt the games because of China absorbing Tibet into their territory. I felt this was a feeble effort that would only take away the joy of the athletes around the world that had trained and worked so hard to be a part of these games. China should have been penalized but this was not the way to do it. Fortunately the games proceeded without disruption.

Tibet-another perspective

The time for protests was when China attacked and conquered Tibet. The international community including our own government allowed it to happen without a murmur. In our case we didn't want to disrupt the flow of cheap toys, etc. to America.

There is falseness to the current turmoil. It was started to bring pressure on China as the Olympics nears. All it will do is irritate and take away from the joy of competition by the athletes and the spectators. President Carter denied our athletes from going to Moscow. He was wrong.

It was also wrong for China to take over this peaceful country. They should have felt the wrath of all peace loving nations. I would still hope that their sovereignty could be restored. There is little chance for that unless extreme financial pressure was brought to bear. In the interim, let the games begin.

April 11, 2008

9. Once again an entity is found responsible for the acts of a crazed person, as if enhanced security could have prevented the tragedy.

State of Virginia $11M Settlement with the families of those killed by Seung-Hui Cho at Virginia Tech

The wanton killing of students and faculty was a tragedy. I can understand the State deciding to cover medical costs for the victims that survived. I can't understand however how the State can be held liable for this tragedy.

We Americans are fortunate to live in a free country where we can come and go as we wish without checkpoints except of course for the ones established after 9/11, but that is a separate issue. It is unrealistic to hold a State or University liable for a random act by anyone possessing the means to kill as he did. Arming all of the faculty and student body and having armed guards roaming the campus would be outrageously expensive and dangerous in and of itself. How about shopping malls, theaters, restaurants, the list is endless. If someone is without fear of their own death that person cannot be stopped.

If a terrorist or some other crazed person kills, that is a tragedy but should not be grounds to sue any institution which has taken security as part of their responsibility.

For me, if a member of my family was killed in like manner and I was awarded money in compensation, I would immediately give every dollar to a worthy cause. Making a profit off of that death would be blood money.

April 11, 2008

10. I express my impatience that the initiative voted for a year ago had not been put into practice. I facetiously suggest that all illegal immigrants had left the State.

Employer Sanctions

We, the people of Arizona voted to place the burden on employers to curtail ILLEGAL immigration in the State. It went into effect 1/1/08 with penalties to be assessed beginning 4/1/08. This was deemed only fair. It gave the employers the time to purge their employment roles and also gave the State time to prepare to enforce the will of the majority.

I have searched the paper diligently and listened to nightly news to see if anything was happening. It is now April 14, 2008. I can only conclude that complete success has been achieved. All ILLEGALS have left for the other 49 States. Now, if those States would enact the same law we did, the problem would disappear. Special thanks to employers and State government for listening to the citizens and doing as asked. It makes my heart feel warm and fuzzy to realize how simple it really is to solve problems.

April 14, 2008

11. I ask the question, why was Governor Spitzer singled out by the FBI? He was listed as suspect #9. There was no mention of suspects' #1-8.

Eliot Spitzer

Have you ever wondered why the FBI was directed to search out and find the evidence that the Governor of N.Y. was hiring prostitutes for his personal pleasure? He was listed as #9. Have any of your investigative reporters ever checked to find out who were #8, #7 etc. I wonder who they were and if they were as important as he was. Was he such a threat to Corporate America that he needed to be cut down? If the FBI could track his infidelity why stop here. Why not continue down the list and punish the others as this man was. Without any personal knowledge I believe he was pursued as a special case to bring him down.

April 25, 2008

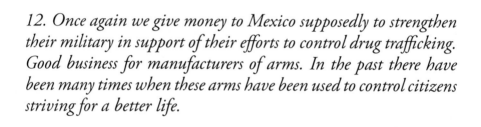

12. Once again we give money to Mexico supposedly to strengthen their military in support of their efforts to control drug trafficking. Good business for manufacturers of arms. In the past there have been many times when these arms have been used to control citizens striving for a better life.

One Billion in Military Aid to Mexico

President Bush is demanding the Congress approve $1 billion to provide military weapons and training for Mexico's military to better fight the drug cartels. You must toughen up and defy your Democratic leadership and vote against this demand. Enough is enough. We continue to flood many Central and South American countries with armament supposedly to combat drug dealers. Do you recall the Iran-Contra fiasco, the School of America training thugs who killed many poor peasants in San Salvador? The drug problem will never be solved by military might only by providing assistance here in this country to wean users from their addiction. Spend the money here not there.

May 1, 2008

13. This was written while Obama was engaged in a tight race with Hillary Clinton for the nomination as the Presidential candidate from the Democratic Party. To me it was depressing particularly in describing the election process.

The Audacity of Hope
By: Barack Obama

I have just finished reading this book. I felt I should since he is nearing his goal of receiving the required delegates to win the nomination as the Democratic Party's candidate for President of the United States. Prior to this I read a book about Hillary Clinton and also two books written by John McCain, the Republican candidate for the highest office.

I have been debating with myself on whether I should attempt to produce a review of the contents. Whatever thoughts that do emerge will probably not do justice to the author. He wrote about himself and his life history to date. He also describes in great detail the life of an elected official including his current position as Senator from the State of Illinois. He expresses anguish over the time spent away from his wife and his two daughters. There can be no doubt about the demands for his time particularly at this time while running for this new office. As sympathetic as I should be, at the same time I believe that when you aspire for lofty positions then you need to sacrifice all other interests in pursuing to the best of your ability the work before you that is important to your constituents.

There are chapters describing the differences between the two major parties, the Constitution, values, politics, opportunity, faith, race, family and the world beyond our borders. He is articulate and shows his intellect. There is a lot of detail to cover each subject. I tried my best to be interested but no matter how factual his writings might be I just couldn't, as I have with other political books I have read in recent years. After reading a few pages I found myself nodding off at which time I would put it down and do something else. I am really sorry to say this as I deeply admire the man and believe he could be the one to rekindle the spirits of Americans. Either my age is showing or I have saturated my brain with this stuff and it is rebelling. I will say this, I found him making many of the same points I did in my last book. To that end I am more in tune with his hopes and dreams than the other two. Those of you receiving this review I would hope would make the effort to read. Perhaps you are better equipped to read heavy material as is contained therein.

May 5, 2008

14. I continue to be alone in wanting an increase in gasoline taxes to invigorate buyers into demanding fuel efficient vehicles. No one ever agrees with me, still I believe I am right and they are wrong.

Governor Janet Napolitano calls for an increase
of 1 cent in the State sales tax

This is her idea to fund transit improvements. She and most all political incumbents either state or federal refuse to take the proper course of action. Raising the gas tax on the state and federal levels would accomplish three things. The higher cost would force auto manufacturers to find ways to increase mileage, would fund the transportation system by the users and help slow down global warming. I realize that this would be unpopular especially now with the cost so high. I have always believed that the beneficiaries of a service should be the ones to pay. If I had had my way we would have started gradually raising the gas tax 30 years ago to levels comparable with Europe. Had we done so we would not be in crisis mode as we now find ourselves?

May 8, 2008

15. How ridiculous is it to continue the costly minting of nickels and pennies when the metal content exceeds the value of those coins.

It doesn't make "cents" to me

Our great and wonderful Congress is pushing through legislation to resolve the problem that it costs more to make pennies and nickels than the face value of the coin. The value of copper and zinc is the problem they are addressing. A penny costs 1.2 cents and a nickel costs 7.7 cents. The proposal is to change the content to steel with a copper coating. If enacted a savings of over $100 million will be realized. While this is a solution, a far better solution is to stop minting pennies and nickels all together. The effect of inflation over the years has made their use impractical. All merchants would need to do is round up the cost of a product to the nearest dime. I am sure if this was done savings approaching $1 billion could be realized. The cost of the raw materials and cost of minting are huge.

Why do they continue to resist. Do they think Americans would be outraged at the loss of these nuisance coins? Are they afraid to admit that reckless spending policies over many decades have reduced the value of our currency? Coin collectors can amuse themselves for centuries until such time as they become extinct.

This is just another of my simplistic solutions to our many problems. I felt I had to write about it.

May 9, 2008

16. I offer a suggestion on how to resolve the health care issue.

Universal Health Care

Knowing that many countries provide health care to all citizens, this has been an issue I have pondered for some time. Last weekend I had an accident that raised my awareness due to my personal experience. On a hike I was leading, I slipped and in the process dislocated my right shoulder. It was extremely painful. Due to the distance from Tucson and other factors it took about five hours before I could be attended to. I have never experienced pain of this magnitude. I have insurance coverage by Medicare and my company so there was no financial concern. I was given excellent and thorough care. Had I been one of the reported 45 million other American citizens without coverage I can only imagine the financial tragedy that might entail. They would have been given the service but when the bills came due it could be devastating for them.

The companies in America pay most of the health care for employees and as in my case for retirees who are not contributing in producing goods and services as they once did. Our foreign competitors do not. How can they possibly compete with this albatross on their necks?

Those who refer to universal health care as being free are of course not correct. Nothing in life is free, but I do believe if the insurance companies need for profit was removed huge amounts could be removed from the process. Care not profit should be the goal. The current health provider companies could still handle paperwork required but the screening process to deny care would be removed. If I could make the decision, I would just expand the current Medicare program to cover all. Patients should be free to choose their doctor or hospital. The best doctors and hospitals would get the highest traffic. This competition should be an incentive to provide the best service. All bills to be paid by the Federal Government. Those with means would be free to add to this as their assets allowed.

Sadly none of the candidates for president will consider my suggestion. They will just tinker with the present profit motivated companies and if others are covered the cost will be astronautically huge.

May 25, 2008

17. This was an astonishing book. Its conclusion is that America could be energy independent but elected officials of both parties refuse to allow it to happen.

The Energy Non-Crisis
By Lindsey Williams

I learned of this book from an e-mail received which contained a video on this subject. It was intriguing enough for me to order a book from Amazon.com. I have just completed reading and now wish to share with others.

He is an ordained Baptist minister and an Alaskan. When the pipe line was just starting to be built in 1974 he requested and was eventually allowed to provide spiritual comfort and guidance to the men and women working on the project. He was not paid but was given executive status which allowed him to be privy to discussions by the oil men and to visit all sections of the construction areas. He does not profess knowledge of the oil business but in his mind was able to glean insight into the process.

Much of it tells of the hardships encountered and the roadblocks continually put in the way which impeded progress and inflated the original cost from an estimated $600 million to over $12 billion. The entire cost was borne by the consortium of oil companies called Alyeska. Specific instances to make his point were;

The detour of the road to Prudhoe Bay was stopped by the ecologists because of a nest of falcons. This would have delayed construction by a month so a by-pass was build at a cost of $2 million.

Toilets were provided at a cost of $10,000 each for remote locations. Refuse was incinerated rather than being disposed of by burying, all in the interest of protecting the tundra.

Permits were required for seemingly all aspects. Once granted some were withdrawn causing expensive delays until re-instated.

Fines of $10,000 or more were written for the smallest of incidences which made no sense to the author.

There were also problems with the unions. As an example he mentioned the need to replace a screw for a toilet paper dispenser. A carpenter, metal worker and laborer all refused on the grounds it was the work of a different craft. Eventually it was resolved by sending all three back together. Mr. Williams calculated the cost at $375.

All of the above were examples of the obstacles needed to be overcome by the oil companies as they fought the Federal and State Governments, unions, environmentalists and public opinion.

As the pipe line was nearing completion the government increased pressure by insisting the welds be re-inspected at enormous cost and placing additional burdens which the author felt were designed to keep delaying completion. It was as if our government leaders did not want the relief this additional oil could provide.

The above I found interesting but the major issue, if there is any credence in his writings, is his claim that our government since this project was started in the early seventies has kept free enterprise from doing its job of providing energy for America. He contends that there is oil on the North Slope exceeding that of Saudi Arabia. He mentions a find equal or greater than the pool presently providing two million barrels per day and that it could be easily extracted with minimal disruption to the environment or wildlife. This is at a location called Gull Island which is just off the shore at Prudhoe Bay. After discovery it was ordered to be capped off, not to be pursued. There is also the matter that natural gas by the trillions of cubic feet is returned to the ground instead of building a pipeline next to the current one and sending to America. He states that there are sufficient reserves to serve America for the next 200 years. He claims it could be completed in six months. I sincerely doubt the time schedule but not the fact that this gas could and should be used by America particularly now with costs going thru the roof effecting all households and business. All of this occurred during the presidency of Jimmie Carter. He opted for the more expensive option of a 3,000 mile pipeline thru Canada instead of 800 miles to Valdez. The great expense was more than the oil companies were willing to spend so to this day the gas is not being provided to America.

Those of you receiving this book review know that I am an envirmentalist and defender of wildlife and also that I believe in global warming. That being stated, I am also a realist. If, by using these resources which are in America,, we could eliminate sending exorbitant funds to OPEC which find there way to support terrorist cells, then we could at least diminish the loss of lives of our troops in this area of the world which is only of value because of their oil resources. The money saved could expand research into alternate forms of energy and speed up the timetable of reducing our carbon footprint.

Why an issue as important as this does not receive news coverage can be due to the fact that what he claims is bogus or everyone's negative feelings toward the oil industry or collusion on the part of news organizations with federal officials or something else. It does seem strange that if there was truth to what he claims that Congress hasn't acted. He experienced these events over 30 years ago. I am requesting that those interested receiving a copy of this letter check your own sources to see if there is a smoking gun here. I am also requesting that some of you take the time to listen to his speech. It lasts nearly one hour. He is persuasive. Go to;

Http://video.google.Com/videoplay?docid=33402746971670011147

After completing my book report I was prompted to search further for answers. I first went to Snopes.com. I entered North Slope Oil and found that while at first oil was shipped to Japan that now all of it goes to the U.S. with current production down to 720,000 Barrels/day from the original 2,000,000/day as Mr. Williams reported. Then I went to Google, again asking about North Slope Oil. There were over 100 articles to read. According to these reports the initial estimate for the pipe line was $900 million with a final cost of $7.7 billion. Mr. Williams had said $600 million and $12 billion. Regardless the cost was far greater than expected due I am sure to some of the points he raised. Other interesting information I gleaned;

For three decades the North Slope has produced 20% of domestic oil production in the U.S.

Taxation has produced $50 billion in 25 years.

In 1999 production fell to 850,000 barrels/day. It is projected that useful flows will continue for another 40 years if other sources are not discovered and put into production.

Vice President Spiral Agnew cast the deciding vote in the Senate in 1973 which authorized the construction of the pipe line. Score one for the Republicans on this one.

In an article called, "Sizing up oil in Alaska's North Slope," it was stated that currently 35 trillion cu .ft. of gas is available and that 50 billion barrels of oil and 200 trillion cu. ft of gas are in undiscovered deposits.

The U.S. consumes 22 trillion cu. ft. of gas per year. Mr. Williams's claim that the North Slope would take care of our needs for 200 years is off the chart.

To this day leases are being granted with some results.

I could find no reference to Gull Island but his claim is inconsistent with the fact that leases continue to be granted. The gas pipeline has not been constructed due to its high cost on the route chosen across Canada. I believe Mr. Williams was right on this one. The much shorter route paralleling the current oil line if approved would get the gas to us whereas it may never happen as currently planned.

I found this exercise to be extremely interesting. I will not explore further unless spurred on by some of you.

May 27, 2008

18. This book is for anyone truly interested in America's history. I learned so much I had never known. I highly recommend it to you.

Douglass
And
Lincoln
By: Paul Kendrick and Stephen Kendrick

This is a very informative book. I found it at the Tucson Public Library. It filled in a lot of blanks for me during the critical years of our civil war. I had known about Frederick Douglass but I was not aware of the great influence he had on President Lincoln.

He was born into slavery in Maryland, endured harsh treatment from his owners and at the age of 18 was finally able to escape and settle in New Bedford, Massachusetts with his wife Anna who he met in Baltimore. She had been freed and provided the funds to secure his freedom. He read everything he could get a hold of and developed oratory skills which he used everywhere he could reach an audience across the Northern States. He, of course, was an ardent abolitionist who could never be satisfied until the four million Negroes were released from slavery and allowed the advantages of citizenship equal with the white population. He lived a long life until 1895 and through all that time struggled to accomplish his goal without achieving it in total.

He was extremely disappointed with the incremental steps taken by President Lincoln. It was not because Lincoln abhorred slavery, as he did, but because of the tenuous situation of the Southern States breaking away after his election and before he even took office. His main goal always was to preserve the union. If that entailed a continuation of slavery he was willing to accept it. He would have tried to keep it from extending into the new Western States as they were formed with the idea that if contained then it would eventually die of its own accord. Once the Confederacy was established and war began again all of his efforts were directed to restore the country. One of Lincoln's first concerns was to keep the Border States from joining the Confederacy. They were Slave States. Any move to eliminate slavery could have lost them and the North would not have had the people or the resources to restore the Union.

Bit by bit as the war dragged on, the citizens in the North were able to accept incremental steps towards freeing the slaves. One of the first steps was to outlaw slavery in Washington, DC. This was another awakening for me as I did not know that slavery had existed in the North. Mr. Douglass deserves credit for continuing to speak and write. He finally came to understand Lincoln and became an ardent supporter. He met with the President on four separate occasions. He found Lincoln to be very open and doing all he could. Had the war been concluded before it did, with a settlement, it would be done with slavery still intact. In September 1862 Lincoln announced "The Emancipation Proclamation" which stated that effective 1/1/63, all those held in slavery within any State rebelling against the government would be "forever free." It was a temporary solution at best as the Border States were excluded and any that re-entered the union would have their right to slavery restored. It also authorized Negros to be admitted to the Armed Services. Thus, as weak as it was, it was a huge step forward, which Douglass realized was monumental in scope.

During the first years the Union Army would actually return escaped slaves to the Rebels. Finally, a regiment was formed in Massachusetts in February, 1863, the 54th. If you have seen the movie, "Glory" it depicted the plight of these Negro recruits as they trained and then fought so bravely at the battle for Fort Wagner, S.C. From this beginning with Douglass's urging more and more Negros enlisted, fought and died. It was now accepted that allowing slaves to enter the North accomplished two goals. The South was deprived of their labor and the North added those capable into the Army. As the war progressed finally Lincoln declared that all slaves who reached the Union lines and enlisted would be forever free. By the end of the war over 200,000 Negros were in uniform, roughly a fourth of the entire Army. Thirty Eight thousand gave their lives. If captured by the Rebels they were killed in brutal fashion. Lincoln threatened to retaliate in kind but could never do so.

On January 31, 1864, the House passed the 13th Amendment by the three fourths required. It would finally and completely eradicate slavery. There was no doubt that the States would quickly approve.

Slavery came to an end in Maryland on 11/1/1864. Douglass immediately returned to the State where he had been a slave, looking for and finding relatives. It was a joyous time.

Lincoln won re-election; the war was winding down but not over when he gave his inauguration speech. It lasted only seven minutes. It was as powerful as the Gettysburg Address, in my opinion. He referred to the fact that both sides prayed to the same God for victory. He stated, he believed that "American Slavery" was an offence to God. He said," God gives to both North and South, this terrible war, as the woe due to those by whom the offence came." He concluded with these powerful words," With malice toward none; with charity for all; with firmness in the right, as God gives us to see the right, let us strive on to finish the work we are in; to bind up the nation's wounds; to care for him who has borne the battle, and for his widow, and his orphan—to do all which may achieve and cherish a first, and a lasting peace, among ourselves, and with all nations." Douglass was overwhelmed. Even in his highest expectations, he had not imagined Lincoln's speech having this kind of power.

April 10th the war ended with General Lee surrendering to General Grant. Four nights later Lincoln was assassinated and with his death his fine words came to naught.

On April 14, 1876 there was a ceremony to dedicate a memorial, The Freedman's Monument, dedicated to the martyred President. It depicted President Lincoln with a gentle hand on the head of a freed slave. Douglass was the only speaker. He began bravely by telling the mostly white audience that Lincoln was first and foremost one of them, a white man, and that he would have sacrificed the blacks if necessary to preserve the union but he finished by saying, "We came to the conclusion that the hour and the man of our redemption had somehow met in the person of Abraham Lincoln. See this man. He was one of you and yet became Abraham Lincoln."

With the death of Lincoln his successor Johnson and the rest to follow in his lifetime did little to provide opportunity to the freed slaves. They were denied the right to own land, vote, have access to education and held down by every means possible. He died in 1895 with only a partial victory.

What is strange to me is that Negros were allowed to fight in the Civil War but never again until President Truman desegregated the Armed Services during the Korean War. It took Presidents Kennedy and Johnson to finally integrate the country. Their struggle for equality continues but great strides have been made. Frederick Douglass, I believe would be satisfied.

June 4, 2008

19. I was outraged that Ann Brown, the Editorial Page Editor, admonished the owners of television and radio to censure commentators who espoused thoughts she disagreed with. I asked if she would want the same done to her.

Censorship is promoted by the editorial staff of the Arizona Daily Star

Ann Brown, the Editorial Page Editor published a major editorial today (6/8/2008) entitled, "Hispanic group right to stand up to hatemongers". She attacks Mr. Lou Dobbs in particular and others including Glenn Beck, Bill O'Reilly and a local radio program on Tucson radio station 104.1-FM, "The Jon Justice Show". What she advocates is that the owners of the networks put pressure on their talk show hosts and censure their comments.

I certainly can agree that any group or individual can boycott as they wish. That is their right. I, in fact have a number of products, stores, stations and countries that I boycott. None of them are aware of my pitiful gesture, nonetheless I feel better for doing it and showing my concern.

What bothers me is the strident attack by the editor stating that Lou Dobbs has lied deliberately. I do not believe this for a minute. He may make a misstatement but I have heard him make a correction when brought to his attention. The truth of the matter is that illegal immigration is totally out of control and mostly from Mexico. You obviously have your mind made up but if you want to be considered an informed editor then you should read other points of view. I refer you specifically to a book entitled,"Mexifornia" by Victor Davis Hanson published in 2007. You will probably assume it is racist and hateful. I am half way thru reading it and I find he is very sensitive to the plight of illegals and how they are mistreated and cheated out of their hard earned wages by one and all.

Their only protection can come by having a viable foreign worker program to give them legal status to work in this country and be paid the going wage and pay all taxes accordingly as Americans must do, instead of cash payments which are the norm today. The policy of the Mexican Government is to export the lowest of their citizens, those with little education. In this way they defuse resentment and minimize the risk of rebellion for their continuing mistreatment in their own country.

How would you like it if the owner of the Star told you what to write in your editorials or worse read them before publishing and amending to their thinking? That is what you are asking CNN to do. Shame on you.

June 8, 2008

20. Another highly recommended book that should be read by any elected official with the responsibility to solve the growth of illegal immigration. It, as I state, is not a hate book but rather a clear the air type explaining what is happening and providing suggestions on how to correct.

MEXIFORNIA
By Victor Davis Hanson

This is a very important book to read by those in a position do solve the problems our country faces with the flood of illegal immigrants entering every day.

Mr. Hanson has the credentials to explore this subject. He is a life long resident of what was once a small town near Fresno, California. His family owns a small grape orchard and he holds a PhD and teaches Classics at the California State University at Fresno. He grew up with Mexican-Americans. He has them as nephews, nieces, sisters-in-law, and prospective sons-in-law as well as friends and neighbors.

This is not a hate book. It is a rational analysis of all the various factors involved in the process. He does strongly condemn the past and present government of Mexico for its lack of leadership in providing opportunities in Mexico for its citizens who are then forced to risk their lives trying to enter America so that they can better provide for their families left behind. It is estimated that $15 billion is sent back to Mexico every year. This is the greatest source of income even surpassing their oil industry. His research has shown that since 1990 the number of poor Mexican-Americans in America has climbed 52%, half of all births are illegitimate, half of all Hispanics do not graduate from high school, less than 10% nationwide have graduated from college with a bachelors degree.

When young Mexicans arrive they are exploited by all sorts of people including fellow Mexicans. It all starts with the Coyote cost to get here. He states most do hard work for cash at $10/hr. and most of that is sent home. They live frugally. Because they keep their cash on them they are sometimes robbed and there are all sorts of fringe players sucking their money from them. Once they reach the age of 45 the backbreaking work becomes more difficult and they become demoralized. It is no wonder that their children have no interest in following in their footsteps. Their children's collective lack of a good education often leads to crime as their way out.

He blames much of the education problems to misdirected efforts which detract from learning the basics. Instead many feel good courses are offered which tend to create in their minds a feeling of being exploited and discriminated against; all the while vast sums are being spent but wasted. The single greatest detriment is their lack of knowledge of English. Finally States are beginning to immerse them in learning English which he hopes over time will correct this problem.

He tries to make the distinction between America which is a melting pot and bi-lingual nations. Over our 200+ years of existence many different cultures have entered and been assimilated. Almost always with difficulty and resentment from those already here, but it was done. A bi-lingual society wherever found in the world has difficulty maintaining continuity. Until these Mexican immigrants master the English language they will never really enjoy the benefits of living in America. The other major theme he espouses is the lack of instruction about our history. If they do not learn of the leaders who created our unique form of government and those who fought and died in the many wars to preserve our freedom, how can you expect them to feel apart of it all. In the various ways used to teach them their Mexican heritage, they cling to a fantasy of how wonderful Mexico is when in reality their parents fled from there to create a better life for their children. He singles out La Raza teaching in colleges and universities that California is an utterly racist state and that only thru protest, agitation and violence can changes be made.

He paints a number of scenarios on where all this may end up, most of them unacceptable. The huge increase in illegal immigration has only occurred over the past 30 years. With leadership, it could be restored to the orderly process that was the norm before this time. He is hopeful that this will occur sooner rather than later.

Please understand that I cannot in this short review cover the content of this book. You must take the time yourself. I am positive if you do you will have a clearer understanding of the scope of the problem and possible solutions. We always seem to throw up our hands and give up. That is not the American way, is it?

I always feel compelled to add my own thoughts when reviewing some one else's work. Europe has open borders between countries that many times are smaller than our States. They do it by verifying legal status when applying for employment. We have the E-verify program which has proved its accuracy. Arizona requires employers to use it. Just this week President Bush signed an executive order making all contractors doing business for the Federal Government to use it as well. It has been reported that 69% of employers nationwide are now using it voluntarily. If this trend continues there will be no work for illegals and they will be forced to return home or fight for menial cash paying jobs. Of course there will be consequences as needed work will not get done. A verifiable guest worker program would fill the gap.

June 10, 2008

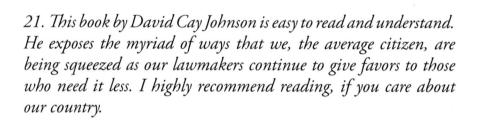

21. This book by David Cay Johnson is easy to read and understand. He exposes the myriad of ways that we, the average citizen, are being squeezed as our lawmakers continue to give favors to those who need it less. I highly recommend reading, if you care about our country.

FREE LUNCH
By David Cay Johnston
(Pulitzer Prize- Winning Reporter)

First off I need to tell you how I came to read this book. Some of you reading this letter remember my good friend and neighbor, Charlie McCarty from Des Moines. He had found out about it and asked his wife Judy to purchase it for him last year. Typical Charlie, he never opened it before his death on St. Pat's day this year. Judy called me a month ago stating that he had wanted to give it to me so she mailed it. I started reading as I prepared for my Alaska trip to visit my daughter and her family. I read it off and on during the visit and completed reading on the flight back to Tucson.

I have been reading and writing for a number of years now as I express my concern with the way our government muddles along seemingly helpless to affect positive steps to reverse the downward slide we are in. He includes the courts as well as all branches of government, Federal or State in his condemnation. Both political parties are to blame but the lion share after reading this book to confirm my own thoughts rests with the Republican Party of today which does not resemble the party I supported most of my adult life. I like most of my compatriots just wanted government out of the way so we could put our efforts towards our objective of making a quality product at a price the public would be willing to pay. We had plenty of competition with other companies doing the same and government only seemed interested in making it more difficult than it needed to be. In those years it was America vs. the world. We supported our employees, communities and did our patriotic duty for our country. That is all gone now. The only measure of success is the bottom line. The owners do all they can to find lower cost countries and ship jobs there without a second thought about the devastation left behind as a result of their decisions. Immediately some one of you will say that the owners are responsible to the stockholders and that their actions are not only justified but to do otherwise would be a dereliction of their responsibilities particularly now with international trade and internets making place of origin less important than before when America was king.

This is where this book opened my eyes to how our government particularly starting with Reagan gave a helping hand to the process by creating incentives to assist these new directions. He asked his famous question during the debate with Carter, "Are you better off now than you were four years ago". With an overwhelming victory he started off to reconstruct the relationship between the government of the United States and its economic system. The solution was to get government out of the way, to let business operate largely free from oversight. As I write this I can still relate to the heady feeling we had during these years. I was naïve enough to think only how this could improve our ability to compete. Never did I think that everything we worked so hard to achieve would disintegrate without our even knowing it was happening.

Now let's discuss the book.

This is an astounding book written with clarity. It was thoroughly researched. He gives names, dates and all relevant data to prove his contention that the rules have been skewed in favor of the rich to the detriment of the poor. The absolute greed is beyond comprehension. I am sure that most if not all of you who take my advice to read this book will have your eyes opened. Some of the issues like home alarm systems which cause law enforcement precious resources which should be put to better and more productive uses, or overly expensive title insurance which effects all home owners, I had never considered as issues.

He states," For a nation whose leaders frequently invoke their belief in the Bible, curious indeed is how the political rhetoric ignores the overriding duty of the New Testament to care for the poor".

There are 26 chapters in this book. While a number of issues are repeated, by and large each chapter covers a different aspect of the blatant give away programs and how the net affect has been so negative for most Americans. Major topics are the health care system, deregulation of utilities, unfair "free" trade with China and other countries, huge giveaways to major league sports, also to large companies like Cabela and Wal-Mart, the fact that there are now over 35,000 lobbyists in the Washington area descending on Congress daily striving to get an advantage and paying tribute for receiving those handouts. Each chapter is short and concise. You can read one and put the book down while you absorb the information. The sum total is staggering in the cumulative affect of one abuse piled upon another.

The most dangerous of all is the unregulated Hedge Fund Industry where for as little as $1 they can leverage $100. The large banks have bought into loaning them money in staggering amounts. A few years ago one fund failed. The Federal Reserve under Alan Greenspan bailed them out to save the banks. A failure of larger magnitude will surely bring this house of cards tumbling down affecting all of us.

Do you still recall Enron led by Ken Lay, President Bush's good buddy. Enron's manipulation of energy costs nearly bankrupted California and nearby States while compiling vast wealth for the few executives at the top.

Chapter 26 "Not Since Hoover" compares incomes of Americans since 1980. While gross national product has grown dramatically the distribution is heavily slanted towards the rich and very rich. The vast majority dipped from 1980 to 2005 when adjusted for inflation while income for the super rich has soared to astronomical levels. He believes that government policies put in place has created this disproportion more than mere chance. It is plain to me that neither party has the stomach to start whittling away at these disastrous policies. In my pessimism I can only see the downward spiral continuing until that fateful day not so far in the future when the ship sinks. On that day everyone will wonder how this great Democracy could destroy itself. Reading this book will at least educate you.

Perhaps change is possible, who knows, but not unless the issues are debated and decisions made to rectify the damage already done.

July 2, 2008

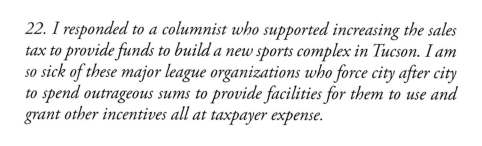

22. I responded to a columnist who supported increasing the sales tax to provide funds to build a new sports complex in Tucson. I am so sick of these major league organizations who force city after city to spend outrageous sums to provide facilities for them to use and grant other incentives all at taxpayer expense.

Dear Mr. Quinn,

I wrote the letter below the day that your Editor wrote promoting the sales tax to provide incentive to attract or keep Major League Baseball in Tucson. My response was quick and short as is required to be published. It was not published. Seeing your colorful and attention grabbing article in today's Star convinces me that the Star will continue to push until they convince voters to approve another increase in the sales tax to provide additional give away to professional sports.

It should be obvious by now that Tucsonans do not support professional sports to any large degree. Just review the lists of bowl games cancelled, hockey, baseball and softball teams that could not attract enough fans to survive. We do support the U of A teams and revel in their successes and cry when they lose. Lute Olson is a household name, adored until recently with the still unexplained debacle of the last season. Regardless the 15,000 seats will be filled with shouting, excited fans as we always do.

If you are a serious reporter read Free Lunch by David Cay Johnston. If you don't want to read it all then just read the chapter on professional sports and how they play one community off against another, always insisting on the taxpayers providing the funds so that they can continue their reckless ways of making huge profits while paying outlandish salaries to the players. The rush of players to the major league teams is making a mockery of college sports with low graduation rates and continual rebuilding as the players leave so quickly.

The new Yankee stadium is a clear example. They took a park used by families and gave it to Steinbrenner. The Seattle basketball team moving to Oklahoma and Glendale luring one of our teams to the Phoenix area or the fact that L.A does not have a professional football team I assume because the city has resisted their outlandish demands or moving the team from Cleveland to Baltimore. I could go on and on.

The owners have no loyalty to the city or State. The same is true for the coaches and players but of course they demand that the fans cheer them on and give them their money.

In my own little way I will continue to resist the Star's promotion of the sales tax.

Thanks for reading.
Jack B. Walters

From: Jack Walters <jackbwalters@yahoo.com>
Subject: Letter to the editor
To: "Arizona Daily Star" <letters@azstarnet.com>
Date: Wednesday, July 2, 2008, 11:46 AM

Your editorial 7/2/08 was just plain wrong.

Professional sports have been tapping the tax payers at an ever increasing rate for the past 40 years. Sales tax, bed tax, concessions on property tax and proceeds from sale of concessions, gifts of land, transportation roads built at no cost and on and on. They always pit one State, county or city against another, always threatening to move if they don't receive all they demand. Public officials cave in place by place only to find that the prize they seek still may move on if better offers are put forth.

The fact that the Arizona Senate did not approve new taxes may not have been due to deep thinking into this subject but rather they were distracted by the kooky gay marriage subject which seems to be more important than practical issues which affect us all.

If these fabulously rich baseball clubs want upgrades let them pay for them or move on. I for one could care less. What I do care about is making all of us pay for the privilege of them enjoying our pleasant winter, spring climate to practice.

July 2, 2008

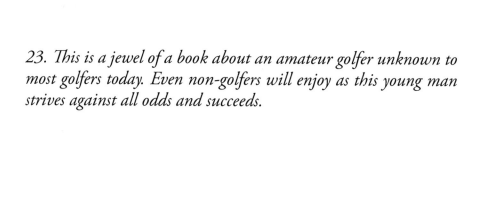

23. This is a jewel of a book about an amateur golfer unknown to most golfers today. Even non-golfers will enjoy as this young man strives against all odds and succeeds.

The King of Swings
By Michael Blaine
July 5, 2008

I got this book at the public library this week. Anyone who cares about golf should read it. It is the story about Johnny Goodman. He grew up in very poor circumstances in Omaha, Nebraska in the 20's. He beat Bobby Jones in the 1929 U.S. Amateur at Pebble Beach and went on to win the U.S. Open in 1933 and the U.S.Amateur in 1937. He was the last amateur to accomplish this feat.

I must confess I don't believe I ever heard of him before. It is a great rags to riches book and gives great details of the holes played win or lose. I really enjoyed reading it. You will too. Jack

24. Another excellent book written by David Cay Johnson. This one exposes the many ways in which the very rich are able to avoid paying their share of taxes needed to support government functions. It is outrageous that they are allowed to continue these practices without being stopped.

Perfectly Legal
By David Cay Johnston

This is the first book written by Mr. Johnston. His second entitled "Free Lunch" I read first. It was so powerful I just had to read this one as well. To tell you the truth, I am almost sorry I did. As much as the other book depressed me this one is even worse as far as exposing the myriad of giveaways authorized by our Federal Government. Both parties are responsible. He calls them the money parties since the money Congressmen receive from the rich is the life blood they need to continue in office.

Not all of the schemes used by the rich are authorized but they might as well be since for decades now the IRS has been crippled to where they do not have the resources to do their job allowing fabulous sums of money to escape taxation. Even those unfortunate to be caught are let off with a fine instead of jail time which they deserve. I will share a few of the most outrageous stories. He tells about a man named Nick Jesson. He founded a successful business in Southern California and became wealthy. A large portion of that wealth is due to his refusal to pay income tax for his company or his employees. He cites section 861 in the tax code which he claims that salaries paid by American owned companies are not taxable. Mr. Jesson was bold enough to taunt the IRS by publishing an article in The New York Times 11/19/2000 stating what he was doing and why. He even boasted that the IRS sent him a refund of $217,000 including interest for payments he had made for the years 1997 thru 1999, the years before he stopped paying altogether. Other business men are mentioned including Dick Celata who owns Kristi Tool Co. He boasts that since inception of his company in 1979 he has never paid income tax. In spite of the public announcement up to the time of publishing this book the IRS has quietly acquiesced to this charade.

Registering a company in the Cayman Islands, Bermuda or other Caribbean Islands has made it possible for billions of taxable income to not be collected. Tax shelter schemes are too numerous to list in this review but they exist and save their clients billions in taxes not paid. Companies have found ways to use the foreign tax credit to shift funds and assets around to minimize US taxes.

There are tax loopholes that allow executives to have their pensions guaranteed while the rank and file employees have seen theirs disappear. All of this legal because of laws passed by our elected officials.

Most of us don't even know about the earned income credit provision in the tax code. It applies to those making less than the minimum wage. For a family with two children making between $11,550 and $13,350 the maximum credit is $4,140. Certain Congressional leaders were so concerned about these poor people cheating that they insisted the IRS audit as many as possible. In 2001 there were eight times as many audits of these families as compared to those making over $100,000.

The alternative minimum tax was enacted many years ago to force the very rich to have to pay at least some tax. This was accomplished by taking away personal and other deductions. The problem for many non rich families today is that it was not indexed to inflation so as each year goes by more and more are forced into this alternate tax system. In 1995 about 414,000 paid this tax. By the year 2000 it was 1.3 million. It is estimated that by 2010 about 17 million families will pay. The problem is that it brings in so much money that Congress doesn't want to give it back. What it means to these families is that the Bush tax cuts are not available to them in spite of the rhetoric to the contrary.

Once again Mr. Johnston has exposed the hypocrisy of Congress and by naming names exposed those deeply involved with promoting processes that deprive our government of the money needed to support it. I know many of you will say whoopee and so do I with the wasteful easy ways they throw money around but the issue here is that those of us still honest and paying our taxes should not carry the burden while others escape tax free. This is a book all elected officials should read and then take the needed steps to correct.

I always feel the need to put my two cents into any discussion on topics such as this. Filing my income tax is fairly simple as it only consists of pension, social security, interest and withdrawals from my IRA plus small amounts of the like from my seven years working in Canada. Even so I resent the lengthy process of calculating how much social security should be taxed and I can't help noting the many deductions that other people are able to make either legally or otherwise. My point is that there is far too much written into the tax code. While I lived in Canada their form if I remember correctly consisted of four pages. Deductions were limited to yourself and family. No home mortgages or interest, furthermore thru an agreement with their Federal Government no Province tax form was required. All it consisted of was a line where your Federal tax was multiplied by a decimal number which meant that that portion of your taxes paid would be paid to the Province. Assuming that is still the case there is not much chance of cheating in Canada.

Read the book and discuss with like minded friends.

July 26, 2008

25. This book was written by Candice Millard. It chronicles an almost unbelievable journey down an unexplored river in South America. It would be astonishing as an adventure book. What increases the astonishment is that a President of the United States would be a part of the group.

The River of Doubt
Theodore Roosevelt's Darkest Journey
By: Candice Millard

What a man. His whole life he was fearless. He was a strong leader who was one of the most popular presidents in the nation's history. When President McKinley was assassinated early in his first term, Roosevelt became president. He was re-elected for a second term then retired. He became disenchanted with President Taft and ran against him as a third party candidate. He called his new party Bull Moose. While campaigning in Wisconsin he was shot in the chest. His eye glass case and manuscript in his pocked slowed the bullet but it lodged five inches in his chest. He insisted on giving his speech while exclaiming "It takes more than that to kill a bull moose". He did collect more votes than Taft but by splitting the Republican vote he gave the win to Woodrow Wilson.

This book is the story of a former President of the United States who after being defeated in 1912, did what he always did after suffering a defeat of any nature by going on an adventure that would tax him physically and included a measure of danger. This trip surpassed anything previously tried. He went on an expedition to discover and chart a river that had never been traveled before. It was called "The River of Doubt". After his return many so-called experts wrote critical reports questioning his accomplishment of discovering and charting an unknown river in the Amazon jungle of South America. Further expeditions to this area substantiated his claim.

There has never been another President to place himself in such a perilous situation. When we think of how our President's today are protected by the Secret Service it is inconceivable to think of this man placing himself, his son and the other members of the group in such danger in an area unexplored and without means of communication of any kind.

The author describes in great detail the many dangers including passing through territory populated by Indian tribes who had never encountered people other than similar tribes. Why they allowed the group to pass was never understood. Years later as more groups entered the area warfare resulted with many deaths on all sides. There were fish, snakes, reptiles and insects of all kinds that they encountered. There were deaths. Roosevelt himself came very close near the end and contemplated taking his own life to save the others as they were nearly out of food and any delay could have been fatal to them all. He didn't and pushed himself to the limit of his strength to keep going.

There were many rapids and waterfalls to portage around cutting through the dense underbrush which continually delayed progress and required incredible feats of strength. Near the end they were living on less than half rations. The author provides infinite detail of the jungle so that the reader can understand the rigorous demands on the participants. Details of the trip were from the diaries of Roosevelt and his son Kermit and the log of the commander of the expedition, Candido Mariana da Silva Rondon. The river trip was preceded by an overland journey from 12/12/1913 to 2/25/1914 which was difficult in and of itself. The river trip lasted two months from Feb.27, 1914 to April 26, 1914 when they reached a settlement. He had lost over fifty five lbs. and had a puncture wound in a leg that festered and had to be opened and drained without any pain medication.

Having completed this book I am in awe that President Roosevelt put himself in such a dangerous situation. It is well worth reading.

August 18, 2008

26. This report is of minor interest. I wrote it as I came to believe that the cameras being installed were to produce income, not to promote safety. I still believe that today.

Tucson Electronic Surveillance Cameras

I have been a proponent of using cameras to catch those who deliberately speed through an intersection when the yellow light is on and they are still not at the intersection or what is worse when the light has turned red before they even reach the intersection. I have stated that a large number of drivers in Tucson have little or no respect for driving speeds or lights which makes a drive in the city a potentially dangerous event.

What disturbs me is that the lights are catching people who are responsible citizens. I am aware of three incidents where friends received large fines and a day in class for being in the intersection while the light turns red. There are many reasons why this can happen. Just this week, while crossing Speedway on Wilmot Rd., there were two cars ahead of us. They stopped abruptly as the first car was turning into the lot for Bookman's and two young boys were walking in the drive. We were still on Speedway as the light turned. Don't know if there is a camera there but if there is, a ticket probably will be forthcoming.

It is my opinion that innocent, responsible drivers are being fined because the system is too finely tuned. An auto standing in the intersection for whatever reason does not present a risk to others. I believe this has become easy money for the city, just another "tax" on our people for the purpose of making money not improving safety, and that is just plain wrong.

Return to the job of catching those I described in my first paragraph which will make our roads safer. Quit solving the cities funding shortfall by this devious program.

August 24, 2008

27. I am obviously upset with the brazenness of the Big Three Automakers demanding bailout funds to reward them for mismanaging their companies.

General Motors demand for a low interest loan from Congress

It is hard to accept the brazen request of the corporate heads of this company to demand a bailout to be given by taxpayers so that they can more easily convert from the behemoths they have been producing and promoting for so many years now for sale to Americans.

This is the company that only a few years ago had designed and built an all electric car that was leased to several thousand Californians. They loved the car. Public officials started placing plug in facilities to assist. It was well designed and attractive. The battery life was not long but for commutes around the cities it was acceptable. It of course had no emissions which was extremely important to reduce the smog problem which is so severe in California. All that was needed was further research on extending battery life. General Motors was ahead of all other companies.

There was a documentary produced entitled, "Who Killed the Electric Car". It is quite evident that the executives in charge of the company at that time realized the impact on profit if these were mass produced. The drop in sales at auto parts stores alone would drastically decrease profit as there were few operating parts to drive this vehicle. General Motors corporate leaders together with the petroleum industry with the continuing aid of our federal government ended this program. The leases were revoked and all the cars were crushed to destroy all evidence that they had ever been produced.

Now they entice us with their new car to be released in a few years called the Volt. They proclaim it will go for 40 miles before the gasoline engine kicks in. It, of course, would be a gigantic step forward. In order to speed up development they want billions from the federal government in low interest loans.

While recognizing the importance of General Motors to our economy and the importance of providing well paying jobs to Americans in development and in the factories, I do not favor granting this bailout. This is not the same as when Lee Iacocca asked for a loan to save Chrysler. He was not responsible for their dilemma at the time. To his credit he paid back every penny loaned to his company and resurrected Chrysler to a profit making entity once more.

General Motors did not emulate foreign manufacturers with hybrid designs; instead they pushed the Humvee, huge pickup trucks and SUV's. Now they have been exposed for their deliberate delaying of the inevitable need to reduce dependence on foreign oil and the need to reduce emissions.

The rapid rise in the cost of oil caught them flatfooted. Americans have responded out of necessity by purchasing the most energy efficient transportation available. I have always believed that demanding increases in CAFÉ standards would not be necessary if the cost of fuel escalated. I am alone in believing that this wake up call, as devastating as it has been was necessary. What the Congress should do now is set a floor price and increase gasoline tax to keep it at a level price so that we don't return to craving the largest and most powerful autos as we did in the 80's. We cannot keep repeating this cycle which only benefits OPEC, Russia and Venezuela.

Either of the Presidential candidates and Congress will of course grant General Motors request regardless of what I may think. They bail out hedge funds, Bear Sterns, Freddie Mae and Fannie Mae, so why wouldn't they continue the trend. After all it is only we long suffering tax payers who are stuck with the bill while the corporate heads continue receiving gigantic salaries and benefits.

What I would support is making grants available to speed up research into battery research, the results of which to be made available to all producers here and abroad. After all, the whole world needs to reduce emissions. Just doing it here will not suffice.

Just another lost cause.

August 25, 2008

28. If you want to better understand life in Afghanistan living under Taliban government, this novel will help you.

A Thousand Splendid Suns
By; Khaled Hosseini

I purchased this book because on the cover it stated that it was a novel by the author of "The Kite Runner". That was a very powerful book describing life in Afghanistan the past 40 years. This new book parallels the same time period only from a different perspective. This was every bit as powerful as the other. I have also read, "Three Cups of Tea", which takes place in Pakistan. This is a true story whereas the others are fiction. I am willing to grant Mr. Hosseini that what he writes describing life during those decades reflects what actually happened.

Life in this country was relatively peaceful until the communists came to power followed by the invasion by Russia. A Muslim country but strict enforcement of Sharia law was not enforced. Some women wore burkas but not all. Some men had beards but not all. Some men had one wife, others had more than one. Men were the authority figures but cruelty was not rampant. Over one million Afghans were killed during the war. When the Soviets withdrew, factions vied for supremacy. This is when barbarous treatment of Afghans began. They had been united against the Soviets but not now. In September, 1996 the Taliban became the ruling party. That is when darkness descended on the land. Their strict interpretation of Muslim law was harshly administered. Page 248 lists the rules all were to obey. Pray five times per day, singing and dancing prohibited, men to have beards, girls forbidden from attending schools, women forbidden from working outside of their homes and to be attended at all times by a male family member, etc.

By 2002 the Taliban had been defeated by the coalition forces and some semblance of normalcy descended upon the land.

The book chronicles the story of two women and their lives during these years. Sometimes they enjoyed happiness but mostly sorrow. It is not a nice story. For me they were just the vehicle required to put people into these years so the reader could sense what it would have been like.

I do recommend reading particularly by people like me who try to make sense out of the world we live in today.

September 2, 2008

29. I really spent time researching the Internet comparing the way we fund elections as compared to other countries. My main thrust was to expose the power of Corporate and Labor groups to influence elections. In light of the recent Supreme Court decision opening the flood gates it is obvious I have lost. The only hope as I see it is to vote against any candidate receiving major financial support from these groups, whether an incumbent or a new candidate. My other suggestion is to mute all campaign interruptions of whatever program you are trying to enjoy.

There is only one answer

I have been struggling for a number of years now trying to find the answer to return our country to an election process that removes Corporations from contributing to candidates and political parties. I have read many books and articles including the two books written by David Cay Johnston entitled, Perfectly Legal and Free Lunch. I am firmly convinced that only by taking out of the election process the enormous funds required can sanity be restored. Billions are spent each election cycle and while more and more small givers have entered the process, big money is still what greases the wheels of Congress to enact legislation for their benefit. Not only are the politicians of all parties beholden to the rich, the lack of time to address major issues is just not there. The time spent raising money detracts from their ability to study, discuss, read and meet with others to find solutions for the many and sundry items on the agenda. How many times have we heard that massive pieces of legislation are voted on based on the advice of subordinates with the elected officials never reading what they are voting for? This is outrageous.

Congress recessed (8/1/08) for five weeks without agreement on legislation to resolve the energy crisis. Both presidential candidates were not there. Perhaps had they been consensus might have been reached. Why must everything important to our country, be put on hold waiting for the next election, after which it starts all over again with candidates competing for the next election without staying on the job and finding compromise solutions to our many problems. In my lifetime it was not always like this, FDR in particular stayed in Washington on the job. He didn't even campaign after his first two terms. He was needed to lead us to victory over the Axis powers. I am not even sure when it started to change. It was probably when television became so important with sets in every household.

There have always been lobbyists. I myself lobbied for my company, usually to prevent State government officials from enacting legislation detrimental to the well being of my factory in Des Moines. Prior to working in Des Moines it never occurred to me that this was something I should be concerned about. My full attention was in the factory. This all started to change, at least for me in the 70's as government started interfering with the manufacturing process. Year by year new laws and regulations were enacted, all of which detracted from our mission of making quality products the public would purchase. I did actually visit Washington on one occasion with other Iowa manufacturers. We were summarily kicked out of a Senator's office. I remember him stating that he had no time for us since we didn't support him in his re-election contest. He was a Democrat and we were all Republicans at the time. During that visit and others to State officials it never occurred to me that money should be handed over. I believed our message was logical and should be accepted on its merits alone. Perhaps that was true before but certainly not today. Those with the most to give have their ear, not the rest of us peons who are just concerned and are only making input because we care. We ask for consideration not for our personal benefit but for the good of all.

I have no illusions that writing this paper will have any influence on those in power. The most I can hope for is that others reading might discuss or share with others and in this way begin the thinking process on ways to resolve. To this end I have searched the internet asking how other countries conduct elections. I will share findings from several for comparison.

Canada

I received a very detailed response from Canada. The complete report can be found by using the web and going to;
http://www.elections.ca/content.asp?section=gen&document=index&dir=c es&lang=e&textonly=false
Canada has a parliamentary system. There are numerous parties. While the Conservative and Liberal parties are the largest, after most elections the party that wins the most districts usually doesn't have a clear majority, which means that the smaller parties are needed to pass legislation which gives them opportunities to add items from their agenda. The election cycle is 5 years but if a no confidence vote occurs then the government must dissolve. A new election is called usually 36 days after the election committee is ready.

Another aspect I like is that a candidate of the winning party with the most votes is declared the Prime Minister. Whereas in our country the candidates for President has in my opinion deteriorated into a very expensive beauty contest. We vote for a person instead of our own personal conviction.

I will now list pertinent items I gleaned from the report;

Contributions are tightly controlled.

Third party expenses are limited to $3,866/district and a total of $183,300 for all districts. This is in effect between April 1, 2008 & March 31, 2009. These numbers are usually revised upward based on inflation.

The limit for nomination expense is between $14,000 and $21,000 depending on the size of the district with an average of about $16,000.

Personal contribution limits are:

$1,100/year for a political party

$1,100/year for a district association, nominating contestants & party endorsed candidates

$1,100/year for independent candidates

$1,100/year for leadership contestants

I know all of these are confusing. In looking thru the list of donors I noticed that some people gave money to more than one candidate. The amounts are indexed to inflation.

The government encourages contributions and provides a tax credit of a max of $750 for contributions over $1,275.01, again indexed to inflation.

Candidates cannot receive gifts except from relatives or as a nominal expression of courtesy or protocol. This statement looked like a loophole to me. I tried for clarification but none was forthcoming.

As of 6/12/2007 all gifts over $500 must be reported while a candidate. Parties cannot transfer funds to candidates.

CORPORATIONS & TRADE UNIONS MAY NOT MAKE CONTRIBUTIONS TO POLITICAL ENTITIES.

During the 39th election, which was the most recent, the expense limits for political parties ranged from $68,158 endorsing one candidate to $18,278,279 for all 308 districts. Limits for candidates ranged from $62,210 to $106,290, again based on the size of the district.

REPORTING OF CONTRIBUTIONS IS MANDATORY

I found it interesting that the process has evolved over the life of the country I assume to keep it within reasonable control.

Of the following countries I will be reporting on, they are democracies with executive, legislative and judicial branches. In the interest of brevity I will only write about their election process. To check on other countries, you just google the name of the country and ask about their government. This will lead you to various web sites to find what you need.

Switzerland

When I started on this country I was excited. They have enjoyed being as close to a pure democracy as any country. The citizens with a petition drive can challenge a law passed by the parliament and overturn it or have it modified.

They are governed by a seven member executive council called The Swiss Federal Council. The leadership changes each year selected from the council membership. The members are selected based upon the largest percentage of votes received by a major party. It had included two each from the Free Democratic Party, the Social Democratic Party and the Christian Democratic People's Party plus one member from the Swiss People's Party. In the 2003 election the People's Party took one seat away from the Christian Democratic Party which normally would be OK except for the fact that there are no restrictions on financing elections and Peoples raised $17 million while the second largest raised $1.7 million. I realize that $17 million is chump change in America, but once it starts where will it end. There is consideration to control but as of now this is the way it is, which means to me that they are deteriorating. following our example with the party with the most income to invest increasing their control as they persuade the electoric to vote as the money dictates. I certainly hope this will be curtailed.

Australia

I was disappointed to learn that Corporations and Unions are allowed to contribute large sums to candidates and parties. In 2004-2005, the Labor Party raised $64.8 million from the corporate sector, while the Liberal Party contributed over $66 million. While again this pales to the huge amounts contributed in America, it is a disturbing trend. Hopefully they will adopt Canada's policy which prohibits corporations and unions from giving funds.

New Zealand

In this country there is an Electoral Commission which allocates funds and time for broadcast election advertising. In 2006 they made an allocation of $3.2 million which parties can use for radio or television advertising, along with 72 minutes for opening addresses and 30 minutes for closing addresses. This was the same as the previous year.

Parties cannot use their own funds although candidates are allowed $20,000. Further, broadcast advertising can only be used five weeks before Election Day.

Wow, can you imagine what a blessing this would be instead of the constant year round haranguing we put up with in America.

Conclusion

There is little reason for me to keep checking other countries. What I have gleaned above is that there are problems everywhere with corporate type gifts. Most of the countries listed control it to various degrees. Canada and New Zealand have the best systems as far as I am concerned. The others appear to be heading in the wrong direction. The one saving grace for them is the quickness of the election process.

America cannot continue spending billions each year with the debilitating effect it has on the efficiency of elected officials. Perhaps in a small way this effort of mine may prompt discussion leading to legislation to curb this obscene process and restore sanity. The campaign finance legislation pushed and passed through the effort of Senator McCain did not accomplish the objective. Another effort must be initiated, hopefully by the next Congress, whoever is in control. I will not be holding my breath as they will not considered it critical as I do.

September 5, 2008

30. This was another I worked hard on to bring to light how ridiculous the Primaries have become costing billions and seriously detracting from elected officials ability to concentrate on the important issues of the day. I offer suggestions on how to improve.

Election Primary is not working

I am writing this as a follow up article to the first entitled, "There is only one answer", and the theme of that one was to remove corporate money from politics. This one deals with the process itself which must be simplified.

We are nearly finished with this season's election process which began early last year and now has 60 days left, after which the process will start over again. It is like a perpetual motion machine; once you start it spinning it just keeps going, as if it had a life of its own.

A number of political entities jockeyed for position in the primary process realizing that their States voting citizens would be also ran votes while the real decisions were made earlier in the process. Michigan and Florida went against the Democratic Parties edict and moved their primaries forward only to find that their votes when finally recognized had been diminished so that they had no effect on the outcome.

I live in Arizona which is one of the last to vote. By that time the field has been winnowed down to two viable choices whereas when it all started there were eight Democrats and eight Republicans. The Democrats were; Joe Biden, Chris Dodd, John Edwards, Dennis Kucinich, Bill Richardson, Mike Gravel, Hillary Clinton and Barack Obama. On the Republican side were, Rudy Giuliani, Fred Thompson, Mitt Romney, Tom Tancredo, Duncan Hunter, Ron Paul, Mike Huckabee and John McCain.

It all starts in Iowa. I lived in Iowa from 1971 to 1993. I was active politically and did attend the Caucasus which chooses the candidates. I never felt good about it. To participate you go to a school or church auditorium and after preliminary instructions, head to an area assigned to a candidate. The total number attending dictates how many votes are needed to get a point count. Once settled in with those you can count on then you roam the place trying to get someone to change their vote and go for your candidate. Once it is concluded then it is announced which candidates received points. When these are added together with the other 99 counties then the results are reported. Why I did not respect the system is because it is usually held on what is usually a very cold February evening. This year it was moved forward to January 3rd. Who wants to be away from home for four hours and drive home on slippery streets and then try for a little sleep before heading to work the next day? The percentage of potential voters actually participating is very small, as I recall less than 10%. When I lived there it was a nearly lily white farm state with a large insurance industry, government and little else. No state could be less representative of America than Iowa. The candidates knowing how important it is to win the first state spend inordinate amounts of time traveling the state. Many, including I recall, John McCain visiting all 99 counties. They must grovel for votes by extolling the virtues of ethanol or they are dead meat.

Next comes New Hampshire, another must win state. Again, it is rural and mostly white, not at all representative of America as a whole. This is where it paid off for John McCain. He had lost in Iowa and was counted out but his town hall meeting process garnered affection for him. He won and the process continued, next to South Carolina and on and on until all states votes have been tallied.

My objection to the process is that these first states essentially decide who the finalists will be. A candidate who I might admire will have dropped out before my turn to vote and it angers me that I am not given the same opportunity as the states mentioned above.

How this came to be, I do not know. I do know that Iowa became the first state in the primary season in 1972. Party officials seem to think that it is cast in stone. If it began in 1972 then it could be changed for the next election. I haven't tried to research what the schedule was before 1972 but whatever it was it could not be more unfair than the current system. This is certainly a windfall for the state, millions of dollars are spent there and considerable media attention is focused on a state that most people could care less about. The same is true for the others. In fact dragging it out for such an extended length of time causes expenditures of billions before it is concluded.

Other countries have limits on campaigning time. In Canada all Provinces vote at the same time so in effect there is no primary just an election with the highest point count the winner of each district. They are not voting for a President. They vote for their representative. The party with the most votes then selects their leader. To illustrate this point, Prime Minister Stephen Harper announced that on Sunday, September 7, 2008, he plans to dissolve Parliament and call for early elections in hopes of strengthening his minorities hold on power. Voting will be done on October 14, 2008. Just imagine a voting process lasting five weeks whereas ours is an ongoing process seemingly without end.

If the process started in January of the election year I suppose we could live with it but it doesn't. I started seriously in 2007. If truth be told it started years before as candidates who lost before sometimes re-appear. This is a boon to all areas of news reporting; particularly television with their talking heads arguing in defense or opposition to candidates. Every word used by a candidate is dissected to search for its true meaning. I can't begin to imagine the revenues they receive from advertisers as well as the parties and candidates, probably in the billions. It certainly represents full time employment for correspondents traveling with the candidates. The states and communities also receive revenue as people flock to these locations whenever any action is occurring. I, of course believe all of this to be wasted funds which if available could certainly be put to better use. You can't turn on your set without your program being disrupted by a commercial most of which are negative in nature.

My suggestion to limit the time and increase fairness is to compress the time. Instead of January, let the voting begin in June of election year with all states voting at the same time. Allow the candidates to travel the country visiting all states if they wish to put out their message asking for support. A clear winner may not be produced so let the delegates to the conventions work it out as they used to do and select their candidate during their convention. There are probably many good reasons why this is a bad idea but using it as a starting point for discussion I am asking that dramatic changes be made for the good of us all.

September 8, 2008

31. I ridicule our Senator for spending all of his time and energy campaigning to become President while totally abdicating his responsibility as our Senator.

John McCain-Ready to Serve

The United States Senate has voted on issues 180 times so far this year. McCain voted 24 times for a percentage of 13%. Most of those occurred on two dates 2/12 & 3/13. He must have been campaigning nearby and stopped in to chat. Just Google John McCain voting record, it will show every vote he ever cast.

He likes to refer to his military service. If he was still in, his performance would be categorized as AWOL (absence without leave), a court martial offense usually punishable by prison time. I guess the good old boy's club does not have any rules like this.

I may be wrong but I have believed we were living in critical times requiring vigilance and leadership. I must be wrong or else John would have stayed on the job and exerted his will to resolve.

Our current President has taken more vacation time than any other in history so I guess the pattern is set. I am sure that after winning the election John will take a much deserved rest until sworn in next January.

Doesn't anyone but me detest the American election process?

September 14, 2008

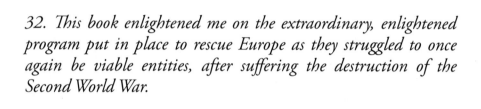

32. *This book enlightened me on the extraordinary, enlightened program put in place to rescue Europe as they struggled to once again be viable entities, after suffering the destruction of the Second World War.*

The
Most Noble
Adventure

The Marshall Plan and the Time
When America Helped Save Europe

By Greg Behrman

We are all creatures of our own past. I admit I am continually drawn back to my youth and the momentous happenings that occurred during that time. I found this book at Bookman's in Phoenix before my annual visit to Lockport, N.Y. to visit family and friends. For my 80th birthday I received gifts of books. They were all worthy of reading. I finally got around to this one. It was like saving the best for last. For those of you born after the war it might interest you if you are a student of history as I am, but unless you were alive it could not be as meaningful to you as it was to me.

In actual fact it filled in voids in my knowledge as the events described mainly occurred while I was serving in the army of occupation of Japan from 1947 to 1949. As a serviceman there were other things to occupy my mind and Europe was light years away from Japan. I witnessed the remarkable rebuilding of Japan. I was not aware of a massive infusion of funds from America. There may have been but other than basic food stuff right after the war it was my impression that it was the Japanese people who got the job done. At any rate little is said about Asia in this book. President Truman and George Marshall believed that if Europe could not be saved as a capitalistic nation that America would be cut off from trade with the continent and our growth stifled as a result. Europe was in ruins. The bombing and ground combat had destroyed most of the infrastructure: roads, bridges, rail roads, airports, utilities and housing. The people were starving and destitute. They were accepting communism as the way out of their misery and countries were on the verge of becoming communist.

Mr. Marshall gave a speech at Harvard University, June 5, 1947. In it after stating the dire condition of Europe, he proposed an aid plan of massive proportions to save it. This was like a shot heard around the world. On April 3, 1948 President Truman put his signature to the Foreign Assistance Act of

1948. He said, "This measure is Americas answer to the free world" and it was, "perhaps the greatest venture in constructive statesmanship that any nation has undertaken". It was forever referred to as The Marshall Plan in honor of this great man who conceived the idea and did what was needed to persuade the Congress to enact the legislation. It was a hard sell. America was in turmoil itself with millions of returning veterans and industry in a massive restructuring from military to civilian goods.

Most of the book describes the many problems encountered and gives praise to a number of men whose skill and devotion shepherded it through. What made it more difficult was that European leaders were called upon to work together as they had never done before. Marshall and the rest were determined that this not be run by Americans country by country but that Europeans had to do the hard work of building a structure which was within reason as far as our funds were concerned. To accomplish this, each country was forced to accept projects for the good of all, not just their own. The ultimate goal was to create a union of countries like America without trade barriers, with free flow of goods and people. Great progress was made but it was many years later that full unification took place. In 1992 the European Union was finally established. It is generally accepted that it would never have been accomplished had there not been a Marshall Plan.

This was a four year program. During that time over 13 billion dollars in goods and services were given to Europe. The author estimates that in today's dollars it would be equivalent to 100 billion dollars. It is important to take this into account so that the enormity of this transfer from Americans to Europeans can be appreciated. Never before or since has there been anything to compare with the generosity of our people.

At the beginning Russia and the satellite states under their control were invited to participate. Marshall Stalin would not allow it. It is stated in the book that Russia took from these countries as much as we gave.

Other interesting facts are;

The CIA (Central Intelligence Agency) was created by the passage of The National Security Act of 1947 to counter communist propaganda.

The Berlin airlift began June 27, 1948, when Stalin closed all land access to Berlin. His goal was to drive us out by starving the 2.4 million Germans living there. He gave in on May 12, 1949 which was the first day trucks began to roll. On the same day the new German Federated Republic was formed. The occupied zones by America, Britain and France were combined into a complete country. Since everyone was wary about Germany rising again as a threat the allies retained veto power should that be necessary. It was never used.

Towards the end of the program on April 4, 1949, NATO (North Atlantic Treaty Organization) was created for the mutual defense of the European nations. This began to drain funds from the economic program but the threat of Russian intervention was so grave there wasn't any other choice.

In June, 1950 North Korea invaded the South which by necessity diverted attention from Europe. President Truman directed General Macarthur to send troops to counter. Macarthur was successful but when the Chinese crossed the border our forces retreated and a stalemate ensued. Macarthur was relieved of command after a fundamental disagreement with his boss, President Truman. Macarthur felt we were fighting Europe's war in Asia but Truman and the European allies did not agree, neither wanted to squander the progress made by getting mired down in Asia. I guess we will never know who was right. I agreed with Macarthur but then my position and 10 cents at the time would only buy a cup of coffee.

I want to conclude with President Truman's inaugural address January 20, 1949. He was so happy with the results of the Marshall Plan that he proposed a new one. He said, "More than half the people of the world are living in conditions approaching misery." Beset by starvation and disease, "for the first time in history, humanity possesses the knowledge and skill to relieve the suffering of these people.' He proposed a "bold new program" of investment and technological transfer to provide resources, opportunity and hope to all the world's peoples. It was called The Point Four Program. It was an inspired speech but unfortunately was never enacted by Congress.

I feel I cannot finish this review without further reflecting on the contribution made for world peace by President Truman. It was recommended that the plan be called the Truman Plan instead of the Marshall Plan. He rejected the thought knowing that with his name attached partisan politics being what it was, that the plan would never be approved. From reading this book I must conclude that he was correct.

Others may disagree but there is no doubt in my mind that his decision to drop atomic bombs brought the war with Japan to an end. The deaths of thousands of our American troops and countless millions of Japanese would have ensued had the invasion been initiated. Having been there after the war I was convinced and other servicemen there at the time agreed on this point.

When you add up all that occurred during his presidency I am amazed at what he accomplished. Very few other presidents have contributed as much. He has never been credited as he should have been. People liked to belittle him since he was not an elitist from Harvard or Yale and did not have lineage tracing back to the beginning of our country.

A friend recently shared little known tidbits of information, which I will add to wrap this up. After President Eisenhower was inaugurated, Harry and Bess drove themselves home to Missouri without Secret Service protection. He had a military pension of $13,507.72 per year. Congress discovered that he was paying for his stamps and personally licking them. They granted him an allowance, and a retroactive pension of $25,000 per year. The only asset he had when he died was the house he lived in, which was in Independence, Missouri. The house was inherited from Bess's mother. Corporations offered high paying positions which he rejected, stating, "You don't want me. You want the office of the President, and that doesn't belong to me. It belongs to the American people and it's not for sale."

On May 17, 1971, Congress was prepared to award him the Medal of Honor on his 87th birthday. He refused to accept it, writing, "I don't consider that I have done anything which should be the reason for any such award, Congressional or otherwise."

I rest my case.

September 17, 2008

33. As you read this article, it will be painfully evident the depths of my disgust with our government giving billions to rescue those most responsible for creating the financial mess we are in. In the middle you will find that it was on President Clinton's watch that the Pandora lid was opened.

Financial Bailout

The Congress will relieve these financial barons of the burden of bad debt. Of that I am sure.

The only way it should be given is if all the executives in the top tier of management and their Boards of Directors be forced to return to their company all compensation including salary and bonuses received for the past decade, the time in which their outrageous, greedy pursuit of profit occurred. I want their corporate jets, penthouse apartments, golf club memberships, box tickets for professional sports and everything else that I have not mentioned. From what I have read some CEOs have already walked away with twenty or more million dollars. Others are protected with their golden parachutes worth millions more. How can we as a government or as citizens allow these predators to continue their fabulous life styles while the carnage goes on?

I continue to see AIG television adds nightly while this is going on. You would think they would have the decency to hold off while they are crawling on their bellies pleading, save me, save me.

On a previous occasion I wrote an article comparing the depression of 1928 to 2008. I concluded that the chips be allowed to fall and that in the end it would sort itself out and people would be able once again to afford purchasing a home. The costs had reached astronomical levels that any fool should realize could not be sustained. I guess that means that all those involved, in my opinion, were fools in spite of the huge profits that were made by those buying and selling. Eventually unless they had gotten out at the right time they were brought down.

How dare anyone compare this to the Chrysler loan given many years ago? Lee Iacocca paid back every cent borrowed plus interest. All the while the loan was in effect he received one dollar per year in salary. At the end an important segment of production was saved. What will we have with these robber barons; they will gobble up any entity weaker than themselves and create another monster that will have to be saved when it happens again.

Is anyone concerned about the other financial institutions that are not included in this bailout? While they struggle day by day to survive shouldn't they also be granted relief?

President Clinton was in office when banks, investment and insurance were allowed to merge. This is when it all became so confusing and uncontrollable. The Republican Party as a whole has been crusading for decades now to eliminate all vestiges of FDR's programs which were enacted to protect the little guys. Even during this crisis, McCain is touting privatizing Social Security, should that happen, this lifeline will disappear, while Wall Street gorges on the goodies placed at their disposal. Company pensions which people like me still live on are no longer available. People are forced into 401K's. How many billions have they lost this week? How many college funds have been ravaged? People like me dutifully put money aside to aid grandchildren as well as parents who put off things they might like to own or do for the sake of their children's futures.

What should really concern us is that this trillion dollar bailout is just the tip of the ice burg. Hedge funds that leverage one dollar against one hundred could tank at any time if they bet the wrong way. Bet is the proper term. These money making entities add nothing to the health of our country. They just suck the life blood out of the economy.

I really feel sorry for McCain, Obama and all the other people running for office. They have lofty goals. There will be nothing left to pay for their programs. The next administration will have its hands full trying to keep America solvent. When I think of the trillions in bonds owned by China and OPEC countries I shudder to think if we will not just be taken over as they purchase our assets at bargain basement costs.

Why do we as Americans allow this to happen? Are we so shallow that all we need is a can of beer and a football game to amuse us? My writing efforts have been a dismal effort. They have accomplished nothing of tangible benefit. That will not stop me from trying to make a difference. I am past the age of getting into the arena and taking them on but believe me I would enjoy it if I could.

September 20, 2008

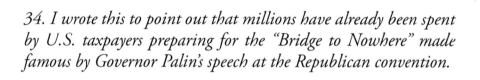

34. I wrote this to point out that millions have already been spent by U.S. taxpayers preparing for the "Bridge to Nowhere" made famous by Governor Palin's speech at the Republican convention.

A Bridge to Nowhere

On a CNN program last night there was a feature on this subject. Sarah Palin got applause when she stated at the convention that she had said "thanks but no thanks" to the Federal Government request for 25 million dollars to build the bridge. I take her at her word for this; however what she didn't say is that 28 million of federal dollars had already been spent on a road from the airport to where the bridge would connect. To be fair this had been granted before she took office. The design was complete and bidding awarded to construct. The program showed aerial views and on the ground of the finished highway that she allowed to proceed. There is no traffic on it. There are fewer than 100 people on the island. Most are there to support the airstrip. The city of Ketchikan is on the coast next to mountains. The island I assume was the easiest flat land available. It takes a ten minute ferry boat ride to reach the airport. I have to assume most users are tourists or fisher people who are not on a tight time schedule. Even when the bridge is finished a car ride could not be less than ten minutes.

I visit Alaska at least twice per year. They still allow studs in snow tires which causes severe grooving. There are many gravel roads in this Wilderness State. My point being that a prudent caretaker of the public's funds could put the 50 million dollars for needed road repair or paving.

I said I will take her at her word. She cannot now ask for federal dollars but with the windfall the State has enjoyed from the spike in oil revenues she will build the bridge with oil revenue.

Do you believe that this person should be given control over billions with this as an example of stewardship?

September 22, 2008

35. This is a long discourse of history beginning with FDR to the present day. Its purpose was to clarify good ideas from bad as we have limped along particularly the last 30 to40 years. The net effect of this bungling is that we as a nation are failing where the opposite could be true. Perhaps you might agree with me.

A History Lesson

As the politicians and media gurus debate ways to salvage our financial system, I believe it might be of some interest to show how it all came about. In the interest of brevity, I will of necessity not elaborate too deeply into each item but rather give this the broad brush treatment. I will leave it to you to fill in the voids.

Let us start during the depression. This followed closely on the heels of the flapper years where everyone had fun. Prosperity was here for all. Let the good times roll. The problem was that everyone thought they were betting on a sure thing. They bought stocks with high leverage, similar to today, with the idea that someone else would pay for bad guesses. It didn't work out that way. When the market started down, there was nothing to stop it and everyone lost, even those not in the market, as credit dried up banks defaulted with ordinary people losing their life savings. The government policy under President Hoover was to just sit back and wait, assuming it would correct itself. It didn't and couldn't because there was nothing to stop the downward cycle. Desperate times for our citizens.

The people overwhelmingly turned to F.D.R. and the recovery began. He was ready on day one and sent a flurry of bills to the majority Democratic Congress. In my book review of his life I enumerated many of them. I will not repeat except to state that his philosophy was to try something, anything, to kick start the recovery. Most programs worked, but some didn't. These he discarded. His overriding thought was that as people received a boost that they not be idle as they received it. He did not want a welfare state just a temporary fix until order could be restored. All of his programs were resisted fiercely by big business but he rejected their advice. Many of his programs clamped tight control on the big money men to keep them from taking control and repeating the cycle.

As the "New Deal" was winding down, along came WWII. This created a boost to industry that provided full employment. As the men became soldiers the women filled in admirably doing work that previously had been considered for men only.

After the war President Roosevelt in his continuing wisdom created the GI Bill of Rights which was made available to all veterans. There were loose guidelines. They could go to college, a trade school, take flying lessons or whatever. In my case tuition and books were paid for. I was also given

$75/ month in living expenses. When I graduated I had a minimal debt to pay. While this was going on, the need to find immediate employment for the millions of veterans was reduced, and an orderly restart ensued. For the next 16 years during the Presidencies of Truman, Eisenhower and Kennedy prosperity was enjoyed by all. As a government, there were surpluses created all the while great programs of assistance were enacted such as The Marshall Plan which saved Europe from going communist and planning the trip to the moon.

All of this stable progress was under Democratic controlled government. Eisenhower was not a true Republican, as were those that followed later, In fact he was courted by the Democratic Party to be on their ticket. He kept things under control. He was called a do nothing president. Sometimes, in my opinion, just letting the process work is the best course of action. We do, of course have him to thank for the interstate highway system. Also, he kept the military industrial types under control.

Lyndon Johnson the successor to Kennedy, with the Vietnam War and his Great Society Programs took the country deep in debt from which we have never recovered.

The Republican Party has done everything it could over the decades to wipe out all vestiges of New Deal programs, particularly those that kept controls on Corporations. They finally succeeded. The only programs left are federal deposit insurance and Social Security. If they are successful in privatizing Social Security, then this too will be gone for future generations.

In the interest of fairness I need to discuss government under President Carter. How it happened or why has always been a mystery to me. Unions were powerful and they were pushing their agendas. Regardless, this was the beginning of the downward cycle of manufacturing in America. We were treated as enemies of the people and many programs were enacted which made life intolerable for those of us on the line. We could no longer devote our full attention to making quality products at a price acceptable to the consumer. Unnecessary cost burdens were added all the while the resurgence of products from the new Europe were being unloaded on the docks at an ever increasing rate. Then came OPEC and the bottom fell out.

If you have read my political journey you can follow my flip flopping from one party to another. During these times I was as stanch a Republican as anyone could be as I resisted a government seemingly dedicated to destroying manufacturing in America.

This was when Reagan came to power with my full support and vote. He told us government was the problem and we agreed. What we didn't know was how swiftly he dismantled financial controls starting the trend to bigger and bigger companies with their strong influence on the market. I guess we didn't care as the Soviet Union was brought down and prosperity was abundant. There used to be programs to keep companies from having monopoly power. The definition, I guess, kept changing, as they have grown exponentially.

All of the administrations to follow both Republican and Democrat kept following this same course in effect allowing markets to operate as they saw fit without oversight. In addition American markets were opened to many other nations, which continued the demise of industry here at home. Legislation was enacted that provided incentive to ship jobs overseas without regard to American workers. Retail giants like Wal-Mart put pressure on industry to relocate in China or other low cost countries.

I want to pause to make a statement. The two decades after WWII were times of unparalled prosperity. I use Firestone as the litmus test. All through those years we expanded on a fast track basis. This was the reason someone like me could advance as quickly as I did. It seemed to start about the time I joined Firestone in 1954. Prior to then the plants had been monolific, solid unchanging, stable. The plant managers all had grey hair and had 30 or more years of service. Wages and benefits improved steadily. Factory workers owned their homes. Some had fishing boats and lake cabins or travel trailers. Nothing fancy, but satisfactory. A good life for them and a solid future for their children were possible. Farmers still lived on their land and worked their acreage. Those who were not of the white race were pulled along with high paying jobs becoming available. Under union contracts there was equal pay for equal work. They were still discriminated against and so were denied other of life's pleasures. That didn't start to change until passage of civil rights legislation in the 60's.

Without unions' health insurance, life insurance, pensions, good wages and vacation time would never have been possible. Even as a plant manager much of the benefits I received were built on the success of union bargaining. The problem of union demands starting in the mid 70's was that they could not or would not accept the reality that our cozy little club had been upset by boatloads of tires being shipped from Europe and Japan and sold in retail stores all across America. By the time they did it was too late. OPEC had already devastated the tire industry worldwide forcing all manufacturers to cut and cut deep. Chaos resulted. In the end American tire manufacturing was reduced by over 50%.

I find myself digressing. The point I want to make is that before the 70's life was good for working people on or off the farm. We were living in nice homes. We as men earned enough to allow mothers to stay at home providing solid support for our children. We were entering a phase that should have kept improving our life style with every passing decade. It didn't continue. Wages and salaries stagnated. Women were forced into the workforce not because they wanted to but because their income was required to maintain the life style we had come to enjoy. For decades now income for average Americans has stagnated. Consumer debt has been relied upon to fill the void that even working mothers could no longer fill. In desperation lottery tickets and gambling of other kinds were tried to provide instant relief, to no avail. Money spent this way only aggravated the situation. Gambling with stocks placed in 401K accounts proved disastrous when severe corrections have occurred including the current crisis. If the money is needed at those times then it was just tough luck.

Our government worships at the altar of bigness. Tax policies encourage huge farms driving average farmers off of their land. Deregulation has created huge conglomerates which lose touch with the basic premise of their mission with profit the only measure of success.

Where we go from here is anyone's guess. I am a pessimist. The money to be made is just more than patriotism can counter. Because of the outrageous request for a trillion dollar payout, the people responsible for creating this mess will still be in control being rescued by taxpayers when justice would have them behind bars after paying full restitution.

F.D.R. would be starting employment programs getting money directly into hands of people willing to work. I guess that is just too simple a concept in today's mega buck world. The fact that his programs worked is just not clear enough for Congress to understand.

I conclude this letter with the title of Lee Iacocca's latest book," Where have all the Leaders gone".

September 23, 2008

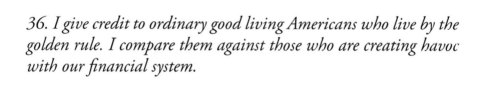

36. I give credit to ordinary good living Americans who live by the golden rule. I compare them against those who are creating havoc with our financial system.

Words to live by

Trying to make sense out of the current meltdown of our financial system is very difficult for those of us not directly involved. There are many theories and enough blame to share, which is enough for me to put that aside in my attempt to state what to date, I at least have not read or seen on a news report. I am referring to who is getting bailed out and the forgotten who are off on the sidelines wondering if in fact we were stupid or not savvy enough to get on the gravy train or just plain gullible.

Let's start with who will be blessed by the bailout and other legislation hurriedly being enacted as Congress prepares to resume campaigning.

American auto makers; Ford and G.M. They get 25 billion to retool. These companies did all they could to delay the inevitable. They built and pushed the least fuel efficient vehicles they could. G.M built electric cars a decade ago then pulled them back and crushed them to remove all traces that they ever existed. Both companies build fuel efficient cars in Europe. If they can do it there, why not here? Lastly is this not unfair to companies like Honda and Toyota who have spent billions on factories in America and as of now are the leaders in fuel efficiency?

The CEO's, their Corporate staffs and Board of Directors who are so highly paid, in my opinion realized that the government would have to bail them out. They get to keep all of their ill-gotten gains and for the most part will remain except for those who chose to take their marbles and go play somewhere else.

Those people who will claim to be duped but none the less should have realized that the homes and goodies being acquired could not possibly be kept without retaining a safety net to cover adverse circumstances. Interest only mortgages, credit cards maxed out. They acted totally irresponsible and in my view should just suffer the consequences and start over. No, no. They will stand in line and be saved.

Now let's get to the purpose of this letter. I want to talk about those who will not receive handouts except in a peripheral way, meaning that perhaps their assets will not be harmed anymore than they already have. These people in their naivete have tried to live their lives using religious principles such as;

Do unto others as you would have them do to you.

Neither a lender nor a borrower be.

A penny saved is a penny earned.

Don't covet your neighbor's possessions.

Live frugally within your means.

Don't be a financial burden to your parents or your children.

As parents, sacrifice as necessary to provide for the children in your household.

Support the charities and your house of worship as best you can.

Prepare yourself and your family in such a way as to be protected in case of emergency including health issues.

Have sufficient life insurance to cover the loss of the breadwinner's wages while your children are still of need.

These are the people who live in abodes that are within their financial capacity. They maintain a zero credit card balance. Should for any reason this not be possible, then they cut back on unnecessary expenditures until they can once again pay off their debts. They may go to Goodwill or other used clothing stores rather than shop the mall.

They don't succumb to the need to have everything their neighbor has.

They don't gamble or buy lottery tickets excessively trying to strike it rich. They don't play with the stock market. They instead look for stable investments which can provide gain with the least amount of risk.

These are the forgotten Americans who have lived by a moral code. All that they will receive is the self satisfaction that comes when you live responsibly.

September 28, 2008

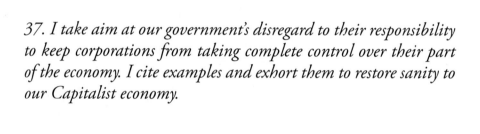

37. I take aim at our government's disregard to their responsibility to keep corporations from taking complete control over their part of the economy. I cite examples and exhort them to restore sanity to our Capitalist economy.

Monopoly

Webster's definition is:

An exclusive trading privilege; the sole right or power of selling something; or full command over the sale of it; ---the possession or assumption of anything to the exclusion of others; ---

I started this letter with the dictionary definition to put my comments in the context of its content. It is my opinion that a true democratic society must have safeguards to protect the citizens from some monolithic entity with sole power over some segment of services whether it is banking, energy, transportation, utilities or other. Our government used to protect us but now it seems nothing is too big for them to be concerned. For example the current financial crisis which has created three super banks; Citigroup, Bank of America Corp. and J.P. Morgan Chase &Co. Wachovia and Washington Mutual Inc. were themselves huge entities who both had been absorbing others until they purchased one poison pill too many and self destructed in the process.

The first order of business for the next Administration and Congress should be to start breaking up these monopolies into smaller and smaller segments at the same time assuring protection from takeover by foreign entities. It will do no good to downsize if the result is a takeover by an overseas entity. The last thing we should allow is foreign ownership of major business any more than has already occurred. As this process unfolds then protections must be installed to keep these companies honest. Excessive CEO pay and benefits should not be accepted as legitimate business expenses which reduce their tax liability. If the Boards want to grant excessive compensation, then so be it, but let them pay the taxes due. Regulations should be established and the agency enforcing them should be adequately funded and not interfered with by politics.

I can envision a final grouping of three or less energy companies controlling everything in the energy field. Make no mistake when alternative sources really start to make a difference they will be ready to buy in and profit from them as they have for decades now with oil.

If the American people don't wake up and demand change, and by that I am not parroting Obama's campaign slogan, I mean real change. If we go back to sleep, the status quo will remain in effect. Only the people can change things for the better. The millions who called or wrote killed the bailout bill. Nothing else did it, only the rage of the people. The same thing happened with the Amnesty Bill last year. It also was sailing through until the people spoke. We do have the power. We can come together and put pressure on them whether we are Democrats, Republicans, Independents or other political persuasion. What I am asking for transcends your political persuasion. Give it a try. Be part of the solution. Don't just sit at home crying, "Woe is me".

September 30, 2008

38. I chastise those risk takers who invested in exotic or growth funds and had a reality check as the stock market plunged to half its value, while I, who had abandoned the market, was spared the extreme loss suffered by many. I should not have written this, as what happened was not funny. It was tragic.

Put Your Money Where Your Mouth Is

I wrote an article on September 25, 2003 with the above as the title. If you look you can find it in my Last Angry Man book. I concluded it by stating as of that date, I had sold all remaining shares of stock and placed what little I had left in Government Bonds and Money Market Funds. From that date my returns have not been sufficient enough to cover inflation but in spite of this I persevered. In light of today's reality check perhaps I wasn't so stupid after all.

October 3, 2008

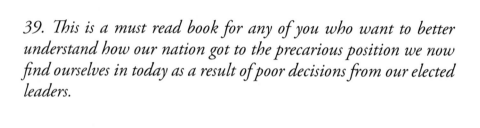

39. This is a must read book for any of you who want to better understand how our nation got to the precarious position we now find ourselves in today as a result of poor decisions from our elected leaders.

Bad Money
Reckless Finance, Failed Politics, and the Global
Crisis of American Capitalism
By Kevin Phillips

Once again I have ventured forth in my ongoing search for answers. I have broken my word before, but I hope I can keep it this time. I'm not going to purchase and read any more books like this. There are many on the market available but after reading this, I cannot conceive that other books could enlighten me more than this one did. The others I wrote book reports about. Some are in my "The Last Angry Man' book. Other more recent you can find by entering my web site at http://jackbwalters.blogspot.com

There is little to be gained by cramming more info into my brain since I am not in a position to do anything about it anyway. It doesn't take that long to read. Wouldn't you think that at least some elected officials would be curious enough to either read themselves or ask staff to read and then report or even call the author in for consultation? This and the other authors present blueprints to follow. Putting the various authors ideas into practice could start the healing process.

Mr. Phillips has enormous knowledge of the financial system and describes in great detail the names of the many types. I will not repeat them since I couldn't interpret them with any semblance of authority. Perhaps you can. I know many of you are very knowledgeable about the industry. You are the ones who should read to add to your understanding.

The main theme that he points to is the emergence of finance as the major industry in our Gross Domestic Product (page 31). He shows a chart that plots from 1950 to 2005.

| Manufacturing | 29.3% | 12.0% |
| Financial Services | 10.9% | 20.4% |

Since the Financial Services Modernization Act of 1999 dissolved old legal separations and constraints, commercial banking, insurance, securities, and mortgage lending have intertwined... They are for all purposes indivisible. (Page 32) is another chart from 1950 to 2005. It shows dramatic increases beginning in the 90's of mortgage backed securities.

For those in the stock market the years from 1982 to 2000 were heady. The Dow increased from 775 to 11,700. Most of this gain is due to unleashing the financial markets and loosening home purchasing requirements which created exaggerated increases in the value of property. The same house tripled or more in value creating the huge bubble which just had to burst at some point. That point as we all know is now.

He makes a strong point that since the 80's investment in physical assets like plant and equipment has diminished while the growth has been in debt. He blames debt for three setbacks. The first was the S&L mess in the 80's (cost 200 billion). The second was the rescue by the Fed of Citibank in 1989. This included a bailout of one billion provided by Saudi Prince Alwaleed bin Tawal. The third was the 1990's bailout of junk bonds by the Fed.

What all of this proved was that the reckless behavior of the CEO's could continue, realizing that the Fed's would bail them out when the boat started tipping over.

On page 41 he has a chart that shows the increase in debt from 1974 to 2006. The numbers are billions.

Domestic $258/$14,184

Total household $680/$12,873

Federal Government $358/$4,885

Total U.S. financial and nonfinancial debt $2,407/$44/744

Another chart on page 45 shows domestic financial debt as a percentage of U.S. GDP. It grew from 12% in 1969 to 107% in 2006.

The crash in 2002/2003 of Enron, WorldCom and Global Crossing were the direct result of President Reagan's deregulation of utilities. They were given free license to do as they pleased.

I have to add his comment on page 47 comparing WWII and Bush's recession that he inherited as he took office. "In a caricature of the U.S. government's WWII advice to the public to purchase war bonds, after 9/11 Americans were told to spend, charge away on their credit cards, or travel to help keep the private economy in a growth mode." What a charade.

Mortgage debt increased 102% from 2001 to 2007, which amounted to $5 trillion. This was the equivalent of 40% of U.S. GDP. He describes this as a lot of soap and air enough to create a huge bubble.

He claims that somewhere around 1988 the Federal Government chose finance as the most important part of our economy, to the detriment of manufacturing.

Stunning charts beginning on page 65 show the unbelievable growth in wealth by the top tier, staggering sums of as much as $85 billion in 1999. You can guess how they have increased in the next decade.

In his chapter entitled Bullnomics he proves that the CPI is continually understated by about 2%. This is done deliberately and of course has an impact on any compensation tied to the CPI including Social Security. I don't know about you but I have felt for a long time that the numbers being reported could not be true, another deceptive practice by your government.

I need to point out that this book was published in 2008 so it is not ancient history but an up to date analysis of current happenings. He predicted a drop in housing value of 15% to 20% this year. He refers to Hedge funds as "The Wild West", for their reckless behavior and the results thereof.

He devotes a whole chapter to oil. Nothing new here, if you don't understand what is happening then there is no sense in repeating.

Just two quotes from his chapter entitled The Politics of Evasion, "the entrenchment in Washington of a staggering array of interest groups, which has engendered a soulless political dynamic of perpetually raising and dispersing campaign funds; and the further, bipartisan trend toward what can only be called a politics of inheritance and dynasty". Sounds like something I wrote recently. He concludes this chapter with the following comment;

"That minimalist description certainly applies to the eight Republican years ending in 2008, during which global warming was denied, market forces and utopias were exalted, sober energy realpolitik was ignored, weapons of mass destruction and nuclear threats in Iraq and Iran were grossly exaggerated to support actual or possible energy-related invasions, and world opinion was offended. Over the last few decades, however, political ineptitude and misjudgment have been bipartisan phenomena. Energy, debt, and currency realpolitik has been missing among Democrats too, lost in their fund raising prowess and heavy petting with hedge funds; naiveté about pseudo- greening of Chinese, Indian, and Brazilian economic growth, and troubling faith in their own parties brand of job growth, and utopianomics".

In comparing our current status to the rise and fall of other dynasties like Spain, Holland and England, he finds similarities in that finance became dominant over real production, advances in science and arts. We don't have much time to put our house in order and at the present time I see a government putting out fires but not tackling the fundamentals that brought us to where we are today.

This is not a difficult book to read if you are willing to study as you go. How to get elected officials to read is the challenge.

October 7, 2008

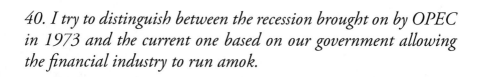

40. I try to distinguish between the recession brought on by OPEC in 1973 and the current one based on our government allowing the financial industry to run amok.

Recession 1973 vs. 2008

There is a difference.

The recession of 1973 was the direct result of OPEC raising their price for a barrel of oil from $4 to $40. This threw all of the developed nations into turmoil. This was due to the fact that America and other countries made the decision to preserve our own natural resources in favor of using cheap Arabian oil. You would think that leaders of these countries might anticipate that something like this could occur and develop backup plans to counter but alas that did not happen. I said at the time that by simply reversing the previous decision and instead of taxing local production to immediately heavily tax foreign crude. This would have added to the misery but within a short period of time positive results would have occurred. In the meantime short term relief could have been given to drivers, airlines, etc to ease the pain. Had we done this by now all nations would be free of dependency on OPEC. Their price would have dropped and all would be well. The difference I am trying to make is that a physical event triggered the recession.

The recession of 2008 is altogether different. This is the direct result of our government removing all controls from the financial markets and letting them go wild. Is there a week that goes by without you receiving another application for a credit card with spending limits in the thousands? After 9/11 we were urged to do our patriotic duty and rush to the mall to keep the Chinese factories in full gear. Where in my day a 20% down payment and a good paying job were required, now houses were given away assuming that ever increasing value would keep the ship afloat. Again, prudent government leaders should have anticipated that a downturn was possible and put stronger provisions into the buying process as a safeguard.

During this deregulation process multi millionaires were created. Good for them but not the rest of us since their gains were at the expense of common sense. They didn't care. Why should they, after all we are all one world aren't we? All our illustrious leaders need to do is restore sanity back into the system. Return to the rules that kept commercial separate from investment and insurance. The companies would need a grace period so they could divest without penalty and they should not be allowed to be swallowed up by foreign entities including countries like China who hold trillions of US dollars. Reverse the trend of huge companies buying up competitors and getting bigger, too big to fail as the current trillion dollar bailout attests to. Reform the tax system so that these huge corporations return to paying their fair share of taxes like we little people do. These are just random thoughts. The list is endless. The solutions are well known to economists. Bring them into the process. In order to remove temptation to fool with it create a commission to pull ideas together and present to the Congress with their only choice to vote yes or no like they do now when reviewing closing military bases.

Wouldn't it be great if one or both of the presidential candidates proposed solutions such as the above instead of stressing great and wonderful new programs as if the current crisis had never happened?

October 12, 2008

41. An article caught my attention about Christians and Jews living in Iraq. The numbers have been drastically reduced since our overthrow of Hussein. I point out that the "surge" wasn't of any benefit to them.

Surge didn't stop
Purge of non-Muslims

Re: the Oct.12 article "Attacks force terrified Christians to flee Iraq's third largest city."

The Star included an article on the persecution of Christians in Iraq's third largest city, Mosul. There have been threats, murders and bombings.

Christians have lived there for 1,800 years according to the article. An estimated 800,000 lived there before our invasion. In Mosul over half of the 20,000 who had lived there have fled.

The point I want to make is that before the invasion Christians and Jews had been living in relative peace. As bad as Saddam Hussein might have been, this was a fact. After nearly six years, not only is the oil not flowing as it should but a purge of all non-Muslims has accelerated. The "surge" didn't help them.

October 21, 2008

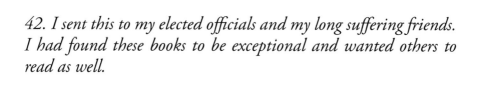

42. I sent this to my elected officials and my long suffering friends. I had found these books to be exceptional and wanted others to read as well.

Blueprint for Success

If I was wealthy enough I would purchase a copy of three books for every member of Congress. If they would read and then use as a guide it would not be long before our country would emerge from the financial nightmare we are suffering from. The books are; "Free Lunch" & "Perfectly Legal" by David Cay Johnson and "Bad Money" by Kevin Phillips. I urge you at least to read and then take the leadership in putting forth an agenda including the information gleaned from the work already done by these two outstanding patriotic researchers.

November 12, 2008

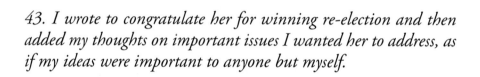

43. I wrote to congratulate her for winning re-election and then added my thoughts on important issues I wanted her to address, as if my ideas were important to anyone but myself.

Representative Gabrielle Giffords

Dear Mrs. Giffords,

Once again I am writing to you since writing to either of our Arizona State Senators is a lost cause. First I want to congratulate you on winning re-election. I believe you have made a great start on your political career. Who knows how far you will go. I wish you the best.

The purpose of this letter is to trigger thinking on your part of things of importance for the next administration to accomplish. You may only have a minor roll to play but on the other hand, you are there, and you are no longer a freshman. You have proven yourself. I would hope you would be bold and assert your thinking into the deliberation process rather than just vote as the leadership demands.

Call on the President to immediately release Border Patrol Officers Campion and Ramos from prison. They should be invited to the White House together with their families and be given a public apology for wrongful imprisonment. They were putting their lives at risk apprehending a proven drug smuggler. The morale and effectiveness of other agents would immediately improve and their effectiveness increase with the knowledge that they could pursue their purpose without fear of prosecution.

Suggest to the President to remove all political appointments from the agencies that were put there to dictate that the agencies follow the political agenda. With this accomplished then they will be free to discharge their responsibilities per their charter.

Suggest that the missile defense systems currently being installed in Poland be quietly dismantled removing this threat to Russia. I am sure he could receive some concession from them such as speeding up the destruction of nuclear weapons or improved accountability of them, anything to make the world a safer place. This has been totally wrong from the start. It is akin to Russia once again placing missiles in Cuba. We wouldn't allow that. Why would we think that Russia would just acquiesce?

Encourage the President to stop all offensive operations in Iraq and accelerate the drawdown of military personnel from that place. The current President is doing all he can to keep this from happening. President Obama contacting the Iraqi Government could keep them from signing the agreement.

Request that he demand the Chinese allow their currency to float which would immediately have the effect of removing their built in advantage by

40%. This could begin the return of less labor intensive industries to America. In addition request that he follow thru on his campaign pledge to eliminate the incentives to moving manufacturing off shore. Take action against countries like S. Korea who severely restrict imports of American goods while they are allowed free access to American markets.

Bailout- You voted against it, but then after changes, you voted for it. This was done in a panic mentality. Now we find that A.I.G. is asking for additional funds up to nearly $150 billion. We are also informed that some banks are using the windfall to purchase other banks, give bonuses and sponsor expensive outings as a reward for great service. I have also read that since the government now has ownership that we the taxpayers will be paying legal expenses to defend the ones who created this mess to begin with. Once you return you and others must address these problems and make necessary corrections.

The cause of the stupidity was the bundling together of home mortgages into salable packages. I don't know how, but if possible this should be outlawed. When a family purchases a home most need a mortgage. They get that through a local bank. The way it used to be is that bank held the mortgage until such time as it was paid off. It was then redeemed and kept as a keepsake or burned in a party. A mortgage should not be considered an object to sell. It should just be between the family and their bank.

Review all of President Bush's signing statements which allowed him to sign a bill and then ignore it.

I care about the environment, wildlife, etc. Return the Forest Service back to protecting the forests not exploiting them for profit. These must be preserved for future generations to enjoy.

I realize we must have American auto makers but I am reluctant to give them billions when the leadership of those companies refused to develop fuel efficient vehicles in this country. They know how. The vehicles sold in Europe are fuel efficient and a number of years ago they did have electric cars on the road. A management decision killed them in favor of gas guzzlers. Removing health care costs as part of a universal health care system like the rest of the civilized nations do would greatly reduce their costs and eliminate this unfair cost disadvantage.

There are so many opportunities to repair the damage of the past eight years. I wish you and your compatriots well. Enjoy yourself and revel in your accomplishments.

November 12, 2008

44. I try to make the argument that the "Big Three" don't deserve the handout that I fully realize will be granted either now or when the new administration takes over. It did happen early in 2009.

Proposed Bailout
for the Big Three Auto Makers

As I take the time to put these thoughts on paper I know full well that even if this handout is not approved by the Congress in session now, that it will be early next year when the new Congress and Administration take control. They will take the feel good position that once again some part of our economy is too big to fail. This is outrageous. Where will it end? The States and cities are lining up for easy money and there are store closings and bankruptcies occurring on an ever increasing frequency.

I will tell you how it will end. It will end when we are no longer able to sell bonds to other countries and become insolvent. I think we are closer than anyone realizes. They keep talking about income tax reductions and no new taxes when we are drowning in debt with interest on the national debt this year approaching $500 billion which is close to what is spent on our military, not including our two wars and space war costs. This is insane. Doesn't anybody in authority realize the dire predicament we are in? I don't disagree that it was the financial industry running wild that drove us over the cliff but that is another story for another time. This letter is about the auto industry.

There was an advertisement in the newspaper this week that Ford will be releasing their new "muscle" car in March. It is a supped up Mustang with a 350 hp. engine, with plenty of get up and go. Just what the public wants. One of the auto executives testifying before the Senate committee yesterday said just that. They built and sold cars wanted by the American consumers. The question is why do they want them? Could it be that advertising has been effective? After all, that is the purpose of advertising. If truth be known I would bet that consumers in Europe would also like them but with gas at up to $8 dollars per gallon they are wise enough to buy smaller more fuel efficient vehicles.

With the current cost of oil at $54/ barrel instead of $147 as it was a few months ago, what is to restrain American consumers from buying the large behemoths these companies like to sell? With a "happy days are here again" publicity campaign the big three may yet prove to be correct and those who have invested heavily in fuel efficient cars may find themselves outside, looking in, as happened in the 80's when oil costs were lowered.

To keep this from happening, the Federal gas tax should be one that lowers and increases depending on the cost of fuel so that costs level out at a high enough level to encourage us to make efficiency serious criteria when buying cars and trucks. That just makes too much sense. Instead billions will be appropriated for infrastructure projects that could and should come from the users. They talk about global warming but when push comes to shove they are out of the office that day. How sad. It is our fault. We demand everything as long as we don't have to pay for it.

The $25 billion already given to the big three to be used to speed up conversion will not be used for its intended purpose. It and the other $25 billion will just be used to keep them afloat until next year when either they will need more or they do indeed begin once again to sell the cars and trucks they are producing now.

Several years ago, Congress, in its ultimate wisdom gave huge financial incentives to buy large SUV's and Humvees. Then finally they gave a small incentive a year ago for 60,000 hybrids. This was gone before you knew it. If they were serious then it would have been open ended but since Detroit wasn't making them, this was used to buy Honda's, Toyota's and Nissans. These were all Japanese models. Even if produced in America by American workers, I am sure Congress was lobbied hard to not overdo it. What will Congress be doing for these companies to reward them for their engineering and development. It appears nothing. The same old story, bail out those who have not tried and punish those that have tried.

For decades the big three and the oil companies have done everything they could to keep from raising mileage. When California and other States tried they were successfully taken to court. G.M. in particular knows how. They had great all electric cars leased in California to enthusiastic users. They called them back and crushed them to wipe out any thought that they ever existed. They make models in Europe that sell. They just don't want to sell them here as their profit margin is so much greater with the larger cars and trucks.

Trust me, this is the old story repeating itself over again and I fear with the same result.

The greatest boon Congress could give, that would help all American producers compete in the world economy, would be enactment of universal health care like our competitor countries enjoy. Don't hold your breath.

In conclusion, the only answer is to let them sink or swim. Use Chapter 11 as the Airlines did. Most of them survived, some didn't. That is the way free enterprise works. Some make it, some don't. Free enterprise includes the right to fail. Under Chapter 11 they would be granted time to delay payments to creditors, re-negotiate contracts, drastically reduce executive compensation, eliminate corpulence such as personal jet aircraft that cost thousands per hour to use, and really get serious about redesign.

There is never any useful purpose for these letters I write except to relieve the pressure I create for myself and to leave a paper trail of what could have been accomplished but never was.

November 19, 2008

45. Once more I criticize extending unemployment benefit checks. It helps keep people afloat but in the end they just demand extensions which are approved promptly. Even today in 2010 extensions are being approved. This never happens to those lower paid persons on welfare. After a set period of time they must find work to support themselves. I keep asking the question "why".

Unemployment Benefits Extended

The US Senate has now approved up to an additional 13 weeks for the unemployed. The House overwhelmingly passed it and President Bush has agreed to sign it into law. It had previously been extended last June. The estimated cost of this latest addition is $5.7 Billion. The average weekly check will be $300/week nationwide. What this means to me is that millions will have received these checks for a year without ever leaving their home. They are not required to work for less than they were making before losing their job.

I have been opposed for a long time. I can't believe there are not jobs out there needing workers. After a reasonable amount of time they should be required to take any job available. I would go so far as to have their pay checks enhanced with a government check to bring them up to the $300 figure, but not working and receiving these funds is just plain wrong.

Everyone in the news media keeps referring to FDR and the programs he enacted. What they never say is that FDR insisted that the men leave their home and put in 8 hours of work in exchange for financial assistance. He did not want them to lose their work ethic. Americans then worked their way out of it. Today we just give handouts to everyone, business and labor. We cannot continue as a viable country if this is our only solution.

November 22, 2008

46. I am critical that the new administrations first order of business is to give a Trillion dollars to jump start the economy. It is not that something should be done but it is that the funds are going to support those who placed us in our current untenable position.

Trillion Dollar Stimulus Package

As I understand it the incoming Congress intends to enact legislation costing as much as a trillion dollars as soon as possible. The only thing I have heard mentioned so far is infrastructure. It appears that there are a number of projects ready to go with only lack of funding to prevent them from being accomplished. I support the idea but whenever funds are thrown at a project on a massive scale like this corruption and waste are sure to follow. It is like believing that the financial leaders could be allowed to operate without oversight since they would obviously exert their own restraint. In you have not been living in a cave, you should realize by now how that turned out.

Does the Congress believe that there are millions of skilled road and bridge workers just waiting for work? How many of those who have lost their jobs in the downturn of the economy, are skilled and capable of functioning efficiently? Are there not winter conditions existing in most of our States that would prohibit construction until Spring rolls around again? Of course they could start in Arizona and the other Southern States. I'm sure the Northern States would be happy to see the funds spent in the South.

Here are my thoughts on how to spend whatever money is appropriated.

Immediately raise gasoline taxes by $1.00 or $2.00/ gallon. Use the funds then for infrastructure instead of appropriated funds. Reimburse all owners of vehicles an amount comparable to this increased burden. These owners can then choose to put money into their pockets by purchasing the most gas efficient vehicles on the market. Let the people control the manufacturers. They will get immediate response instead of the song and dance routine of Congress with their CAFÉ standards and Detroit fighting them every step of the way.

Immediately cover the total cost of health care that manufacturers and business now must provide. This will remove this costly burden and improve the competitive standing vs. the rest of the world's businesses who do not pay these horrendous costs. Once this is done, then Congress can finish the job by providing health care to every American citizen.

Make funds available to any company in the business of producing energy, whether American owned or foreign, as long as the production is done in America by American citizens or immigrants in our country legally. Since the sun is the ultimate energy source this is where the emphasis should be placed. The urgency of becoming energy independent is so critical, I would also allow funds to be made available to any other feasible type to help us achieve independence as we move to solar as our final goal.

There are many other places where funds could be spent. I will not enumerate further other than to say that any money available should be shared equally with all Americans, rather than enrich those who have brought us to this sorry state of affairs, including those who purchased homes they could not afford or went deep into credit card debt to enrich their lifestyles. Try to remember that there are some Americans who have lived within their means. We don't understand the mentality of rewarding the wanton behavior of these people. We are citizens too. We are the forgotten ones. We do exist and we also vote.

December 9, 2008

2009

2009

Listing in order by date

1. I requested a response from my elected officials on the reasoning for not including Wachovia in the bailout program. To my understanding, they were right on the edge. Perhaps with a loan as provided to others they might have recovered as a viable institution. Letting Wells Fargo gobble them up just made a huge bank bigger. Where does this end?

Wells Fargo-Wachovia

I am writing requesting a response on why Wachovia was not included in the list of banks who were the beneficiaries of the multi- billion dollar stimulus package approved several months ago? I have read that 92 banks were included. Why was the only recourse for Wachovia to be bought out by Wells Fargo?

Why does my Federal Government seem to favor larger and larger corporations? I have read that some of the funds granted by these huge mega banks have been used to buy up smaller banks. I have no way to confirm but you should be able to. I have also read that bonuses and other benefits are still being paid out to the high officials of these corporations as if their performance deserved it.

These corporations that are too big to fail, in my opinion, are too big. Returning to the days of local banks would be far more preferable than these monstrosities which are so big they can create havoc with the economy as they have done and are continuing to do.

January 11, 2009

2. The slaughter of wolves in Alaska using aircraft and helicopters I feel is cruel and offensive. They are seriously disrupting the balance of nature.

Aerial Shooting of Wolves in Alaska

What is wrong with Alaskans? Why were they persuaded by Governor Palin to support aerial shooting of wolfs and their cubs? This is the person who felt qualified to be a heartbeat away from being President. With a mindset that she possesses, I can see her enthusiastically sending our troops into harms way at the slightest provocation. If she has so little regard for wildlife why should she care about human life?

I urge you to reverse this decision and demand that this barbaric practice be stopped before she can accelerate the killing, as I have been informed she is determined to do. Show the world and me that Alaskans are better than this.

January 12, 2009

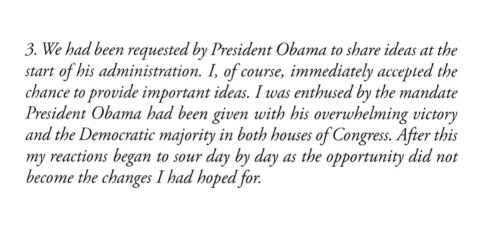

3. We had been requested by President Obama to share ideas at the start of his administration. I, of course, immediately accepted the chance to provide important ideas. I was enthused by the mandate President Obama had been given with his overwhelming victory and the Democratic majority in both houses of Congress. After this my reactions began to sour day by day as the opportunity did not become the changes I had hoped for.

Open Letter to President-elect Barack Obama

There have been many challenging times for our country in my lifetime. The first that I experienced was the last years of the great depression. Being born in 1928, all I have is a general feeling that something was not right. I can't actually claim that I experienced hunger because I don't believe I did. My father held down two jobs and my mother also earned income in addition to being a housewife. The second, of course was WWII. It started when I was 13, so my memory is still vivid. Then after that came the "police" action in Korea, the Cold War with Russia and by the war in Vietnam. All of these were disturbing times. People with means built bomb shelters, vast expenditures on armament took away funds that could have been used to better our people and others around the world. I won't say it was wrong, but usually after a war is ended there is a peace dividend. For all of the reasons listed above, no dividend was granted. Deficit spending increased year by year. We totally departed from any semblance of fiscal responsibility. When OPEC raised the cost of oil in 1973 from $4/barrel to $40/ barrel, the entire civilized world's economies were thrown into disarray. Being the manager of a tire factory, I and others close to me were punished by this event. Before things settled down my company was nearly ruined. The installation of missiles into Cuba could have resulted in nuclear war. Desert Storm was a successful war against Iraq supported by many countries including Arab States. Then came 9/11 and a whole new chapter opened. Now we were at war with an enemy without borders, an idea, not a country. A new war was started which will cost in excess of one trillion dollars. All the while this is going on; China grew exponentially taking millions of jobs and industries from our country, creating astounding negative balances of trade. President Reagan had a number of accomplishments but one of them created the beginning of our current financial crisis. That was de-regulation, which was right to do, but corporations didn't self police themselves as he had expected. As a result it has been deemed necessary to "bail" out huge mega banks to the tune of $700 billion dollars with more on the way.

This is where we find ourselves as President-elect Obama gets ready to accept the authority granted to him by the majority of voters in the last election. When he ran for this office, his theme was change. There were any number of issues he enumerated that were to be enacted, most of which I agreed with, which is why he received my vote. Now he will find that much of what he hoped to achieve will not be possible as he is forced to take our country deeper into debt, so deep

I question whether it will ever be possible to regain solvency. Printing more and more dollars merely cheapens the currency in circulation now. I know it is worthless for me to suggest a course of action because my thoughts will never be seen except by those few I am in contact with. Never the less I feel compelled to try.

We have all seen the oratorical skills Obama possesses. I still believe that deep down most of us are patriots who would sacrifice if they believed it was for the common good. This is his time. He could, if he is willing to take the risk, be one of our all time greatest presidents, but to accomplish this he must be bold and include the best ideas from both parties. McCain didn't lose on Republican ideas. He lost because the Republican Party has lost their ideals of limited, frugal government. I would like to see Obama incorporate the old time Republicanism with Democratic Party concerns for the working people and those in need. The following items are just a few thoughts to illustrate what I mean.

1- Reduce or eliminate entirely business tax for corporations and businesses in this country, at the same time increasing taxes on corporations doing business overseas. This would have the immediate effect of increasing jobs for Americans. The costs might balance out, but even if they didn't, putting our people back to work with decent wages would be a good expenditure of funds, far better than the billion dollar giveaways to huge corporations. They would be able to fend for themselves rather than ask for handouts. It would probably have to be fazed in gradually so as not to disrupt the system, but if corporations realized it was happening they would adjust. Think about it. Wouldn't this be better than the current policy of providing incentives to move our jobs offshore, and by this I don't only mean manufacturing jobs but also service jobs?

2- Take over the cost of health care so that this unfair burden is removed from American or foreign businesses operating in our country. This again would greatly increase our competitive ability to compete.

With the first two enacted, jobs would be created in all fields of endeavor not just road and bridge repair. Most needing employment do not possess the skill or physical ability to perform these construction jobs.

Instead of appropriations for infrastructure use increased gasoline taxes instead. Give a corresponding tax deduction other ways to counter this increased burden. Only in this way will we ever wean ourselves from oil dependency.

Drill, drill, drill. This was the slogan for the other party. It was not wrong. High taxes is the reason the oil companies have searched the world over when it is well known there are proven reserves in Alaska, N. Dakota, Colorado and off shore. Most people are upset with the exorbitant profits of the oil industry so this will be a tough sell. To compensate merely increase their foreign taxes as stated in #1 above. I, of course, support all other forms of energy still in the beginning stages of being successful. Proper financial incentives will get them going in a hurry. It could be exciting to watch.

Enact strict regulations to curb the abuses in finance that triggered the current crisis. Break up the mega corporations to smaller less disruptive and powerful than are in existence today.

Remove all political positions from the agencies so that they will be free as they were, before this last administration, to carry out their mission as they were legislated to do.

Remove all signing statements President Bush added to legislation passed which had the effect of stating he could ignore if he felt it would restrict him from doing what he wanted.

Reverse the many anti environmental directives Pres. Bush has enacted which are detrimental to preserving our wilderness, wildlife and environment. He has been pushing hard these last few months to reward the fat cats who benefit from degradation.

I could go on but when you try to do too much it all gets lost so I will end here except to say, please bring our troops home from Iraq and Afghanistan as soon as possible.

January 15, 2009

4. I wrote an article of protest against State officials for sanctioning a hunt near Globe, AZ by out of State hunters who belong to a group that fly around the country killing meat eating animals. It was published but only after the hunt had been completed and they had left, so the intended target never knew anyone was opposed.

Predator Hunt near Globe
This was published in the Arizona Daily Star

It was reported in the Star that this week hunters from all over the country are convening in Globe to kill what they refer to as "predators". The definition describes animals that eat meat as compared to others who graze. It is all legal and sanctioned by the Arizona Department of Game and Fish. In fact the hunt is specifically encouraged by Randy Rabb of Fish and Game. They are after foxes, coyotes, bobcats and mountain lions. These are all magnificent animals that I have encountered on hikes in our wilderness areas. I have never felt fear but did give them their space.

There are legitimate reasons for keeping the numbers within reason just as there are to keep deer from overpopulating. You can put me down as one of those wimps who cannot understand the joy of killing. Yes. I eat meat, which comes from slaughtered animals, but under most circumstances they were raised for this purpose and were killed humanly.

In my opinion the predators in this operation are those doing the killing and their cheerleaders from Game and Fish Led by Mr. Rabb. By the way Mr. Robb, if things ever get tough here, I am sure you could find employment in Sarah Palin's Alaska. She loves to kill using aircraft just as the San Carlos Tribe does.

February 9, 2009

5. In one short month I have become totally disillusioned with our new President together with the majority of Democrats in both Houses of Congress. I am completely at odds with their feeble efforts to revive our economy and putting people back to work making decent wages in the private sector.

I am disappointed

I have submitted a number of thoughts to our new President. You can read some of them by visiting my blog at http://jackbwalters.blogspot.com. It is predicted that tomorrow the stimulus package he is seeking will be approved.

Our government under President Bush foolishly gave the huge mega-banks nearly one trillion. There were no restrictions. Huge bonuses in the billions have been handed out to those responsible for the depression we find ourselves in. They have even had multi million dollar excursions for their high ranking management without regard to the fact that they were rescued by us, the taxpayers of this country. They continue buying up smaller banks and have not opened up credit to business or individuals, as they promised to do.

I have reviewed the content of the new bill to be enacted. I find little in it to create jobs in business and industry. There will be construction jobs and government jobs but not production. Most of it is to provide unemployment benefits for the entire year of 2009. No doubt that it will be extended for another year beginning in 2010. Let me be clear, I am not opposed to helping those in need, but what is missing is a clear cut program to put people back on the job. It is as if our leaders have given up, and have accepted that jobs already transferred to far away places like China and India, are gone forever. I refuse to accept this idea. I had hoped that President Obama would take bold steps on our behalf but so far he has not. Even his promise to pour funds into alternative energy are not included in this bill in large enough amounts to do anything other than make us believe we are finally serious about breaking away from OPEC and other energy rich countries who do not have our best interests at heart.

In the House version there is a statement about buying American products with this money. I can assure you that it will be stricken from the final document as being offensive to our trading partners and starting a trade war. If there is to be one, then bring it on. We cannot survive as a great power, if we become totally dependent on other countries to provide us goods and services at reasonable cost. We must take care of ourselves first and foremost. A recent example is Russia cutting off natural gas to the Ukraine and Europe in the middle of severe winter weather conditions.

Here is my take on the two parties who are debating this package.

The Republicans are asking for tax cuts, but not the right ones. They should be using whatever leverage they have to lower domestic business and industry taxes, not individual. To compensate they should increase taxes on business and industry that has been sent to other countries. They should be supportive of any program to remove medical costs from industry as the other industrial countries do to increase our competitiveness.

The Democrats are doing what they think is good business and that is to give away funds to as many voters as possible to assure their loyalty at the voting booth. They do not want us to make it on our own. They want us to be dependent on their largess to exist.

This will not work as there are still many of us who do not want handouts. We believe in the free enterprise system and only want government to take care of national interests and get out of our way. By this, I don't mean there should not be regulation of business. They have proven that left on their own they have created havoc. What I mean is they should do all they can to improve our competitiveness with the rest of the world.

Our leaders continue stressing the need to stimulate us to go shopping. I was disgusted when at the start of the Iraq war our previous President said the same thing. Should we once again forgo reason and spend till we are deeper in debt than we are now, all we will be doing is sending these dollars to places like China and creating jobs there.

The talking heads on television warn us about protectionism. They stress the need for free trade. What this does is shame us into believing that we must keep turning the other cheek and walking the extra mile. They are wrong, dead wrong. How many times must it be said that what we need is fair trade.

Here are a few examples for consideration. Airbus in France receives massive funds from their government. Because of this Boeing and our other aircraft manufacturers are put at a severe disadvantage. Places like Japan and Korea make it extremely difficult for our domestic auto manufacturers to bring their products into those counties. China provides low or no cost electricity to industry. They keep their people's wages extremely low, do not provide health benefits and have little or no concern about safety, pollution or anything else to improve the lives of their citizens. They maintain a 40% advantage by refusing to allow their currency to float. If Obama really cared he would take immediate steps by raising tariffs on Chinese goods until equity is achieved. Wal-Mart and its millions of customers would scream bloody murder. I say, so what.

We can, and we must bring business back home so that good paying jobs are once again available for willing workers. To spend nearly a trillion dollars and still not create a favorable business climate which could create real jobs is just plain wrong and in my humble opinion stupid.

February 9, 2009

6. My message here is that the Medical Profession should censor the Doctor who provided the wherewithal for these multiple births to occur.

Fertility Doctor is Responsible

Nadya Suleman is just a blatant example of millions of American's who find ways to stick taxpayers with paying for their lifestyles. The real culprit, and the one who should be held responsible, is the doctor that performed the implant procedure that resulted in the multiple births. He should lose his license for reckless and callous disregard of the consequences of a woman having the possibility of multiple births, a woman who already had six children, three of whom required support for disabilities and who was without financial support of her own.

The medical profession should be required to institute guidelines on who should be allowed to have implants.

The State of California should start legal proceedings against the doctor and the AMA for dereliction of responsible ethics. Let them pay for the support of these children, not the rest of us.

February 12, 2009

7. During the Bush Administration news media were not allowed to photograph caskets being unloaded of the remains of servicemen killed in Iraq or Afghanistan. My theory was that they didn't want the American viewers seeing the cost of the wars they had initiated. This was one issue I expected President Obama to correct. Instead he has stated that it is under advisement, so instead of correcting it will be delayed until who knows how long. That is wrong according to me.

Restriction from publishing photos of flag draped coffins arriving at Dover Air Force Base

President Bush ordered secrecy with regards to the remains of our service people who had given their lives for our country. He didn't want to have our citizens reminded of the true cost of war.

According to news I have read, the new administration is taking this under review. They have expressed concern about the families involved. This is just a cowardly way of not making a firm decision. No names are given to the press. They were just pictures of the coffins as they were unloaded with our flag respectfully draped over them.

What is it about leadership in our country today, where every decision is deferred until everyone has had a say. I can remember when it was said that President Clinton waited until poll results were in before deciding. When I was a Plant Manager I made decisions as quickly as possible. We didn't have time to waste. If the decision didn't solve the problem, then we would make another decision and move forward.

February 12, 2009

8. Dr. Bowman wrote a powerful letter as if he were the incoming President of the U.S. listing his priorities and goals. It was powerful, dynamic and in agreement with most of my thoughts that have been expressed in one manner or another for the past eight years. I'm sorry that I could not make it a part of this book.

February 12, 2009

I have e-mailed this paper to those on my list. I believe it is the most powerful message ever written on this subject. Last spring Dr. Bowman was in Tucson. I had the opportunity to go to his meeting, listen and talk to him. He is very inspiring. I agreed with 90% of what he said then and I agree the same amount about the contents of this paper. I only disagree on some of his examples like his comments about the atomic bombing of Japan. If he is right and we did not need to bomb, then that is blight on our leaders but from my perspective, the Japanese hard line military leaders had no intention of surrendering regardless of loss of life of their citizens. The conflict would have gone on with great loss of life to them and our soldiers.

I agree completely with his premise about "Just War". You may recall my poor efforts as expressed in my book in letters such as, " History- as it might have been", "We are all god's Children or no one is", The Impending War with Iraq" and others. I find similarities between what I have written and this.

I am mailing this to Pastors I know currently and others who were my pastor's years ago, with the thought as Dr. Bowman stresses, nothing will ever change unless our church leaders discuss this with their congregations. All I can do is write and hope somehow by osmosis something sticks.

This paper is long and requires concentrated reading to understand and become inspired. I hope you will take the time.

9. This theory should be the basis for our leaders whenever contemplating military actions.

Just War Theory
(From Mr. Brian McLaren's book," The Secret Message of Jesus")

The just war theory gave seven criteria for a "just war": a just cause for the war, a legitimate authority declaring war, a formal declaration of war, the goal being a return to peace, recourse to war only as a last resort, a reasonable hope of success, and means proportional to ends. The theory also presented three conditions for the prosecution of any war that met the seven criteria: noncombatants must not be targeted, prisoners must not be treated with cruelty, and international treaties and conventions must be respected. In this way, just war theory sought to balance competing demands: commitment to nonviolence in the way of Jesus and responsibility to protect neighbors from violence in the way of Jesus.

March 26, 2009

10. This book puts the life of Jesus into a clear document that illuminates the Scriptures as no other book I have read was able to do. I highly recommend it to you whether you are of the Christian faith or not. It also includes the "Just War Criteria" which is spelled out in the previous article.

The Secret Message of Jesus
Uncovering the truth that could change everything
By; Brian D. McLaren

Pastor Don Janssma recommended that I read this book. I had given him a 15 page article written by Dr. Bob Bowman. It condemned our practice of using war as the preferred way of resolving issues between nations and theologies. He articulated what he referred to as the just war theory. It immediately resonated with my current thinking and was so profound, I sent copies to other ministers I have encountered in my life's journey. I did this because he specifically requested that those in a position to spread the word as Pastors can, espouse this theory to try to convince their parishioners to refuse to support wars that do not conform to this concept. I had never heard of it before and credited Dr. Bowman with authorship. On page 155 of this book the theory is mentioned word for word and this book was published in 2006. Perhaps Mr. McLaren picked this up from some other source. The important thing is the theory itself not who first wrote it. I am attaching a copy as an addendum to this report for your information.

The author goes on to say that while the above idea is better than nothing, he believes we should strive to find peaceful solutions to settle conflicts between nations and theologies. He promotes spending ever larger sums from our budget by addressing the underlining causes of conflict.

This book provides a clinical review of the life of Jesus, his statements and actions. It is easily read and understood. He provides clarity where often there is confusion and interpretations that are not in accord with the truth. He points out where Christianity has strayed by taking phrases out of context rather than staying true to the whole body of scripture. He makes sense of the use of parables and the fearless way Jesus took on the reining authorities while breaking bread with prostitutes, tax collectors and other outcasts.

Of particular importance to me is the issue of life after death. Mr. McLaren points out that the kingdom referred to is also here and now as well as in our after life. Only recently have some evangelical churches broken away from the doctrine of subduing the earth to being concerned with saving our environment. We are required to do good works not just so we can be rewarded but because that is what is required of us. I have always believed that the promise of life after death has been used to calm people into accepting their fate, as miserable as it might be, while those with wealth enjoy life to the full, here and now.

I strongly recommend all who read this review to read this book. The last chapter asks that we join together in study groups sharing ideas, using the book as reference and then as a result put into practice what we believe should be done. I have not attempted to write portions from the book as I cannot agree with what to put in or leave out. The only way for you is to read it yourself.

I write this with trepidation as I do not consider myself to be qualified to make statements about Jesus since I have been a skeptic most of my life. The reason for that is that I cannot accept that people professing to be Christians live non-Christian lives. When self interest rises up they do what is best for themselves rather than the good of all.

What a wonderful world this would be if the principles of Jesus were adhered to. Perhaps hatred between peoples and other religions would cease so that all resources could be put to work improving instead of destroying. It is possible but only if we care enough to make it happen.

My above comments represent the feeling I have after reading. Yours may be different. I look forward to discussing with anyone who also reads this book.

March 26, 2009

11. I just cannot believe that the major countries cannot find the will to stop these pirates from capturing naval vessels of all types. Instead they pay millions in ransom for the release of ships and crews. Another clear example that our military forces are not functioning as they should without being under the thumb of civilian authority as our forces have been in Iraq since the war began.

Muslim Somali Pirates

We have had problems with Muslim pirates in our early history. It started when Jefferson was president and continued until Madison was president. The Navy and the Marines brought it to an end. The words in the Marine Hymn refer to it; "to the shores of Tripoli". I used google to find information about the Barbary Pirates. The point is that force was required to stop piracy. I am convinced that force must be used in sufficient magnitude to stop it today.

Some have told me that the problem should be handled by the ship owners. That is probably right. There seems to be reluctance on their part. Over $200 million in ransom has already been paid and hundreds of crew men are held hostage from many different nations, with no end in sight. If there is a maritime rule that prevents merchant vessels from protecting themselves then perhaps it will take action from the United Nations. I believe all nations suffering from these pirates should come together and present a unified coalition. America does not have to do it alone.

Putting armed personnel on board with permission to repel hijackers with force would put a stop to this in short order. A better response would be to strike their bases wiping out their pirate "navy" and destroying facilities used to generate these attacks.

They are vowing revenge against America for the killing of three pirates and capture of the fourth. In my opinion that opens the door for America to use our naval forces to point out the futility of them carrying out their threat. As long as easy money can be made what other than force can put a stop to this outrage.

It is embarrassing to see us humbled by a rag tag collection of bandits.

April 12, 2009

12. The article I write about was another clear indication to me of the lack of concern for US manufacturing.

Federal Government encourages expansion of jobs overseas

In writing about this subject, I feel I am aping a broken record as I have railed against our government before for continuing to create a favorable climate for American business to move jobs out of our country. An article in the Arizona Daily Star on 4/9/09 got my attention. The title was," Now More Than Ever, Lobbying Payoff Is Huge". There were a number of examples. The one I am zeroing in on is where the lobbyists were able to convince our "leaders" in 2004 to push through a one time tax holiday on profits earned abroad. The lobbying expense was $282.7 million. The savings was about $100 billion which resulted in a 22,000% return on investment. Most of these savings were given to Pfizer, Merck, IBM, Hewlett- Packard and Johnson and Johnson. In 2004 the Republicans had total control so when they cry crocodile tears take it with a grain of salt. I really don't expect anything better with Democrats in charge.

You can't fault these companies from seeking improved profit but you can blame the Congress and Administration from failing to protect American jobs by continuing to make it more profitable to move jobs offshore. We are not talking about lower foreign wages or better quality workmanship, we are talking about our own government making it difficult to produce in our country by having high business tax rates here at home and lower tax rates for American companies operating off shore.

Tomorrow is tax day. Across the country people are organizing protests of high taxes by using tea bags to get government's attention. It will be to no avail, as government will take it in stride and when the rallies are over, return to what they do best and that is to serve the interests of big business and foreign countries and continue to ignore American workers. All our workers can expect is balm in the form of unemployment compensation, temporary health cost relief and other giveaways, but not a new climate where real jobs can be created so Americans can feel proud of their support for their families and not the debilitating situation of living off the dole.

April 14, 2009

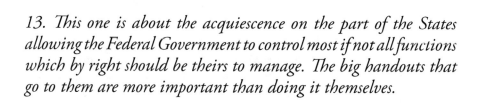

13. This one is about the acquiescence on the part of the States allowing the Federal Government to control most if not all functions which by right should be theirs to manage. The big handouts that go to them are more important than doing it themselves.

Federal Government Usurping States Rights

State Governments over the years have acquiesced by giving authority to the Federal government the right to interfere in States business. The writers of the Constitution clearly never had this in mind when it was approved. The Federal Governments authority was clearly defined.

I decided to put thoughts to paper after listening to the Governor of Texas yesterday rail at the loss of authority and proposing creating a Commonwealth separate and apart from the USA. This of course will not happen but what I hope it will do is energize State elected officials to begin to fight back with the positive result of curbing the abuses.

The reason it happened is quite simple. Only the Federal Government can print money. Most States have constitutional provisions which demands balanced budgets. The Feds have used the power of the purse to demand adherence to their requirements. There are myriad of examples. In the current stimulus package the States must use the funds provided as dictated. This is why the Texas Governor and other Republican Governors are protesting. The problem with this protest is that they are making their protest political, trying to denigrate President Obama's program to score points with the electorate. Just once wouldn't it be nice, if the countries good as a whole was the driving force, not partisan politics. Oh well, don't hold your breath. Politics it seems is the life force that is all important. Sorry, I digress from my subject.

Transportation is another. The Feds don't just allocate funds based on population or other criteria. They provide a huge bureaucracy to oversee and control how the States spend the funds. No Child Left Behind is a huge multi billion dollar bureaucracy that requires tabulation of results from the time children enter the school system until they graduate or drop out. This one in particular offends me. All school districts across America are making painful decisions to lay off teachers because of shortfalls in tax revenues. (This would be the first program to be cut if it were up to me.) What good are records if students are being deprived of the instruction necessary to develop? The only reason it exists is because of the funds provided.

I could go on and on but to what use? The Governors, together with their Legislators, must join forces to stop it. It can be done. Think of the costs that could be saved.

April 16, 2009

14. President Obama goes back on his campaign pledge to review NAFTA and CAFTA agreements after being chastised by South American leaders. It seems as each month goes by another pledge is ignored. I am now more than discouraged, I am irate.

Wall Street Journal Editorial-4/24/09

It was reported with glee that President Obama announced quietly on Monday that he was repudiating a campaign promise and would not press for new labor and environmental regulations in the NAFTA agreement.

Supposedly he was rebuked at the Summit of the Americas last weekend. Then the report went on to question his willingness to spend political capital to defeat protectionists in Congress.

In my mind this is a betrayal of his pledge to the American workers who only want a level playing field. I can remember Obama lauding the American worker during his campaign. When it comes time to put up or shut up he does that latter.

He can give billions to the capitalistic fat cats but cannot or will not take a stand to improve the lot of working people. The word 'protectionist" is inflammatory. It implies a mind set of closing our borders to trade. I could state over again the unfair trade practices that have driven factories outside our country as the only way they can make a profit, but I won't in this letter, except to say that with our trade imbalance so far out of whack anyone with a brain can see that we cannot continue down this road to bankruptcy. We already owe trillions to foreign governments to where they can dictate policy.

One last point, the issues that should be revised would improve the lives of workers and their families in Latin America, so it would be win, win. The only ones to lose would be the fat cats referred to previously. Once again they win while we all lose. Where is the "CHANGE" promised? Guess we will have to wait for the next candidate. Hope we are still a viable country at that time. I don't think we will be. The clock is running out of sand.

April 28, 2009

15. This book exposed the growth in power of corporations. It is worth reading.

The Post- Corporate World
Life after Capitalism
By: David C. Korten

Mr. Korten previously wrote a book entitled "When Corporations Rule the World". This new book suggests how much improved the world could be if they no longer had control. I will probably punish myself by reading his other book. Whether I do or not, it will probably not change my current opinion. There is no question in my mind that money rules and all else is merely what's left. All governments are seemingly powerless to resist the mega bucks controlled by international corporations. He mentions in passing the enormous influence and power of organizations such as: the Council of Foreign Affairs, the Bilderberg, the Tri- Lateral Commission, and the Business Roundtable. He also lists the World Bank and the International Monetary Fund and their control over third world countries.

The theme of this new book is to point out that there are many groups of caring, thoughtful people around the world that are fighting back. He lists a number of success stories. He points out a goal of substituting life for money and how when considerations other than wealth are used that improvements can be forthcoming.

This is not an easy book to read. I will recommend it nonetheless to those who care as I do.

I would like to close this review with information contained about how and when Corporations were granted the same privilege as persons. It came about with a unanimous decision by the Supreme Court in 1886. There was a case involving Santa Clara County vs. the Southern Pacific Railroad. In the discussion it was inferred that a private corporation is a person and entitled to the legal rights and protections the Constitution affords to any person. This was not the basis for their decision but has been used over and over again to grant individual rights of citizens to corporations.

This decision is responsible for the growth in power and wealth of corporations at the detriment of our people. It would be great if some group put forward a test case to try to overturn. Since this happened so long ago our government leaders must have concluded that it is proper. I doubt if it will change, which will maintain the status quo where corporations, due to their enormous financial power will continue to dominate and control whoever we elect to government positions.

May 3, 2009

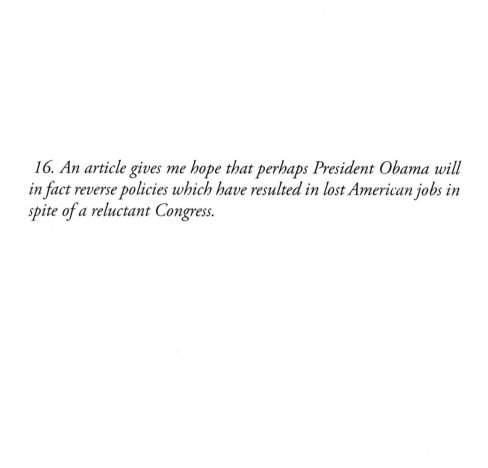

16. An article gives me hope that perhaps President Obama will in fact reverse policies which have resulted in lost American jobs in spite of a reluctant Congress.

Letter to my Congress People

President Obama is addressing the issue that is of utmost importance to the recovery of our country. For decades the Federal government has done the bidding of big business and created incentives to shut down factories in our country in favor of sending them overseas and then allowing them to cheat on taxes owed forcing citizens to support our government's needs while they get off scot free. It has had a devastating impact on the lives of our people trying to support their families with reduced income. I read that some Democrats in Congress are uneasy with this and are reluctant to support him. I sincerely hope you are not one of those. This is your time once again to step to the plate and take the bold initiative that is being presented to you. I and others like me will be watching.

May 5, 2009

17. My letter was meant as support for the Sheriff who dared to speak the truth.

Sheriff Clarence W. Dupnik,

I had intended to write in support of your brave, honest appraisal of the illegal immigration issue but held off until reading the article in today's Star where a number of Democrats have signed a letter demanding an apology. I sincerely hope you will not cave in to their demand. They are out of touch with reality, not you. They can stick their heads in the sand if they want to. The position you took is supported by the majority of voting Arizona citizens. They and I are not racists. We are only demanding that our elected officials get control of this issue and take steps to restore some semblance of order. In my opinion government only puts forth lip service without any real intention of stopping the constant inflow from our neighbors to the South. Representative Giffords is reported to have said they just want to come to flip hamburgers. She wants to overturn the employer sanction legislation we voted for two years ago. Homeland Security Director Napolitano was furious to discover that her agents had raided a business; I believe it was in the State of Washington. You can be sure there will be no more raids on her watch.

The letter implies that you spoke without data to support your statement. Who better than you, who deal with this on a daily basis, can understand the results of uncontrolled illegal immigration on our county?

You are not in the minority. It is only the government elected and judicial officials that are out of step. Trust me, when the push comes to grant citizenship to the millions who have settled against the law, there will be a groundswell of anger just as there was when Senator McCain and President Bush tried. We, or should I say I, would be supportive of expanding work visas if there was a shortage of labor one place or another, but with unemployment nearing 10% I doubt even that could stand the test of reality.

May 5, 2009

18. I take issue with the author of an article that attempts to put the growth of Muslims in Europe in a benign context.

Study finds religion not a big stress factor for Muslims in West
(Associated Press article- 5/8/2009)

What a bunch of hogwash. The article claims that Muslims do not consider religion as important as jobs. If that is so then why have only 10% integrated themselves into British Society, 46% in France and 35% in Germany? These are the percentages listed in the article. I doubt if they are true. Everything I have read in books and news media tells me that they deliberately keep apart and do not allow integration into society, preferring to stay in conclaves living by their own laws and defying the countries laws and customs.

This article is nothing more than balm to soothe us and keep us asleep while their poison spreads country to country with the ultimate goal of ruling the world. They are doing a commendable job of it. Certainly no high ranking official in our government has a clue. They continue to fiddle while the fire keeps burning higher and higher.

May 8, 2009

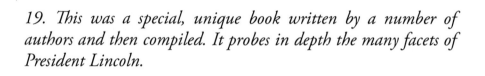

19. This was a special, unique book written by a number of authors and then compiled. It probes in depth the many facets of President Lincoln.

Our Lincoln
New Perspectives
On Lincoln and his world
Edited by Eric Foner

This is a new book published in 2008. It is unusual in that Mr. Foner did not write it. He compiled chapters written by different researchers. Each of them wrote about Lincoln in the various aspects of his life. Instead of an overview, each of them concentrated on one subject. For example the first chapter is his role as commander in chief while the ninth chapter covers his religion.

As most of you have probably done, I have read countless books about Lincoln. Fortunately, the ones I have read were positive. I was hurt to realize in the final chapter the number of negative books that have also been published. I find it sad that in current times so many have tried to cheapen the lives and accomplishments of so many of our greatest leaders in American history.

The growth and skill of this man as he steered the Union through its darkest years is a marvel to recall. He was always opposed to slavery but at the same time early on did not consider Negroes the equal of whites. This began to change as he allowed leading black leaders the opportunity to visit with him in the white house and changed completely when the blacks in the Union Army acquitted themselves in such outstanding ways beginning with the Massachusetts' 64th Infantry's attack on Ft. Wagner in South Carolina. After that he not only pushed for their freedom but also for all other rights of white citizens including education.

If you are open to read another Abraham Lincoln book, you will not be disappointed. I found this in the Tucson Public Library.

May 10, 2009

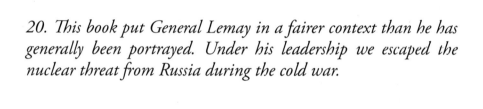

20. This book put General Lemay in a fairer context than he has generally been portrayed. Under his leadership we escaped the nuclear threat from Russia during the cold war.

Lemay
By: Barrett Tillman

Those of you old enough to have seen the movie, "Dr. Strangelove", will recall the heavyset General with his jowls hanging down and a stogie in his mouth. This was a caricature of General Curtis E. Lemay. Everyone enjoyed the movie. It was designed to show the sickness that we lived with during the cold war. America and Russia poured our collective wealth into thousands of nuclear warheads and the delivery systems to send them on their way. Should that have occurred hundreds of millions would have died and there was concern that perhaps the world would cease to function as the result with the sun blotted out by the mushroom clouds.

While the movie was outrageous, it was not fair to General Lemay. This was a man who devoted his life in defense of our country. He was born in 1906 and early on developed a love for flying. He went through the lean years before the war and was ready when war broke out. He is credited with designing the box formation used by our B-17's in Europe to defend against German fighter planes thereby saving countless American lives. He was transferred to the Pacific with the first B-29's and is credited for making them into the weapon they became. He sent hundreds into low level fire bombing missions over Tokyo and other major cities causing the deaths of hundreds of thousands. He then sent the planes that dropped the Atomic bombs on Hiroshima and Nagasaki. It, of course was not his decision, that decision came from President Truman, but it was he that carried it out. At that point the war was over. I am one of those that believe the war would have continued on with great loss of American lives had the air war not done its job. Brutal, yes, but then all warfare is brutal. The difference between average men and General Lemay was that he did what he had to do to end the war.

He was in command in Europe when Russia shut off all land transport to Berlin. It was he who started the airlift and kept improving it until such time as Russia relented.

He was the man who organized SAC, the Strategic Air Command. Under his leadership it continued to expand and improve throughout the cold war. Because of his leadership a nuclear war did not happen. Russia realized the futility of sending bombers or missiles our way. It would have meant the complete destruction of the Soviet Union.

He went from here to Washington advancing to Chief of Staff of all armed forces doing whatever he could to keep America strong. He retired in 1965 after serving 37 years. The world had changed and he was out of step. He, like General McArthur wanted to use our full potential in Korea and was denied. He wanted once again to use our full potential in Vietnam and was denied. The Bay of Pigs fiasco angered him and it was he that insisted on bombing the Cuban missile installations in Cuba. He was convinced that Russia would back down. Thankfully the embargo was effective and it was ended peacefully.

If you read this book you will be amazed at his accomplishments during his service years and beyond. All Americans should give him the honor and respect he deserved.

May 14, 2009

21. This was a report on one of my "Bucket List" accomplishments. Just thought I would share with you.

My Sky Dive Experience

May 18, 2009, yours truly finally accomplished his goal of parachuting, as they say, out of a perfectly operating airplane. Ironically it was exactly one year ago that I had scheduled a dive with hiking friends: Gary Fabiano and Silver Wilkie. The day before, I was guiding a group from the club to four peaks in the Tombstone area. While attempting the final climb of the day I fell and dislocated my right shoulder. It was a painful experience. The next day Roxanna drove me to Eloy to be with Gary and Silver to cheer them on. They both accomplished it and thoroughly enjoyed the drop.

Gary promised to go again with me. He left town for the summer and it took quite awhile before I had confidence in using my right arm. We would talk about it from time to time until finally we agreed on a date. Ursula Pillar was going to join us. At the last moment Gary had to cancel because of an appointment with his eye surgeon and Ursula decided not to go as she was preparing for a visit to Germany to visit her daughter. That left just me with Roxanna as the driver when lo and behold Mike Harris said he would join us and video tape my drop. This was important as he is a skilled sky diver with 330 drops to his credit. Having his quiet confidence was calming to me.

Actually I was never scared. I looked at it no differently than a person putting confidence in a physician and allowing him to do whatever is required. Sky Diving is no different. I should explain that I was not parachuting by myself, it is called tandem. I was strapped in front of a fine young man. His name is Jason Sanders. He like the others takes people like me up five or six times every day. They know what they are doing. I had complete confidence that it would be a thrill which I would live to tell about.

The airport is named, Sky Dive Arizona, located in Eloy, about forty miles North of Tucson. It is world famous. There were teams from the Air Force Academy practicing on the same day. We remember, a year ago there was a large group from Asia. I checked in at 9: 30 AM, watched a video and then signed documents holding them and the rest of the world blameless in case of injury or death for any reason. This was the worst part as they described the various things that could go wrong. We made friends with three young students who would be jumping with me. Our turn came at 11:30 when we met our instructor. We stepped into our harness which was adjusted to fit but not tightened, then at noon we were led to an open wagon, climbed on next to our instructor and driven to the airplane. I was first on which meant that we were the last to jump and the last to land. As we reached 13,000 ft. we unbuckled our seat belts and for the first time Jason pulled me to him hooking up the clamps and tightening the straps until we were essentially one person. We hitched our way closer to the door until there were no more people. He shoved me to the opening, grabbed the bar and swung out the door. At 120 miles per hour, that is quite a rush. After dropping 3,000 ft. he signaled it was time for me to pull the rip cord. I pulled, but I was also aware of his hand on mine making sure it was done sharply. We were pulled upwards and then started our gradual descent. He put my hands on the control rings so I could move from side to side. It was then he asked if I liked Roller Coasters. I replied no. If I had said yes he would have had us tumbling about. I had absolutely no interest in doing that, so we just floated quietly to earth. At about three thousand feet he took the rings from me so he could assure a safe landing on the grassy area in front of the Academy. I held my legs up so he could land on his feet. We did but then I sat down. He got me up and released me at which time I started towards Roxanna and Mike. I felt dizzy but did not get sick. The pressure on my ears just wouldn't release for quite awhile afterwards. We treated Mike to lunch and returned home.

Just another bucket list item checked off.

May 20, 2009

22. This is the second important expose book on corporate power over the countries of the world.

When Corporations Rule the World
By David C. Korten

I wrote a review of Mr. Korten's second book recently, entitled, "The Post-Corporate World". In it I stated I would probably read his first book as well, and I just did. He points out with clear examples the obvious truth that huge mega-corporations today truly rule the world. I personally have been a believer for some time now. It took awhile as my life's career was working for a large corporation for which I had and still do respect and support. I did not want to believe what had occurred in the 60 years following the Second World War.

To digress, corporations up until the late 30's had done much the same as today, but they were exposed and tamed by the Roosevelt Administration. He referred to them as "Robber Barons". In his new deal he took drastic steps to bring them under scrutiny and control by enactment of legislation. One of the controls was the Glass-Steagall Act enacted into law in 1934 to reduce the risk of bank failure. It prohibited banks from engaging in the insurance business. In 1998 President Clinton together with a Republican Congress joined forces in repealing this law. Huge mergers of banks and insurance companies were created. Since then investment companies have been added to the mix. The disastrous result we are currently paying the price for, as we taxpayers bail them out to the tune of trillions of dollars with no end in sight.

The framework for corporate takeover started with the best of intentions at a conference in Bretton Woods, New Hampshire July 1-22, 1944. Out of that came The World Bank, the International Monetary System (IMF) and the General Agreement on Tariffs and Trade (GATT). The purpose was to create order in the world economy so that goods and services could be made available between countries without artificial barriers. It was signed by 44 countries. As corporations increased their power the effect has been to decrease sovereignty of countries including our own. In effect corporations rule with impunity. He provides many instances to support his theory.

He points out the obvious that governments all over the world including America have been doing their bidding with their power increasing year by year. He proposes solutions and shares the names of organizations that increasingly are fighting back. Make no mistake, in America it is not one party as compared to the other. They are both under control of the money machine.

Read this book and get involved.

May 24, 2009

23. Since I have taken my theme from the movie "The Last Angry Man" I finally got around to reading the book used for the picture. It was well done. You would enjoy.

The Last Angry Man
By Gerald Green

This book was written in 1956. I had seen the movie starring Paul Muni when it was released in 1959, but in those days there wasn't any spare time to read novels, I was too busy getting started in my career at Firestone. I purchased it recently and read it during quiet times on my recent trip to Alaska, which included many available hours on airplanes or in airports as you will easily understand.

Some of you are aware that I copied the name for the book I wrote and published in 2006. On the back cover I told the reader that I borrowed the name from that long ago movie.

This is a well written book with 494 pages. It describes the life of a young Jewish boy's struggles to improve his lot in life. His name was Sam Abelman. He was born in Rumania and immigrated with his family in the 1800's. They settled in on the East side. His father was a tailor. The author provides interesting background on how hard life was in those early years. Somehow he was able to receive his medical training and became a General Physician. Throughout his entire life he fought against injustice, avarice, greed, bullying verbal or physical. He had no tolerance for fools. As a result his life was a struggle until the end.

He comes to the attention of a TV writer who gets approval to create a new program entitled America, USA. Sam is to be the subject for the first edition. Thru interviews we learn about his life's struggles. At the end, as the reporter is wrapping up the information, he makes the observation that Sam Abelman was the last angry man.

This is a well written novel which I hope you will read.

June 21, 2009

24. I consider this one of the most important articles I have written. It is my effort to get the reader to understand that where we are today did not have to happen and had it not "The Golden Age" would still be occurring. Our country and our people would not be deep in debt. Millions more would be gainfully employed instead of receiving what has become a perpetual handout, which to me is part of a deliberate strategy to force dependency on government instead of doing it ourselves as it should be. Take the time to read this one and let the message soak in.

The Golden Age of America

You would probably think this occurred during the roaring 20's. I disregard that period as being false prosperity, it was reckless and out of control, much like the fiasco we are trying to dig out from at the present time. High leverage and no accountability led Americans like Lemmings over the cliff.

The golden age I am referring to occurred during my life time and lasted from about 1947 to 1974. These were the years following WWII. The growth was real, solid and dependable.

I'm going to ignore the effects of the war in Korea (or police action) as it was referred to, and the Vietnam War. Both of these conflicts had a negative effect on the prosperity of Americans to say nothing about the millions of oriental lives taken together with over 100,000 Americans and billions of dollars wasted. It took rioting students to bring the latter to a halt. I have stated that the IRAQ war would never have occurred if the draft was still in effect. Since the current generation of students weren't involved they just ignored it, and so it goes. Putting that aside I want to talk about the good things that occurred during these years.

Before FDR's death he convinced the Congress to enact the GI Bill of Rights. This provided opportunities for returning GI's to learn new skills and stretch out their horizons. This one simple act took the pressure off of business and industry, as there were not sufficient jobs available for the millions of returning veterans. It must be remembered that America's factories had quickly converted from peacetime products to producing weapons and material to support the war effort. Manning those factories were men not qualified for military service and the women of America. Do you recall the name, Rosie the Riveter? These women gladly returned to their home responsibilities to make room for veterans. I might also add that President Eisenhower deported millions of illegal immigrants back to Mexico. I believe it was in the early 50's. It was simple then. It is only complicated now as our leaders have no intention of sending them home regardless of the unemployment status of millions of American workers.

The GI Bill was to expire in September 1946. I turned 18 on 7/30/1946 and immediately enlisted in the Army Air Force. When my enlistment was over in 1949, I took advantage of this opportunity and entered college at the University of Buffalo. I graduated with a degree in Electrical Engineering, married my wife, Carolyn and started my career with Firestone in Akron, Ohio. You can multiply my experience by millions of other veterans. The point I want to make is that these men receiving higher education and spreading across the country was unprecedented. Prior to the war only the children of doctors and lawyers went on to college. The rest stayed in the communities where they were born, worked for the local factory and retired after 35 or 40 years never straying far from home.

During the four years of war civilian goods were just not available. Civilians put their extra money into war bonds. There was a pent up demand for goods and services. These bonds were cashed to purchase. With increasing speed the factories converted back to civilian goods. The influx of new GI graduates greatly helped in spurring on development of new products. Salaries and wages increased on a steady basis. Families could now afford to purchase homes where previously most lived in rental units, including my own family. Year after year prosperity spread from State to State. There were of course pockets of despair and the Negroes for the most part were not as prosperous as the rest of us, but even here they had jobs paying wages they had never seen before.

President Truman is credited with the Marshall plan which sent goods and agricultural products to Europe at a critical time. This also increased production here at home. The net effect was increasing capacity with more good paying jobs available. These were happy times. People moved to the suburbs, bought fishing boats, campers and vacation homes. They were able to put aside college funds for their children. We were determined that they would be able to inherit a better life. This continued until the early 70's when chinks started to develop.

Once again using me as an example, the opportunity for growth was astounding. The tire industry blossomed. New plants were built all over America and Canada. Because of this, men like me were given advancement opportunities. It seemed as if it would never end. These were heady times but solid not flaky as recent times. Salaries and wages steadily increased. Houses grew in value at a steady rate. All was well with the world and then it was over. If you did not live thru these years you cannot possibly understand.

I have many former union friends but would be remiss if I didn't make the point that unions became so powerful, they could shut down whole industries to realize their demands, the granting of which made it more difficult to produce quality products at reasonable cost. It was during this time that rebuilt factories in Europe and Japan started exporting products to America. At first it was a bother but later on became a real threat. We could no longer compete as many of our factories were aging with high wages and benefits and with decreasing productivity. Then along came President Jimmy Carter. He and the Democratic Congress started enacting punitive legislation such as OSHA, DOT, and EPA.

These, while of some benefit, added enormously to our cost of production.

In spite of all of the above, our country was still growing and still prosperous. The Golden Age finally came to an abrupt end with the creation of OPEC. They instantly raised the cost of oil from $4 to $40/barrel. The whole industrial world was affected. In my own company, six huge factories were immediately shut down. The tire industry to this day has not recovered to where it had been previously. We might have grown to overcome this huge financial setback but there were other forces at work. The Northern States were depleted first by sending factories to the Southern States where unions did not have power. This went on for some time until the next step was initiated and that was to desert America entirely. Decisions were made to send the latest equipment overseas whereas previously they would have been installed in USA factories. This ushered in the era of huge corporations making profit only decisions without consideration of the problems created by lost, good paying factory jobs here at home. This led to entire factories being shut down and reassembled first in Mexico and later the Far East i.e.; Thailand, South Korea and China. The unions already weakened continued losing influence. This was accelerated during the presidency of Ronald Reagan.

As the men lost their status as breadwinners, millions of housewives entered the work force, not because they wanted to, but because the families were desperate to maintain the standard of living they had grown to accept as their right. Men worked two or more jobs. None of these had the wages and benefits that they had become accustomed to.

Even with all of the above, families continued to lose ground. It is my contention that this is when drug use intensified. They were used to cloud reality.

Government, whether Democrat or Republican, was either too stupid to realize what was happening or just didn't care. I have heard politicians say that manufacturing can never return. I deny that categorically. All Americans need is a level playing field. As it is now the cards are stacked against us. Corporate taxes in America are far greater than factories located overseas. Health care costs are borne by factories here but not elsewhere. How can we ever compete? The so-called free trade agreements have created havoc both at home and abroad. Their real intent is to foster huge profits for corporations with total disregard for Americans or for the citizens of the country where the factories are installed.

The military/ industrial alliance exerted their influence forcing America to spend billions and yes, trillions on an annual basis to create the illusion that we were a super power. Europe and the other industrial nations took a different route. Without ever declaring it as a plan, they reduced their military to a reasonable level consistent with backing away from wars as the way to settle disputes. Having their countries devastated during two world wars, they have said no more. The funds thus made available were used to improve the lives of their citizens which included universal health care. This alone reduced the cost of production and kept their industries viable, even though high wages are paid to their workers.

I sometimes wonder what life in America might have been like had the golden years continued. I think my generation would have opted out of the work force at earlier times, probably to play golf year round in Arizona or elsewhere. The void of us leaving would have created opportunities for younger people to take our places. Children wanting college educations would not have to go deep in debt to do so. The tension people live with today would not exist. Drug usage would be lessened as well as crime. We would be a more content society. We would probably donate funds on a larger scale to assist poorer people around the globe, etc. etc.

Can we ever return to those solid years? The answer is yes and no. Yes, if our government would take the steps necessary to remove the barriers that make it nearly impossible to compete on the world stage. No, if the status quo remains the same. I will be honest here even with the creation of a level playing field, those industries that are labor intensive will not return, but there are many where labor costs are not the principle cost of doing business. Those would come home. With competition as it is, we will never regain our #1 status, but the hemorrhage of jobs being lost would slow down and hopefully some would return. We will never know if we don't try.

My thoughts on regenerating the golden age would include the following ideas;

Reverse the taxation policies from encouraging companies to send jobs overseas. This would include closing tax loopholes such as using the Cayman Islands as a pseudo headquarters.

Universal health care, to remove this pediment from our factories.

Eliminate star wars funding immediately.

Begin an orderly but systematic withdrawal from our over 4,000 military bases around the world, starting with Korea.

Renounce war as our first reaction to disagreements with other countries.

Reform the election process. As it is today corporations exert enormous pressure on those seeking public office. Ban them as well as unions from contributing campaign funds. They do this in Canada, why not here? Restrict primary campaigns to six months before the voting day. Limit TV exposure to specific hours and thereby eliminate round the clock campaigning. How can anything worthwhile ever get enacted when our elected officials need to spend so much of their valuable time begging for contributions? It has reached the point where the candidates of the two parties are indistinguishable except for social issues like gay rights and abortion rights.

Spend whatever funds are necessary for us to become energy independent. Make sure these funds are spent in American factories here at home.

I could go on and on but to do so would only bore you. The point is that Americans today could be enjoying a higher standard of living but the huge mega corporations have seen different. In their pursuit of obscene profits they have abandoned Americans to second class status except for those few at the top. We only have ourselves to blame as we let it happen without so much as a mild protest. I believe it will take us going to the streets in peaceful demonstrations in order to get the attention from our "leaders". The news media will not help. They make too much money with the way it is. I would support, but am too old to lead something like what I envision will be necessary. Don't think it can't happen here. Just look at the bravery of Iranians who have taken to the streets in defiance of what they consider to be a rigged election.

Think about it. Will you be the one?

June 25, 2009

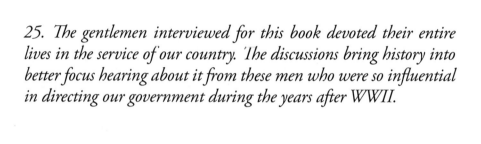

25. The gentlemen interviewed for this book devoted their entire lives in the service of our country. The discussions bring history into better focus hearing about it from these men who were so influential in directing our government during the years after WWII.

America and the World
A book report

I found this new book at the Wilmot Public Library. It was published in 2008 before the election for president had been completed. It was interesting for a number of reasons. The first was that it wasn't written. It consists of taped interviews. The moderator was David Ignatius. The principals were Zbigniew Brezezinski and Brent Scowcroft. Both of these men served many years for different presidents as National Security Advisors. The second is that even though they were of different parties, they agreed on the main issues of concern. Topics discussed were the Cold War, the Middle East, relations with China and other immerging powers, mistakes made over the years and the successes. They have advice to give to the incoming president, whoever he or she might be.

From my lofty position of knowing all things, I found I disagreed on a few of their positions such as;

They feel that those of us critical of illegal immigration are racists. We don't agree. We believe that for a government to exist there must be rules and laws to follow, otherwise you have chaos. These people flooding into our country, deliberately breaking our laws, have caused great financial distress on law enforcement, medical facilities and undercut the wages that citizens could be earning. We just want order not wanton disregard.

They believe that those of us who want to preserve employment in manufacturing are protectionist. Nothing could be further from the truth. We just want a level playing field. China, in particular breaks every rule in the book with impunity.

They champion our military involvement in the Middle East, whereas I want an orderly withdrawal so that the people of those countries can choose their own destinies without having to suffer under our military occupation.

What I did agree with was their hope that the incoming president would reverse the damage done by our last president and vice president. A statement made was,

"The new president will come into office in a world that is very angry at the United States. I can't remember, in my lifetime, a time when the world was more hostile to the country".

All in all, if you are a person interested as I am and keep searching for the truth; you will find this book informative, particularly as they recall decisions made during their tenure.

July 9, 2009

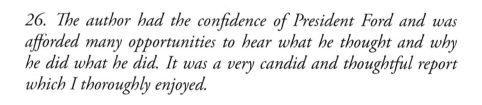

26. The author had the confidence of President Ford and was afforded many opportunities to hear what he thought and why he did what he did. It was a very candid and thoughtful report which I thoroughly enjoyed.

Write It When I'm Gone
By; Thomas M. DeFrank
Remarkable Off-the-Record Conversations with Gerald R. Ford

Mr. DeFrank is a reporter who was assigned to follow Vice President Ford in 1974 during the time leading up to the resignation of President Nixon. He became a trusted friend who did not betray confidences. As the years passed by during the Presidency of Ford and the years following they began meeting on numerous occasions' right up until President Ford's death at the age of 94. The only proviso was that the content would be held for publishing after his death.

For those of you interested in American history and politics, you may be surprised at the opinions he held for other political persons. For example, right up until the death of President Reagan, Ford held him responsible for losing his bid for re-election to Jimmy Carter. There had been a bitter nomination battle between them, and after Ford won, Reagan did little to help Ford get elected. In contrast Ford worked tirelessly on Reagan's behalf when he ran against Carter.

I won't share more than the above. Read it and you will better understand this wonderful, courageous, loyal person who worked hard for his party, his country and the numerous charitable endeavors he supported.

For recreation, he was an avid golfer, which proves that he was OK.

July 22, 2009

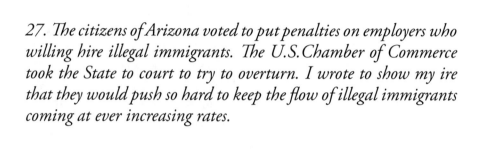

27. The citizens of Arizona voted to put penalties on employers who willing hire illegal immigrants. The U.S. Chamber of Commerce took the State to court to try to overturn. I wrote to show my ire that they would push so hard to keep the flow of illegal immigrants coming at ever increasing rates.

US Chamber of Commerce
Asks Justices to kill Ariz. Rule
Article written by Howard Fisher-Capitol Media Services
In the Arizona Daily Star-July 28, 2009

In his brief to overturn our program, Attorney Carter Phillips makes the point that there were over 1,000 immigration bills and resolutions introduced in all 50 States so far in 2009 alone. He complains that they place an undue burden on employers and all should be found to be interfering with the Federal government's immigration program.

I would predict that the Chamber will be successful. What the Court should review is the complete lack of commitment on the part of the Federal government to do their job. They should review the underlining reason why citizens, state and local governments are taking matters into their own hands to resolve because the Federal government will not. I was upset with President Bush and Senator McCain when they pushed for amnesty. The response from citizens was enough for them to back off and wait for a better time. Now I realize that President Obama, Speaker Nancy Pelosi and the rest want the same thing.

Further, I have read that the health system revision being proposed does not specifically deny coverage for illegal immigrants and therefore they will receive coverage.

The State of California has the largest illegal population. The cost to support them has nearly bankrupted the state, but even there, they pretend that all is peaches and cream.

The Court, the Administration and Congress had better understand the anger building in American citizens, 10% of whom cannot find employment. There will be an up roar if amnesty and complete surrender to special interests is tried.

July 28, 2009

28. I wrote to this columnist to let him know my disagreement with his article which was about the black professor and the white police officer.

Opinion by Eugene Robinson

Your opinion article in today's Arizona Daily Star, entitled," Rising number of Powerful minorities change race mix".

You ended the article by throwing down a challenge. "Any body wanna bet". I accept. I am 81 years old and white. Any time I have ever had the occasion to talk to a police officer, I always addressed him as "Sir". This is my way of letting them know I appreciate all they do for me, putting their lives on the line, never knowing if they are dealing with a crazed person.

Your precious professor took offence at the officer questioning him, as if to say, I am important, you are just a lowly peon. How dare you challenge me? I know Obama personally, etc, etc.

You know that in the past there were lynchings, blacks had separate drinking fountains and were told to move to the back of the bus. That was then, this is now. It is time for you and other educated, articulate people of color to put that aside and deal with the here and now. We are getting tired of being told how bad whites are. By the way, to my knowledge I never dealt with a black man any different than a white man, so don't put me down as a racist. Put me down as someone who believes we should all be treated the same regardless of race, or for that matter standing in the community.

President Obama is doing the right thing trying to close this episode, but I will not forgive him for jumping to the typical black position that race was involved.

July 28, 2009

29. I went back thru my records and listed the many times I had felt compelled to make my thoughts known on the issue of illegal immigration.

Illegal Immigration articles written by me beginning 4/25/05

The first group was put into my book "The Last Angry Man".

4/25/05-Open the Borders North and South

6/6/05- Problems with Mexican government

7/18/05-Encounter with illegals

11/8/05-Ernesto Portillo Jr. 12/29/05-Vincente Fox letter

1/24/ 06-Eureka, Solution to our immigration problem

2/21/06 Ernesto Portillo Jr.

3/28/06-Amnesty

4/6/06- Thoughts, item 4

4/19/06-Confrontation at the border

5/27/06-Senate bill 2611

5/28/06-Memorial Day Wal-Mart style

6/15/06-Arizona Daily Star articles retort

The following are included in this book

5/21/07-A call to action

6/29/07-Illegal Immigration, my recommended solutions

9/16/07-TUSD Sickout

10/16/07-Eliot Spitzer granting drivers licenses to illegals

11/19/07-Ernesto Portillo Jr.

12/21/07-Ernesto Portillo Jr.

4/14/08-Employer Sanctions

4/16/09-Empoyer Sanctions

5/5/09-Sheriff Dupnik

7/28/09-US Chamber of Commerce

This list written July 28, 2009

30. This long article was my first attempt to make known my concern with the monstrosity being pulled together on health care. I point out a number of obvious things that could and should be done and I also ask for restraint and wonder why it has become so cumbersome. What I would prefer is taking it apart and voting up or down on the many facets of the health care issue.

Health Care Thoughts

Why must everything be so complicated? Sure there is a problem in this country. How can we ignore some 45 million people not having access to affordable care? I am concerned as are many of you who I receive e-mails from that the reforms planned are ballooning out of control. The legislation being debated will probably contain a thousand or more pages of details which no one in the Congress or Administration will ever review much less understand. Health care in America today is complicated enough as it is. I am always frustrated with the myriad of forms I must sign no matter how routine the procedure might be. Have any public officials taken the time to review the systems in place in other countries, many of which have been in effect for decades? Why must we start from scratch? If there are flaws in any of these, then it should be relatively easy to make whatever changes are necessary.

This is what I truly believe.

The Insurance Community and the Drug Companies will come out stronger than ever and more obscene profits will be theirs for the taking. Our Congress and Administration will do their bidding, where to my way of thinking they should be bypassed and in the case of the insurance industry they should be redundant, completely put out of business. Why would we need insurance if a Medicare type system was made available to all instead of just seniors? Perhaps their role could be to supplement just as my former company does for me now. Those who could not afford, at least would have basic care.

I would rescind the Drug Companies right to advertise to the public as they so obscenely do today. Every time I am watching some program, on they come with Viagra or some other miracle drug that you must talk to your doctor about. Most of the ads tell all the bad things that the drug could do to you. It is just sick. In a recent article written by Christopher Lane he reveals that only two countries around the world allow this; New Zealand and America. He quotes an August 2007 New England Journal of Medicine article that the total cost for 2005 for all drug-related marketing in 2005 was $29.9 billion, with $4.1 billion spent on Direct to Customer advertising. The authorization to allow DTC advertising was granted while Clinton was our President. Think about that as you contemplate which political party has your best interests at heart. This should not be construed as an endorsement for the Republican Party. If that party means so much to you, then tell me what wonderful things they did during the eight years when they had total control.

One pillar in the plans being discussed is mandatory benefits to be paid by employers. Doesn't anybody understand that this is totally wrong? I have harped on this subject for years now without result. My basic premise is to relieve businesses in America from this cost burden, particularly their obligation to retirees like myself. The burden to cover my medical expenses has to be paid out of product sales for which I no longer contribute. Eliminating these would immediately increase the profit they could make while producing goods and services here in America. Jobs would come flooding back that were lost to China and elsewhere, tax revenues would increase dramatically enabling our country to afford health care, pay down the debt or whatever else is deemed important.

I would rein in the huge costs the Doctors and Hospitals pay to protect them from excessive law suits. There undoubtedly are abuses which should be punished but there are also frivolous law suits, many of which are settled out of court to limit the cost, even when completely unfounded. The Democratic Congress is indebted to the Trial Lawyers for campaign funds and I can assure you this will not be discussed. President Obama at a medical convention recently told them that it was off the table.

Medicare fraud is rampant. I have seen a report that so far this year alone it exceeds $33 billion. Putting more people and resources to work to drastically reduce this amount would provide billions to be put to work helping people instead of enriching thieves.

Do not provide government paid procedures having anything to do with sexual enhancement, cosmetic surgery, tummy tucks, etc.

Limit free or subsidized health care to citizens and legal immigrants.

I have one final thought, why must it be all or nothing? Why not chip away at it? People without insurance can still be served at the Emergency Rooms. Not preferable and terrifically expensive but still it is an option. Why not take the creepy crud approach and lower the age to receive Medicare by one year each year until it covers all age 50 and older while at the same time covering children up to the age of 18. That would leave those in their prime working years not covered now but perhaps later. I only suggest this as the Trillions in costs being discussed will no doubt derail any meaningful program and something is better than nothing.

I am mailing a copy of this to my elected officials as well as e-mailing to friends and others. If you agree in part or all, I request you let your voice be heard as well. Sitting back and hoping for the best just won't do.

July 29, 2009

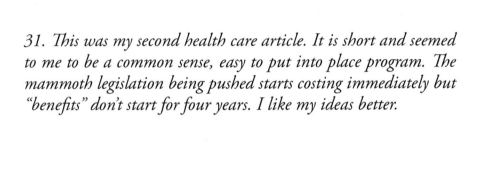

31. This was my second health care article. It is short and seemed to me to be a common sense, easy to put into place program. The mammoth legislation being pushed starts costing immediately but "benefits" don't start for four years. I like my ideas better.

Health Care

86% of Canadians approve of their government health care system. Their costs are 1/2 ours and they live longer. They do not place the cost burden on industry which gives their companies an edge when competing with us.

We don't have to adopt their plan. Thanks to LBJ we have a system. It is called Medicare and Medicaid. All that is needed is to lower the age for joining Medicare to 50. We also have CHIP for children; it was expanded earlier this year. Expand it again to cover all children regardless of family income to the age of 18.

Drop the end of life counseling, it is a distraction. Cut down on fraud which robs Billions each year and make people pay for frivolous lawsuits.

Control costs without adding 100,000 Federal employees. Those between 18 and 50 will have to wait till the next time. One step forward is better than doing nothing.

August 13, 2009

32. My third about health care. I point out the most glaring problem and that is putting the cost burden on business and industry in America.

Needed-Private Sector Jobs

I have searched in vain in newspapers, TV news and opinions and radio for discussion on what I consider to be the #1 fault with the health care legislation being proposed. Placing the cost burden on business and industry will decrease their ability to compete with companies in countries where the cost is borne by all taxpayers not industry. Campaign pledges should not be so sacred that our leaders pretend that another 47 million people can have health coverage without all of us contributing.

If business was freed from this burden they would be better able to compete and good income jobs would be created. The individual taxes would go a long way to cover the shortfall.

Would someone please tell me why I am wrong?

August 16, 2009

33. Another great look at behind the scenes of history. Mr. Schlesinger Jr. kept thousands of pages of his personal notes which his sons reduced to a readable book after his death. You will learn a lot by reading.

JOURNALS
1952 – 2000
Arthur M. Schlesinger, Jr.
By; Andrew and Stephen Schlesinger

Mr. Schlesinger was a prolific author and historian. For over 50 years he was in contact with the most influential politicians, artists and world leaders. He would be considered an intellectual. He died at the age of 89. Prior to this he had asked his sons to write a book using his personal notes. Since there were over 6000 pages, their task was to choose the most important and condense to fewer than 1000 pages. They ended up with 958.

It would be impossible to write a review. What I have chosen is to list comments I found interesting. Should this trigger interest on your part be prepared for long hours of intense reading?

Page 37 - A quote from HST when asked for advice by Adlai E. Stevenson as he sought the presidency, "Do you want to know what the issue in this campaign is?" He went to the window and pointed at a passerby. "The issue is who's looking after that guy? The people down in Washington aren't looking after him. They're looking after themselves. What we have to tell the country is that we Democrats intend to look after the ordinary guy."

Page 156 - President JFK observations about comments made by President Eisenhower at a press conference. JFK said, "The thing I liked best," he said, "was the picture of Eisenhower attacking medical care for the old under Social Security as "socialized medicine" and then getting into his government limousine and heading out to Walter Reed."

Page 286 – A conversation with Jackie Kennedy. She took Arthur aside and said, "Do you know what I think will happen to Bobby if he is elected president?" I said no. She said, "The same thing that happened to Jack... There is so much hatred in this country, and more people hate Bobby than hate Jack. That's why I don't want him to be President... I've told Bobby this, but he is fatalistic, like me."

Page 336 - Stalin was very much impressed with Roosevelt; you could almost say he was in awe of Roosevelt. He saw in Roosevelt the power of the USA, but he also saw in him the New Deal: he knew that something had been happening in America which did not fit the categories and which he had to take account of....

Page 362 – Nixon continues to get away with murder. Now it is the progress toward a Vietnam settlement.... What is saddest of all is that if Nixon had been willing to make these concessions in 1969, we could have had the settlement then; and 20,000 Americans and God knows how many Vietnamese, now dead, would be alive.

Page 612 – Describing a British film... But its vision of an electronic world in which nothing works, of cities drowned in filth and litter and divided between the stupid rich and the aimlessly poor, of an intrusive, incompetent and brutal state bureaucracy- all seemed peculiarly convincing. I find I have no faith, none at all, in progress. I do not expect a better future.

Page 660 – He comments on the debate between Dukakis and Bush. Bush regurgitated his demographic crap about liberalism, the pledge of allegiance, the ACLU, etc..... I have thought that George Bush knows better but I am beginning to wonder if he really does.

Page 670 – With reference to the book "The Satanic Verses" by Salman Rushdie- Last Thursday Waldenbooks, claiming the need to protect its bookshops and employees from Muslim fanatics, ordered the removal of the book from its shelves. This provoked him to fire off a letter.

Page 673 - So democracy has won the political argument. The market has won the economic argument. The elections this year in the Soviet Union, the demonstrations this week in Tiananmen Square—all signify not just the survival but the triumph of democracy in its century- long struggle against the totalitarians. For the historian, an exciting time.

Page 684 – With reference to American troops sent to Panama-As one opposed to presidential wars undertaken without congressional consent, to unilateral U.S. intervention in the hemisphere and to sneak attacks by superpowers on small countries, I am deeply unhappy, but I am very much in the minority.

Page 701 – With reference to the first gulf war- The most unnecessary war in American history began on the 16th.

Page 832 – Starr's report lived up to anticipations. It is indeed the most salacious public document in the history of the republic... Starr, who is already exposed as the nation's number one pornographer...

Page 857 – The Florida roller-coaster rushes on. Very odd succession of sensations: in the morning, Bush is winning; in the late afternoon, Gore is granted a reprieve and is still in there. I suppose Bush will win in the end. But if he wins when votes are still uncounted, it will be regarded as a steal.

August 17, 2009

34. I use history to try to make the point that the new administration and Congress were blowing the fantastic opportunity granted by the voters. They will not get another chance anytime soon.

Analogy

While pondering the health care issue being debated vociferously between the Democratic Administration, Democratic controlled Congress and the minority Republicans, for some reason a statement made by General Patton came to mind.

His 3rd Army had been making great progress pushing into Germany when the decision was made to cut off all supplies including fuel and ammo for his tanks. He had just arrived at the scene of an all night battle. He noticed the Germans were using carts. The statement was that he had the right instrument (3rd Army) at the right place at the right time. Nothing could have stopped him except the decision to give full support to General Montgomery as he drove up the coast. The V-2 rockets were creating havoc in England. Patton was not allowed to use his full resource and the moment passed by. The Germans had time to move their forces and the drive once resumed met heavy resistance.

The majority of American voters put the Democrats in charge expecting the "change" promised. There are only 18 months left before mid term elections. Traditionally the party out of power gains seats. The overwhelming power the Democrats have now will vanish. Nothing of great importance will be accomplished particularly in health care. Their time is now. They have the power and the issue. In my humble opinion they are blowing it. They have caved in to the mega health industry with only a possibility that a public option could be part of the package. No other major country on earth has allowed the private sector to reap obscene profits while denying care as best they can. The cost for most American families is prohibitive. Many do without protection because the cost is out of reach.

Let me make this point clear. I want Doctors, Nurses, hospitals, clinics, and all other health providers to make a good living or profit. The investment in education and facilities must be rewarded. When the original concept of insurance was created the thought was to pool resources to lesson the impact on families and companies. Somewhere along the way the industry realized they could increase their profits by denying care for pre existing conditions, delaying payments and vastly increasing the cost with their incessant paperwork.

It is obvious to everyone by now that the minority party will not agree with any proposal put forth by President Obama and his co-horts. It is time to fish or cut bait as the saying goes. Go all out for the best and lowest cost proposals which will at last provide care for all our citizens. This will cause serious downsizing of the private insurers. Perhaps the blow could be cushioned by letting them handle the paperwork. Their problem is of minor importance as compared to citizens. They had their chance and like the huge banks they blew it with their lust and greed. Tough.

We as a nation cannot continue the irresponsible excessive spending that started with Bush and continues with Obama. If this continues we will become a third world country with only our military to create the premise that we are a super power. In other countries the individual taxes are the source of funds. Pretending this can be done by just taxing the rich and business is nonsense. Maybe a referendum is in order. Let the people decide to increase taxes to pay for health care. We must remove this burden from business to give them a fair chance to compete worldwide. Good paying American jobs will solve our debt problem and pay the costs. Another source of funds could be any of the following;

Cancel the Bush tax cuts for the super rich which are scheduled to expire a year from now anyway. That is assuming the Administration and Congress has the guts to do so.

Bring our troops home from Iraq and Afghanistan, these are wars which can never be won.

Eliminate the "No child left behind" program; this is only a paperwork nightmare which only improves the student's ability to pass tests. It does nothing to improve learning.

Make drastic cuts in funding for the CIA, Homeland Security, Star wars, stop the installation of the missile system in Poland, cut funding for the Energy and Education Departments, cancel the Senior Drug program, replacing it with our government using it's leverage to lower drug costs across the board, etc, etc. These could lower annual costs by a trillion or more.

The Democratic proposals are seriously flawed. If approved, as much as a trillion dollars will be added to the national debt. Why can't they just create the process and let it be implemented piecemeal. In the 60's president Eisenhower got legislation approved to build a super highway system. Fifty years later look what has been created. He knew that once started no subsequent administration or Congress would ever be able to stop it. The same would be true for health care. We already have the superhighway built. Its names are Medicare and Medicaid. I have proposed this before. Start lowering the age of eligibility from the current 65 and at the same time move towards covering the children who are still without coverage. This would be relatively easy to do since the procedures are already in place. As to the question of these programs and Social Security running out of funds, the simple solution is to create a committee charged with advancing solutions which the Congress can only approve or reject without amendment. That is how it was done before.

No one has to re-invent the wheel.

August 23, 2009

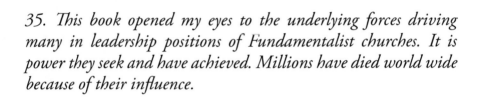

35. This book opened my eyes to the underlying forces driving many in leadership positions of Fundamentalist churches. It is power they seek and have achieved. Millions have died world wide because of their influence.

THE
FAMILY

THE SECRET FUNDAMENTALISM AT
THE HEART OF AMERICAN POWER

By; JEFF SHARLET

Mr. Sharlet immersed himself into the heart of the fundamentalist movement to find out personally what was happening. In addition he did deep research into the beginnings and gives great detail and insight. There are numerous endorsements from reputable news outlets and individuals, sufficient to assure me that the content was verifiable. He lays the program open to scrutiny and proves at least to someone like myself that he is telling the truth.

The book was released in 2008. A friend, knowing my inquiring mind, recommended it to me. I purchased it to read while on my annual visit to family back East. I finished it before landing in Tucson. It was a tough read, not just because of the small print and length but because of the content.

Most of you who will read this report will not be pleased. Rather than get angry with me, I ask you to check it out for yourselves and read other books that might counter this one. While I don't take issue with the millions who seek support by attending fundamental churches, I do take umbrage at the driving force of the leaders, who as the author states, are more interested in power than in helping the poor. There are numerous references to their admiration of fascist regimes including Hitler in the thirties, stating that where two or three are gathered together great results can be achieved. This was in reference to Hitler and Mussolini. This was not necessarily supporting the ends they achieved but rather the totalitarian process which is more productive than a democracy with the many factions to be listened too. Page 130- What was desired was a "God-controlled Fascist dictatorship".

The other theme that runs throughout the book is that the poor will be with us always and that real progress will only be achieved by ignoring the poor while keeping the power and influence in the hands of a select few individuals whose only requirement is devotion to someone called Christ. Not the teachings of Jesus which we try to adhere to but some vague person of power. The quote about "bringing a sword not peace" is repeated several times.

These people provided leadership supporting using our armed forces or by supplying weapons to dictators around the world resulting in millions of dead people, women and children included, all in the attempt to eradicate communism. Our government leaders such as Ford, Reagan, H. Clinton and many others are implicated in the search for a world order under the banner of Christianity. Places like East Timor, Chili, El Salvador and others are documented.

On page 260 there is a quote by Senator Sam Brownback. It was, "Washington right now is a town where if you're going to be powerful, you need religion. That's just the way it is".

My personal opinion is that religion as the driving source can be dangerous whether Christian or Muslim. Spending our capitol and the lives of our troops in the field because of religious beliefs is wrong. Only when we band together as people of God, whoever he or she is called, will we be able to rise above hatred and move forward creating a better world for all.

I wonder who, if anyone will take the time to read this book?

September 12, 2009

36. I am ashamed to be reminded that the United States is the biggest exporter of armaments in the world. We send weapons all over the world. The tragedy of this is that the countries purchasing arms for the most part are poor and need these funds to better the lives of their citizens. What a crime. How can we be proud of this achievement?

America's Contribution to the World's Economy

There were two articles in this week's Arizona Daily Star that caught my attention.

It seems that we as American's can only handle one crisis at a time. The health care debacle consumes everyone. I include myself in this remark. I have written a number of letters which were shared with my House Representative and others who I felt might agree. I didn't bother with our Senators as they have shown repeatedly that they have no interest in the subject other than handing a defeat to President Obama.

The subject of this letter is America as the number one exporter of death. Our most profitable industries are 'defense". Millions are employed in the only industry we have left that is protected from foreign competition. Good wages are paid to employees in, I would venture to guess, every State in the Union. It has always been my belief that this was done deliberately so that voters in all States would become irate should their cushy jobs disappear.

9/13/09- AZ overseas arms sales on rise by Enric Volante. This article starts by stating that arms sales last year boomed to more than $1 billion. Arizona deliveries rose 72% from 2006. Raytheon led the way. The biggest buyers among at least 25 countries included Egypt, Pakistan and the United Arab Emirates. Secretary Clinton finalized an agreement to clear the way for large sales to India. Raytheon officials stated that they do business with more than 40 allied nations.

9/15/09- "The poor get poorer; leaders buying arms" an opinion piece by Andrés Oppenheimer. Overall defense spending in Latin America and the Caribbean grew 91 % over the past five years to $47.2 billion in 2008. While this is going on the World Bank estimated that the number of poor in Latin America will grow to six million this year. In Latin America the United States has competition for arms sales from Russia and France.

My opinion is firm in that America should provide assistance to any country that wants to improve the lifestyles of their people. Just a small portion of these enormous funds channeled in such a way as to minimize corruption could make a huge dent in the outrageous poverty billions of people are forced to accept today. Perhaps, just perhaps, these people might look at America in a positive light. Wouldn't that be better than the bitterness that drives them to become "terrorists"?

Weapons flooding into the Middle East I am convinced will one day, if not already, be used against our armed forces in the area. Three nations already possess nuclear capability with others closing in. It is just a matter of time before the holocaust begins. This is where the bible tells us it will begin. We are certainly doing our part to help make this prophesy come true.

As to South and Central America, they have many problems to resolve. Buying military aircraft and missile systems will not resolve them. One false step and chaos will be the result with us and Russia taking sides. This is just what we need, another world war between us. Will we never learn? Will we never get past the macho image we like to project of being the #1 Super Power as far as weaponry is concerned?

I have no illusions that a change will occur. Those of us who voted for our current president had hoped he would back away from using our troops as our means to resolve problems. We are still in Iraq. We have increased our forces in Afghanistan. The missile system is still under construction in Poland. War appropriations continue spiraling upward.

It is amusing to me that those who claim we are a Christian nation are the most militaristic in their approach to the world. I wonder how they will react when the chickens come home to roost. Perhaps they won't care as the chosen ones will be lifted up to heaven leaving the rest of us to pay the piper.

It probably won't make a difference at that time if we have a health care system or not.

September 16, 2009

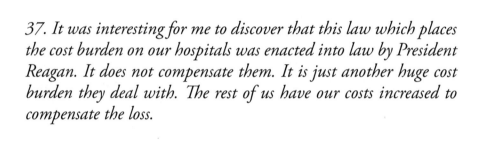

37. It was interesting for me to discover that this law which places the cost burden on our hospitals was enacted into law by President Reagan. It does not compensate them. It is just another huge cost burden they deal with. The rest of us have our costs increased to compensate the loss.

Emergency Medical Treatment and Active Labor Act of 1985

This letter is in response to an e-mail received from a friend who is like me in that he searches for facts to explain or help understand current events. He alerted me to the Act mentioned in the title. While we argue about stupid end of life issues during the current discussion about health care, it is important to review past actions to understand how we got to where we are today. An important part of history occurred in 1986 with the passage of this Act. It mandates that all hospitals are required to provide treatment for all without consideration as to their ability to pay. This sounds so nice. On review the Federal Government did not see fit to reimburse these facilities leaving private and public hospitals to pick up the costs.

This is another constitutional matter, in my opinion, where the Federal Government has usurped the rights of the States by dictating policy without regard to costs private citizens are forced to bear. Guess who actually pays? You guessed right, it is you and me, tax paying suckers who live our lives trying to do what is right.

Google Wickipedia and you will see that over half of all emergency cases are uncompensated. This includes over nine million illegal immigrants. So when our current President says they won't get free health care, he is wrong because nothing in the legislation being debated changes the current law, at least to my knowledge.

I will be sending this particularly to those who are most opposed to legislation currently under consideration. They flood my e-mail box with hate filled rhetoric about our President. Let me be clear, the legislation is an abomination. Forcing all citizens to purchase from the thieves in the health care industry or be fined is so ludicrous that it defies understanding. Also adding mandated costs on industry by providing a portion of the cost or be fined will only continue driving all manufacturing out of our country.

Now here is the punch line. I didn't know, and I'll bet you don't know either who was President when this Act was signed into law. Hold your breath, it was Ronald Wilson Reagan, the hero of all the wild eyed right wing conservatives, who can't wait until sanity is restored and the current occupant of the White House finishes his term in office.

If you are one, I challenge you to defend your hero. I can't wait to hear from you.

September 19, 2009

38. This book lets us know how so few fighter pilots were able to stem the onslaught of the German Air force during the Battle of Britain.

With Wings like Eagles
A History of the Battle of Britain

By; Michael Korda

Another prize found at the library. It was published just this year. I found it extremely interesting. It is not what you might expect. It did quote from a few pilots about their dog fights but for the most part it concentrated on the strategy and planning that helped to make the pilots efforts successful.

Students of history will remember that all of the Allied countries drastically reduced the size and quality of their armed forces after winning the First World War. This continued into the early 1930's until it became apparent that Hitler was rearming at an accelerating rate. Until then the RAF consisted of bi-wing fabric airplanes not much improved since the war. The author gives credit to a few leaders that started the modernization which resulted in the production of Hurricanes and Spitfires plus the network of radar sites which were most valuable in allowing for better utilization of the limited fighter force.

Stanley Baldwin was the Prime Minister up until 1937 when he resigned. He was one of those who believed that bombers were more important than fighters but could not accept the havoc bombing would inflict on innocent civilians of any country. It was easier to get Parliament to approve funding for fighters to be used to defend English cities. His attempt to speed up production was what brought his downfall. Before he left the radar network was in place and the first Hurricanes were reaching fighter command. He also appointed Sir Hugh Dowding as Air officer Commanding-in-chief of fighter command. This was the man who directed throughout the battle while facing extreme criticism and to whom it was said by Winston Churchill, "To him the people of Britain and the free world owe largely the way of life and the liberties that they enjoy today". Stanley Baldwin was replaced by Neville chamberlain. We all remember Chamberlain for giving in to Hitler and proclaiming, "Peace in our time". This author goes out of his way to give him credit for continuing the production speed up of modern fighter planes without which England certainly would have been defeated.

2,000 young fighter pilots were all that stood between Hitler and victory. Their victory like the defeat of the Spanish Armada and Nelson's victory at Trafalgar is etched deeply into the national conscience as the most important victories in their long history. September 15th each year the "Battle of Britain" is commemorated. That was the final decisive day after which the threat of imminent invasion was over. They had held out long enough so that worsening weather made an invasion impossible. Hitler then turned his attention to Russia. Had these young men, with the courageous support of the men and women on the ground, not been successful, history would have been altered. America would not have had England as a base to assemble our soldiers. The Axis Powers perhaps would have prevailed.

I would be remiss if I did not end this with Churchill's famous words spoken August 20, 1940; "Never in the field of human conflict was so much owed by so many to so few".

If history is important to you, I strongly recommend this book to you.

September 24, 2009

39. This book brings to light the unbelievable cruelty that took millions of lives during the 20th Century. It was a revelation to me.

A Century of Horrors
Communism, Nazism, and the uniqueness of the Shoah
By Alain Besancon

This is a very short book, only 94 pages. It was originally published in French in 1998. The English translation was published in 2007.

There were several purposes. The first was to bring to light the carnage inflicted on innocent people during this century. The second to point out how readily we understand the Nazi slaughter but know so little about what happened in Russia and China under Communism and third the definition of the word Shoah.

His claim is that the number killed under Communism ranged from 85 to over 100 million. While the millions killed by Germany have been well documented, those under Communism are clouded in mystery as the borders were sealed and there doesn't seem to have been concern on the part of the Western countries to find out and perhaps stop it. It has always been the case that a tragedy to a person or even in the case of the World Trade Center where over 3,000 died is deemed of great importance but when the number is in multiple millions the human mind is not capable of grasping the enormity of it. These were not only Jews but also other ethnic groups.

A large part is devoted to the ongoing hatred of those of the Jewish faith. We see it today with the leader of Iran threatening to wipe out all in the State of Israel. There are deep references to religion in general with specific emphasis on the 'chosen" people and their part in the crucifixion of Jesus.

Shoah is the word the Jewish community prefers as compared to holocaust. Holocaust indicates sacrifice. Shoah means catastrophe which they feel is more appropriate to describe the senseless paroxysm of evil that occurred.

This is not light reading. In my mind hatred between people's and religions is ongoing. It can only end in complete tragedy for all mankind. That is the conclusion I reached after reading. How tragic that we cannot accept all people as equals.

September 28, 2009

40. Few of you will agree with me about this documentary. I felt Moore did a great service by exposing what Capitalism has come to be in recent decades.

Capitalism-A Love Story
A documentary written, produced and directed
By Michael Moore

I went with a like minded friend on opening day. I have seen all of the films produced by Mr. Moore. They have all been excellent but this one surpassed them all. He spared no one, the fat cats raking in their plunder and the politicians from both parties who do their bidding. He asks all of us if we intend to accept our lot forever without taking action to put an end to the carnage that the huge mega companies have foisted on an unsuspecting citizenry.

While, theoretically we have the power of the vote, in reality it amounts to nothing because they are able to use scare tactics and hot button issues to pit us one against the other, nullifying any opportunity to bring common sense solutions to resolve the many woes we face as a nation.

There was one news item which shook me and that was when President Roosevelt sent in the Army when the union workers were on strike with G.M. early in his first term. I can't tell you how relieved I was to discover that they were sent in to protect the workers from local law enforcement and goons sent to harass the people. Another great segment was seeing him give his speech in 1945 asking for a second Bill of Rights to be enacted on behalf of all Americans. One of the items was universal health care for all. Others were the right to an education; the right of gainful employment at a wage sufficient to support a family and live in dignity. It was obvious that his health was deteriorating. He died shortly thereafter. His dream died with him. Nothing ever came of his ideas.

Both Clinton and Reagan come in for scorn as they collectively wiped out any vestige of regulation standing in the way of corporations who wanted and received unfettered rights to do as they please. Some of you adore Reagan. He does not come out too well. His Chief of Staff, Don Regan standing next to him, is caught on tape whispering in the President's ear that he is talking too long. The implication is that Reagan was the spokesperson to convince the electorate that all was well and to go back to sleep because daddy is protecting you while all the while the thieves were at work.

He documents that Wal-Mart takes out life insurance policies on their employees with Wal-Mart the designated beneficiary not the person's family. Millions are garnered for the company.

He shows families being forced out of their homes after being conned into using their homes like bank vaults and not being able to pay back as the interest balloons. He shows whole areas of communities with bordered up factories and houses. He even interviews a realtor who has named his company Vulture Condominiums. He buys up vacated homes for pennies on the dollar and resells garnering huge profits. This company is not alone. Many with excess funds are doing the same all over the country benefiting from the misery of others.

Two judges in concert with a contractor in Pennsylvania were given millions for sentencing juveniles to the privately owned correction facility. They were eventually found out and punished for it with jail time of their own.

He exposes the pressure that was brought to bear by Secretary of the Treasury Paulson and President Bush which resulted in the passage of the 700 billion dollar bailout with the smiling leadership of Rep. Pelosi and Senator Reed. He goes on to disclose the abuse of the use of those funds in granting lavish bonuses, parties, purchase of private jets and buying up other banks so they could keep getting bigger while we the taxpayers are treated like the saps we are for allowing this to happen.

President Obama is not spared as it is confirmed the huge sums given to him by Corporations during the last election. He has continued the mega funds give away to these same corporations during his administration. Moore doesn't mention it but I will. The Health Care Bill being debated is just another huge present to the health and drug industries. Those of us who voted for him were hoping for another FDR. So far I have been disappointed.

He closes the film by showing him stringing yellow tape around the headquarters of places such as The Bank of America. The tape has crime scene written on it. He uses a bull horn asking them to surrender peaceably. He can mix humor into a dreary subject.

I know full well before even mailing this that 90% of you will not go to see it. That is a shame as we must band together to tell our elected leaders that enough is enough. Seeing this film would open your eyes.

October 3, 2009

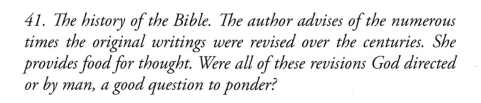

41. The history of the Bible. The author advises of the numerous times the original writings were revised over the centuries. She provides food for thought. Were all of these revisions God directed or by man, a good question to ponder?

The Bible
By; Karen Armstrong

This is another difficult book to read and understand. It is something like a text book that I imagine might be used in a Seminary to create discussion with students. I will defer to Pastor D. assuming he reads it to interpret the content.

This is an astounding effort by Ms. Armstrong. She follows the origin of the Old and New Testaments as they were created and passed on generation to generation. Mark was written in 70, Mathew and Luke in the late 80's and John in the late 90's. She makes the point that these men in their writings separated the Jewish community into good and bad. The bad meaning they did not follow Christ. These words written have been used over the centuries as justification for the persecution of Jews.

We tend to think of the Bible as if it was always as we know it today. She details the endless revisions made over the centuries, revising texts, eliminating books or adding. Whether these revisions were God directed or the work of men is the question she raises.

Until Luther and the printing press, it was something that only scholars and priests could read and study. Luther broke away partly because he was incensed by the papal policy of selling indulgences to swell the coffers of the church.

In the 1600's people like Zwingli and Calvin wanted their congregations to be acquainted with the entire Bible whereas before they only read portions. Science and Astrology were pointing out facts about the natural world. These men could accept advances as religious activities. Galileo was silenced by the inquisition at about the same time and forced to recant his conclusions that Earth was not the center of the Universe.

The Puritans who ventured to the new world likened their journey to the Exodus. They gave their colonies biblical names like Hebron, Salem, Bethlehem, etc.

In 1859 Charles Darwin published "On the origin of Species by means of Natural Selection". This created havoc continuing today. Dwight Moody founded the Moody Bible Institute to bring people back to the faith. The Rapture theory was ardently articulated by Nelson Darby during the same time period.

She mentions the role people like Pat Robertson and Jerry Falwell have had in our time. Their goal was to replace the secular administration with a

Christian government run along strictly biblical lines (Page 216).

Let me conclude by admitting my ignorance as far as ascertaining if the content is totally factual or not. Her work was praised by noted organizations and knowledgeable persons. I believe her intent was to prove that the Bible is a living thing in that meanings have changed generation to generation. I liken it to our Constitution. It too is not a dead document but living and changing over time.

If you have the time and willingness to concentrate while reading and want to learn more about the history of the Bible, this book will do it for you. I found it at the Tucson public Library.

October 8, 2009

42. *This documentary dwells on the use of Bio-fuels and the potential that may yet become viable as an alternative to oil.*

Fuel

This is a documentary film now showing in a few theaters around the country. For those living in Tucson it started at the Loft today. I went to the matinee. There were six others who watched it with me.

It is a film that took 11 years to compile. Josh Tickell was the director and the energy behind the production. Growing up in Louisiana surrounded by the petroleum refineries he witnessed first hand the staggering pollution to the environment and the health problems as a result. His own mother had 9 miscarriages.

He discovered that Bio Fuels could power any vehicle with a diesel engine. He visited Europe. Germany and Sweden in particular have made great strides in converting. Sweden has a goal to be 100% free of petroleum products in another decade.

One part that confused me was that progress was being made in our country until about four years ago when the press starting with Time Magazine came down on it as being the wrong thing to do which killed the progress being made. I will try to check it out. It is strange that I missed this. I think it had to do with using crops for fuel.

The hopeful part is that technology is starting to blossom giving hope for the future. As usual the politicians come out as villains. Just like the banks and the health industry, the petroleum industry spends big bucks getting them to do their bidding. He asks us to make our voices heard and pay attention and vote out those who refuse to make the decisions we all are waiting for so that we can climb out of the hole we are in.

That's enough. I sure hope some of you will see this film and become more active.

October 10, 2009

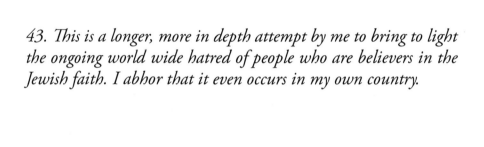

43. This is a longer, more in depth attempt by me to bring to light the ongoing world wide hatred of people who are believers in the Jewish faith. I abhor that it even occurs in my own country.

ANTI-SEMITISM

I have been thinking quite a bit lately about the resurgence of anti- Semitism in the world today. The following are my thoughts after reading the letter written by Mr. William E. Grim, an American of German descent telling about his personal observations gleaned by visiting Germany. He is not a Jew.

Everything I have read regarding this subject makes the truth of his words acceptable to me. If you disagree strongly or even mildly then I ask that you send information to me so I can learn from reading it.

In 1945 the civilized world was stunned to realize the enormity of the Holocaust and the slaughter of over 6 million Jews and another 6 million of persons found to be inferior or not willing to conform to the tenets of Nazism. It is starting all over again. It is like a virus that just can't be killed. It pops up here and there and eventually consumes all in its path. The Jewish people it seems are blamed for all sorts of problems. They are an easy target. A funny thing happened after the war when they settled into the Holy Land. They were attacked again and again and guess what instead of allowing themselves to be led to the slaughter houses they fought back and won each time. For them there will no second chance. The first war they lose the curtain of death will descend on them. That will trigger world chaos. It cannot be allowed to happen.

A few days ago I forwarded an e-mail entitled "The Speech" given by the current Prime Minister of Israel. I thought it was brilliant. Some of you responded about how horrible the Jews have been in their treatment of the Palestinians. I cannot dispute the truth of this. In particular those who fled during the wars with neighboring Arab countries were not allowed to return. In addition many were forced off their land to make room for Jews immigrating to Israel from Europe. I will not equate this to the extermination of over six million Jews by the Nazis during WWII.

Now that they have a homeland they are determined to stay against the entire Arab world whose goal is to rid the world of all Jews. The Arabs are supported again and again by the majority of countries in the U.N. The U.N. never condemns the Palestinians from sending missiles indiscriminately into Israel. They only condemn Israel when they fight back.

Early in Mr. Grim's letter he refers to Mein Kampf, the famous book written by Adolf Hitler. It was published in 1925. I read this after America entered WWII to try to understand what was happening. The one part I will never forget was his condemnation of all Jews. He used the Bible as reference. Go to Mathew Chapter 27, verse 25 and there it is written, And all the people answered, "His blood be on us and our children". That was his justification for the slaughter that followed as soon as he acquired the power to do so. He called all Jews "Christ Killers". It worked. The German people allowed them to be rounded up and deported to places unknown. Whether they knew of their fate is a question to be answered. They happily acquired the homes and properties as their own.

A book written by Bruce Bawer in 2006 entitled, "While Europe Slept" exposes the threat to Jews everywhere in Europe by the rapid increase in the Muslim community which he estimates at over 20 million just three years ago.

I have just re-read the letter I composed to the Israeli Embassy in Washington 6/11/03. It was entitled, "Open Letter to the Israeli Government". My basic premise I still believe was right. The only difference is that Bush is no longer President, Obama is. Regrettably he is pushing hard for a separate State solution, which I claimed then and now, can never be. All of the territory must be encompassed under one government with charity and understanding between those of different beliefs. If in fact the current Israeli government is pushing to create a Jewish State then they will fail. A homeland for displaced Jews is one thing. Discrimination against other faiths is another. What I had proposed was assimilating portions into the new nation and letting the natural process of improved lives for all create the climate necessary to sustain the process.

I decided to check out the internet, so I Googled "Anti-Semitism". You could do the same. There are many opportunities to research history up to the present day even here in America. I copied a few that caught my attention. Most I gleaned from Wikipedia. There are hundreds of other sources. I do not have the wherewithal nor energy to explore every word to see if 100% correct. Should you see something that bothers you as to accuracy I would be pleased to hear from you. I have sent out retractions in the past and will no doubt also in the future with this or other subjects.

The following are from those sources:

Recently Professor Dietz Bering of the University of Cologne defined anti-Semitism as, "Jews are not only partially but totally bad by nature, that is, their bad traits are incorrigible.....Jews bring disaster on their "host societies" or on the whole world, they are doing it secretly, therefore the anti-Semites feel obligated to unmask the conspiratorial, bad Jewish characteristics".

Henry Ford wrote many anti-Jewish articles in his newspaper "The Dearborn Independent".

There is a large section entitled "New Testament and anti- Semitism". It points out the many instances where the Gospel writers expressed Jews in unfavorable terms. I had pointed out one in the paragraph at the top of page two.

Martin Luther wrote a book "On the Jews and their lies". He advocated the murder of those who refused to convert to Christianity, writing that "We are at fault for not slaying them".

The Roman Catholic Church in the 19th and 20th centuries was strongly anti-Semitic.

Saudi textbooks today teach Muslim children to "hate" Christians, Jews and other non believers. A line from a book stated that " fighting between Muslims and Jews will continue until judgment day". In 2005 the US expressed "serious concerns" over anti Semitic passages in Pakistani text books.

Finally there are recent articles about incidents in America which proves to me that those of the Jewish faith are not safe even in our country, so we can't just say it is a problem somewhere else.

I guess all I can ask of you receiving a copy of this letter is to take any opportunity to stand up for and offer protection to Jews whenever a situation presents itself. In my life I have known a number of people who are professing Jews. I have considered them friends. I don't discriminate based on a person's religious beliefs.

October 13, 2009

44. Mr. Quinn wrote an extensive article advising shoppers in Tucson that the lowest cost food products could be purchased at their local Wal-Mart store. As you will see I shared my thoughts with him by copying articles I had written over the past few years about Wal-Mart. I never heard from him or the editor of the Star, not that I expected that they would respond.

Dear Mr. Quinn,

I read your very prominent plug for Wal-Mart in today's paper. It will no doubt convince many to leave the grocery stores they have been using to take advantage of the pennies to be saved.

You mentioned that there were 10% who refuse to shop at Wal-Mart. As you will note, should you read the following letters, that I am one of those. Who knows maybe my personal boycott has inspired others to follow.

You and those who employ you may believe you are doing a public service but I see it otherwise. Providing support to this gigantic enterprise will contribute to the demise of the other stores, who pay decent wages and provide good benefits for their employees.

Yours truly,
Jack B. Walters

The following letters were written by me over the past four years.

Boycott Wal-Mart

The Walton family's wealth grows exponentially. It now exceeds $100 Billion. As their fortune grows it is on the backs of workers throughout the world. Every time you see the commercial with the happy bouncing ball reducing the cost of items, you can be sure workers somewhere have taken another hit. Their arrogance is beyond belief. They are attacking communities all over California attempting to by-pass elected officials and bring ballot initiatives to the voters, some of which have been successful. The strike against the groceries was for increased health care and eventually was granted. The reason the owners fought this was not to deny benefits for their workers but to survive. Once Wal-Mart enters the arena, they know they cannot compete with the low wages and low benefits Wal-Mart employees receive.

Farmers worldwide who grow the produce are also forced to sell at their cost or worse because of the pressure brought to bear by the enormous purchasing power this huge monolith can exert.

You would think that $100 Billion is enough, but it just proves that greed is still very much in vogue these days.

Will anyone be willing to join me in my personal boycott so that it becomes something more than an empty gesture? Pay a few cents more and support the other merchants and their workers until such time as the Walton family sees the error of their ways.

Jack B. Walters
March 18, 2004

Memorial Day Wal-Mart Style

Since shopping on Memorial Day weekend is not one of my activities, it took a like minded friend to alert me to the advertisement placed for this weekend. No reference anywhere to the real intent of this weekend. It is all about Mexico with their flag prominently displayed. All ads are in English and Spanish. They were obviously catering to the new immigrants including those here illegally. It was probably smart marketing but it also was a disservice to those of us who care about our heritage and those who gave their lives for us.

Jack B. Walters
May 28, 2006

Enforce big-box ordinance
Published in the Arizona Daily Star-August 1, 2006)

The Star continues to push for the City Council to make an exception to the big-box ordinance (Chicago big-box decision may impact Tucson". July 29, 2006). It ignores the fact that the ordinance was initiated to protect the markets in existence in town.

Wal-Mart, with its immense leverage, can undercut any competition. Its only positive attribute is the low cost of its products. The poorer of us enjoy this advantage. If people had better-paying jobs they might not be so needful.

Wal-Mart epitomizes evil in my book. The destruction of local manufacturing jobs, the driving out of well established local stores, the low wages it pays to farmers, and the fact that all of us have to pay extra to support its employees are the reasons I refuse to shop there.

The City Council should enforce the ordinance as written.

Jack B. Walters

Take This Job and Ship It
By Senator Byron L. Dorgan
August 2, 2006

I have just finished reading this excellent book which cuts deeply into the stupidity of our government's trade policies which are detrimental to the best interests of American workers while at the same time doing little to improve the life style of workers in the countries that are included in these agreements. The only winners are the huge corporations that have a stranglehold on elected officials. Big business equals big influence. The obscene size of contributions overwhelms the conscience of those who are in elected office and who are supposed to be looking out for all of us.

The recent letter I wrote to the editor was inspired to a large extent by his stories about Wal-Mart's continuing effort to force American industries to shut down their US factories and relocate to China or some other very low labor cost country. These are the same countries that exploit child labor and ignore the impact on the environment.

I will not imitate the book contents other than to state that I highly recommend reading it and then do what you can to throw the bums out who are so derelict in their duty.

Sincerely Yours,
Jack Walters

45. *An editorial writer had written a column that pointed out correctly that the emissions from the Navaho Station were not the cause of air pollution since the prevailing winds are from the West and for the most part, are not over the Grand Canyon. I wrote as I felt he was misleading his readers since air pollution is a problem that must be dealt with no matter what part of the country is most affected.*

Navajo station needs emission control reprieve

You went to great lengths to make your point that pollution from the stacks head east away from the Grand Canyon. That is completely beside the point. Let me take you back a few years. Near the end of the Clinton administration the EPA was taking a number of facilities like this to court to force them to add the equipment necessary to curb pollution. When Bush took office, one of the first things he did was put a stop to these efforts and for the eight years he was in office nothing was done. To the Obama administration's credit, it would appear that the EPA has once again been allowed to do their job of improving air quality in our country. There is no reason that the Navajo station should be exempt, anymore than the others that put massive amounts of pollution into the air on a daily basis.

You question whether the technology has been proven. After so many years have gone by, I just cannot believe that the technology doesn't exist required to solve this problem.

Of course, it will increase our electrical costs, but so what. Either we want clean air or we don't. You can't have it if nothing is done. What about Global Warming? Either this is a problem or it isn't. If it is, and that is my position, then we need to start addressing it rather than continuing to delay for additional decades. I don't believe we have that luxury.

October 26, 2009

46. Let me begin this by referring you to the article I wrote on Oct. 18, 2007. That is a part of this book in the 2007 section. I had written a follow-up letter. My first had been written July 1, 2004. That was also added at the bottom of the latter one. This one you are about to read represents a partial apology since my original assumption I found was incorrect. I say partial because of my strong feelings that my thoughts are correct. There are two other letters immediately following this one pertaining to the same subject. I hope you will read as well.

FDR'S words quoted on the WW II Monument in Washington, D. C.

On July 1, 2004 I wrote an extremely critical letter condemning the people responsible for the quote from FDR's Declaration of War Speech which appears on the World War II monument which was dedicated by President George W. Bush on May 29, 2004. I accused them of deliberately leaving out the words "so help us God". After discussing with others and rechecking with Snopes I find that I was partially wrong. I say partially because I still feel that they were insensitive and chose another phrase that was more politically correct.

This is the phrase they used;
PEARL HARBOR
DECEMBER 7, 1941, A DATE
WHICH WILL LIVE IN INFAMY…
NO MATTER HOW LONG IT
MAY TAKE US TO OVERCOME
THIS PREMEDITATED INVASION,
THE AMERICAN PEOPLE, IN
THEIR RIGHTEOUS MIGHT,
WILL WIN THROUGH
TO ABSOLUTE VICTORY.
PRESIDENT FRANKLIN D. ROOSEVELT

If I had been on the commission it would have read as follows;
PEARL HARBOR
DECEMBER 7, 1941, A DATE
WHICH WILL LIVE IN INFAMY…
WITH CONFIDENCE IN OUR
ARMED FORCES, WITH THE
UNBOUNDING DETERMINATION
OF OUR PEOPLE, WE WILL GAIN
THE INEVITABLE TRIUMPH.
SO HELP US GOD.
PRESIDENT FRANKLIN D. ROOSEVELT

The first two lines were at the beginning of his speech. The rest was five paragraphs from the end. The sentence I want is the second from the end. Now you may ask what is the difference. I will reply that his final words which ended with a prayer were the words that inspired all of our people to come together to defeat the Axis powers. If there was someone who was an adult living at that time on the commission, then I just cannot understand why he or she did not feel as I still do about his speech and that sentence. People born after can be excused I guess, based on how screwed up we have become. The greatest generation caught fire hearing those stirring words. As we die off no one will remember. I think that is just plain wrong.

October 23, 2009

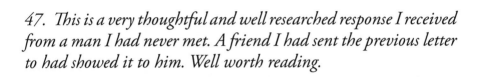

47. This is a very thoughtful and well researched response I received from a man I had never met. A friend I had sent the previous letter to had showed it to him. Well worth reading.

The first document, dated July 1, 2004, is a letter that you wrote stating that you had confirmed that FDR's Pearl Harbor speech at the World War II memorial had been altered, that the commission had committed sacrilege and had tried to rewrite history by deleting the phrase "…so help us God." You demanded an apology from those responsible, and you requested that everyone reading your letter ask their members of Congress to correct what you referred to as a distortion of history.

In stating that you had confirmed that the FDR speech was altered, you did considerable damage in misleading your readers who might have otherwise checked out this misinformation had they not trusted in your research? We can only hope that very many of them did not proceed in contacting their Representatives and Senators and in flooding the American Battle Monuments Commission (ABMC) with complaints.

That, of course, is all water under the bridge. We all make mistakes. But what concerns me is your second letter dated October 23, 2009.

You had previously demanded an apology for the wrongs you believed were committed, but when you discovered your own error, you gave no apology to your readers or to the ABMC. Instead, you accused the ABMC of being insensitive and of yielding to the pressure of political correctness by selecting a portion of the speech other than the one that included the phrase "…so help us God.".

You wrote that you don't understand why they did not feel as you did about the FDR speech. I am surprised that you didn't attempt to see if you could find out what their reasons were before you wrote this second letter.

You are entitled to your opinion, and I must admit that I also might have chosen the paragraph from FDR's speech that ends with "…so help us God." However, your second letter has prompted me to do some research that have changed my mind. I now agree with the commission's choice on the inscription. Here's why.

First, let me say that the choice of the inscriptions at the memorial was not a trivial decision made by an incompetent. According to an August 2, 2006 letter from Michael G. Conley, Director of Public Affairs at the American Battle Monuments Commission.

The inscription selection and review process involved two American Battle Monuments Commissions (one appointed by President Clinton, one by President Bush), a Memorial Advisory Board, military service and civilian historians, the Library of Congress, the National Park Service, and the Commission of Fine Arts. The inscriptions were chosen based on content alone-for their reflection of the American spirit that fueled the victory of democracy over tyranny. The inclusion or exclusion of religious references was never an issue, nor was it ever discussed.[1]

Among those associated with the memorial, who were old enough to remember FDR's speech or who served in the military, were such names as, Senator Bob Dole, General P. X. Kelley, USMC (Ret), Lieutenant General Julius W. Becton, Jr., USA (Ret), Major General Patrick H. Brady, USA (Ret), General Frederick M. Franks, Jr., USA (Ret), Major General John P. Herrling, and John William "Bill" Murphy. [2]

Certainly, some of these citizens must have been inspired by FDR's speech, just as you were, and they would have objected to the inscription if they believed it to be incorrect or unsuitable.

Remember that the purpose of this specific inscription, at this specific location in the memorial, was not to honor Franklin D. Roosevelt's ability to inspire the American public or to acknowledge their faith in God. It was to accurately preserve the memory of Pearl Harbor. Those responsible for selecting the inscription had a very good reason for choosing the way they did. It was because of the words "No matter how long it may take us to overcome this premeditated invasion..."

They believed that the words "premeditated invasion" more specifically related to the events at Pearl Harbor and to the start of the war than the paragraph that ends with "...so help us God." Rather than distorting history, the inscription is an heroic, and far from politically correct, reminder to all future generations, and especially to those who would try to rewrite history, of how the war started and who was the aggressor.

Director Conley described this decision, as follows, in his letter to Congressional Representative Gary G. Miller on January 20, 2006:

The entire speech contains more than 450 words. Because of proper letter sizing and inscription area, we had to manage between 35 and 40 words in total to achieve both the aesthetic effect and evocation desired. The inscribed sentence was selected because its phrasing ("No matter how long it may take us to overcome this premeditated invasion... ") directly relates to the rest of the carved inscription, which commemorates the attack on Pearl Harbor. [3]

Many people who heard Roosevelt's speech remember the expression, "... so help us God." They believe that it was one of Roosevelt's most inspiring phrases and that leaving it out does not portray Roosevelt in his best light, but highlighting Roosevelt's ability to inspire was not the purpose of the inscription.

I remembered having seen a copy of Roosevelt's original draft with his handwritten changes on it. I wondered if the "...so help us God" phrase was part of his original dictation or if President Roosevelt had inserted it later.

I found a copy of the original draft and was surprised to see that the original version contained neither of the two paragraphs in question. The paragraph about winning through to absolute victory was added by Roosevelt in one of his changes to the first draft, but there was nothing resembling "...so help us God" in the original version of the speech, or even after Roosevelt had revised it.

As it turned out, the entire paragraph, "With confidence in our armed forces with the unbounding determination of our people we will gain the inevitable triumph so help us God." was written and inserted into the speech by Roosevelt's aid, Harry Hopkins.[4]

Grace Tully, who was Roosevelt's secretary and who took the dictation from Roosevelt, tells about the event in her book My Boss, (1949). You can read an excerpt from her story at Eyewitness To History.com [5]

An external voice in the matter regarding the high points in FDR's speech is that of Halford Ross Ryan, Professor of Speech at Washington and Lee University. In his book U.S. Presidents as orators, published in 1995 before the memorial controversy, Ryan commented about the "absolute victory" phrase:

"No matter how long it may take us to overcome this premeditated invasion, the American people in their righteous might will win through to absolute victory" arguably one of the most elegant lines in the address, was inserted by FDR on the first draft. [5]

So, even from a literary standpoint, the "absolute victory" paragraph seems to have been the better choice.

Regarding your statement that FDR's final words were a prayer that inspired all of our people to come together to defeat the Axis powers, I disagree.

Roosevelt's speech might have inspired all of our people to come together to defeat the Axis powers, but it was no prayer.

On December 8, 1941, neither President Roosevelt, nor the Congress, nor the American people were in a prayerful mood. It was anger that inspired Americans that day. It was the same kind of anger that inspired King David to swear, "So help me God, Adonijah shall pay for this with his life."[6] Without that anger, the American public might not have responded as they did.

It was a great speech, and I believe that the excerpt selected by the World War II Memorial Committee to tell the Pearl Harbor story was appropriate.

Those are some of my thoughts on this matter, and this is about as far as I can go with the amount of time I have available. I hope that some of my comments and references help to change your mind about the World War II Memorial.

I also hope that, if you haven't done so already, you visit the World War II Memorial in Washington D.C. and enjoy our country's tribute to her World War II veterans.

Sincerely,

Gilbert J. Mros
Minneapolis, MN
October 26, 2009

48. This was my response to the letter received in the previous item. I am happy to report that our relationship did improve a little later and we correspond from time to time. In my years of writing the response from Mr. Mros was the best researched I have ever received. I will not bring this subject up again. I have done all I believe I can do. There is no chance whatsoever that my thoughts will ever lead to a revision on the monument.

Dear Mr. Mros,
October 28, 2009

You went to great lengths to prove me wrong. The research including the names on the commission proves your capability to use the internet is impressive.

Before I respond I would like to share the history I have with Glenn and Bill. Glenn and I met over 50 years ago in Pottstown, Pa. We were both in the early years starting our careers. I determined early on that he possessed an intellect superior to my own. I was the impetuous one, ready and able to take action sometimes with disastrous results. For the most part over the years he has accepted my personality. We were in fact the mirror image of Felix and Oscar. I will let you guess which one was Glenn.

I met Bill at the Puncochars one night when I was visiting them. I took to him right away. He also is an intellectual with talent as an inventor and scientist. In his note to me he described the last meeting with them and you as wonderful. I can only assume that you are as intellectual as they are. I am sure the conversation was stimulating and important.

You and I have gotten off on the wrong foot. I am not sure we can recover, not that it is important, since you are there and I am here with little chance of meeting. Having said this I will now address the issues you raised.

My 2004 letter- that was five years ago. I can remember reading the speech and also listening to it. I was so focused on his final words I erred in that I did not accept the paragraph chosen. With political correctness the vogue these days I assumed they didn't use it because of the reference to God. The only reason I sent out what I considered a correction is because the subject had come up recently and I went into Snopes and other places and finally accepted that I had erred. As far as the readers of my book are concerned I doubt very much if any of them took the time to contact their legislator. That is something that I seem to be the only one who cares enough to do, so I doubt that anyone was flooded with comments. I can assure you that I never received a response from my letter.

You say I did not apologize. The fact that I sent the second letter to those who had received a copy of my book was intended as an apology for erring. I guess according to you I needed to kneel down and beg forgiveness. The recipients of my book are friends. I never charged them for it. They are not some group unknowing to myself. I was embarrassed that I had made a mistake. Where you find fault with me is that I still believe that the commission erred.

I was 13 years old when my family and I gathered around the radio to hear these stirring words given by one of our greatest presidents. The phrase that stuck included the "So help us God" part. Neither Glenn nor Bill was old enough to understand and I will guess that you weren't either.

You state that at first you agreed with me but then read why they chose the other phrase including premeditated invasion instead, and that it fit in with the theme better. I did not understand that this was a Pearl Harbor Memorial. It says WWII, so I assumed in was for the entire conflict. Therefore I will not apologize for my second letter. The words I picked were far more important. I will concede that my reference to it ending in a prayer was not correct. It was more of a threat than a prayer, but either way those words inspired a nation.

49. I sent this letter to my hiking friends and others. I had accomplished a personal goal that was meaningful to me.

1,000 SAHC Peaks Climbed

November 2, 2009 I reached my latest objective of climbing 1,000 peaks on the SAHC Peak list. I guess I am one of those people who need goals to spur them on to accomplish something. After reaching the highest award of 400 different peaks in March 2008, I kept climbing whenever I could and bit by bit the numbers increased until this new goal came in sight.

I started climbing mountains shortly after arriving in Tucson in the fall of 1993. Wasson Peak in the Tucson Mountains was my first. I fell in love with the beauty of the desert and the joy of reaching the summits and then looking down on the spectacular landscape which Southern Arizona possesses. The original top achievement award was the 315 which were peaks identified within 75 miles of Tucson. This took me to remote mountain ranges and onto 4 wheel drive dirt roads to places 99.9% of Arizonans have never seen. All of it is spectacular. We have seen all forms of animal life including bears, lions, coatimundi, fox, antelope, deer, lizards and lots of snakes, mostly rattlesnakes. We enjoy seeing them. We keep our distance and let them live. We also never litter. We have great respect for the wilderness and try to enjoy it without leaving a trace that we have been there except for the practice of hiding a bottle in a rock pile on top with our names written in. It really has no significance. It is just something we enjoy doing.

Once I reached the 315 goal I started leading hikes helping other friends reach their goals. In addition I would go on hikes led by others particularly to the newest peaks that were added for the 400 award. The distance from Tucson was increased to 100 miles to find enough named peaks for this purpose. I never really intended to try for the 400 but while I was off on a family visit Roxanna opened a member account for me on the web site created by John Yau and had started putting in my peaks. Once I accepted her idea I spent a considerable amount of time going through my records and when I brought it up to date I found I had 345 separate peaks already so I accepted the challenge of adding 55 more. I owe a deep debt of gratitude to those who cheered me on and particularly those who guided me to these new very remote areas. The ones most responsible were Doug Howard, Brian Larson and Ron Meech. There were others of course but these three really took on the challenge and I will be forever grateful for their encouragement and extreme effort extended on my behalf.

I must now admit that in recent months I have climbed Saddleback in the Catalina's on a weekly basis as club hikes. Erika Hartz leads a hike to Blackett's Ridge usually every Monday and Friday. To reach it you pass by Saddleback, so every time I hiked with her, I took the side trip to the peak. Many do not think highly of this as far as difficulty is concerned but at my stage of life it still takes considerable effort for me to climb. It is 6 ½ miles and about 1,700 ft. of elevation gain and takes me about 3 hours and 20 minutes roundtrip to complete. Particularly in the hot summer months we are grateful to finish before the extreme heat builds up so we leave very early sometimes using flashlights. Another aspect of aging is that my pace is slower now. Erika has allowed me to start ahead of her main group and I usually hike with Roxanna so Erika doesn't have to accept responsibility for me. If I end later, I will call her at home and advise of my safe return.

This past Saturday Ron Meech led a hike with 15 hikers to Harts Butte, Helvetia BM and Weigles Butte in the Santa Rita Mountains. The wind was unexpectedly fierce and each of the peaks were extreme bushwhacks including rocks, many of which were loose. I was very conscious that I held up the group from the beginning but particularly the last peak. I honestly didn't think I could make it, but because of Ron's patience, the understanding of the group and Roxanna and Jim Terlep hiking with me step by step, I did reach all three. Jim steadied me numerous times as fatigue affected my ability to maintain balance. I wanted these to close in on my objective. They were 997, 998 and 999. This was the fourth time for me to climb these peaks, but the only time it was so difficult to finish. For the sake of friendship with Ron and the other hikers, I will limit the times I hike with the group to hikes I am fairly confident I can finish without delaying the hike.

Now that I have cleared this point up I want you to accept this letter as a feel good report on what for 16 years has been my main source of amusement and accomplishment. This morning Jim Terlep came in support of my 1,000th peak. We met him at the route leading to Saddleback peak. Erika and her group were also waiting for me to lead them to the top. Once there, we all signed the register. Roxanna provided treats at a tailgate party in the parking lot to celebrate my achievement.

I am not sure what I will do, going forward from today. There are trail and canyon hikes offered, but being a dedicated peak bagger I would like to continue on those I feel confident I can do at a reasonable pace. I have had unbelievable experiences over the years and have made many friends. I could write another book just about those adventures but I won't.

(K.O.H) Means keep on hiking,

50. Within a week after my previous bragging letter, I discovered that I had a serious blood clot in my right leg. In the months following no more peaks have been climbed. I am active but cautious as a cut can have serious consequences. Good thing I accomplished my goal when I did.

My Thrombosis
November 18, 2009

I have been diagnosed as having a deep thrombosis. It is in my right calf and consists of a totally blocked vein about ten inches in length.

I have been going downhill for some time now but refused to accept my problem as anything other than laziness. The last two Saturdays in October, I pushed myself to the limit. I climbed Mildred peak to within 20 ft. and just couldn't finish. I was exhausted, and then the following week I did the three peaks I reported before in my 1,000 SAHC peak letter. I followed that with my thousandth on Monday. As it has turned out it is good I did as I will not be climbing any mountains for many months. Right now I am restricted to short walks on level ground, no hiking, golfing or any other exercise. I am not even allowed to drive.

Let me return to the sequence of events leading to the treatment I am now receiving. After reaching my goal I fell apart, even when golfing I got extremely tired. Finally last weekend I mentioned to Roxanna about the pain I was feeling in my right leg. She looked at it and said I should call my doctor as she noticed newly formed varicose veins. I should have gone right to emergency but I waited and called my doctor Monday. He got me right in and as soon as he looked he sent me to emergency where I spent over seven hours. They took an ultrasound and discovered the problem. I was treated before I left. For three days a nurse has been calling twice per day giving me a shot in the stomach and I am taking coumadin tablets. I was critical of the doctor when she told me that it was rat poison. I replied that I didn't really have to know that. The purpose for the shots is to get the blood thinning process started, after which the pills should be sufficient. I will be on them for six months or perhaps forever depending on how long it takes to dissolve the blockage without clots breaking off. That is the danger I am in. A clot could go to my lungs, heart or brain. Sure hope that doesn't happen. A result of having blood thinned is that you become susceptible to bleeding, even a bruise will result in internal bleeding. This will restrict my activities once I begin again to those relatively safe, meaning no bushwhack hikes.

The doctor in the hospital gave hiking credit for the condition I am in. She said this would have happened 15 years ago otherwise. I should explain. While in college I was in a car wreck that nearly took my life. I was thrown out on a gravel road. Mt right femur was broken and the back of my right leg sustained damage resulting in varicose veins. This area is where my current problem is located. In other words it would have happened sooner or later.

So there you have it. Wish me well. I will be tough to live with if inactivity continues as it is now. The way I feel right now I don't want to do anything, but that will change as those who know me well will attest to.

51. With all the talk about our excellent health care system, this article shows how low we rate in regard to deaths of infants.

High infant death rate in US
Associated press article 11/4/09

In the late 60's my family and I were living in Calgary, Alberta, Canada. Our youngest son was born there. A nurse started calling on my wife early in her pregnancy and continued for several months after birth. She provided information and counseling. Since this was our third child, my wife well understood the process but none the less it was appreciated. For a first time mother it would have been extremely valuable. This service was provided without cost to us.

We have it all wrong in America. Compare this minor expense to the tragedies that were mentioned in this article. Is it even possible to apply a cost evaluation when so many lives are lost who could have been saved?

Hooray for our health care system.

November 4, 2009

52. This book confirms how outstanding our troops continue doing their duty under extreme circumstances.

THE STRONGEST TRIBE
By Bing West

Mr. West is a reporter who became imbedded with our military in Iraq beginning in 2003. The book ends as 2008 begins. He provides detailed information about our policies and procedures in conducting the war throughout these years. The title was from a statement made to him by an Iraqi. It was meant as a tribute to the fighting ability and total dedication of our soldiers in carrying out their mission.

As a person who was totally against starting this war from the beginning and still today, this was difficult reading. I spent most of my reading time over three weeks to finally finish.

Before even starting to read, I knew that my opinions wouldn't change after reading. As far as I am concerned it was a fiasco from the start. It became a dark pit into which billions were poured together with the blood of thousands of our military men and women, for what purpose?

His concluding sentence hit me directly. "No nation can sustain its values by claiming to support the soldier while opposing his mission. The truth is that the nation determines the mission." In the many articles I have written since the war began I have continued to praise our soldiers while condemning the leaders who put them in harms way, presenting them with a nearly impossible job to do with their hands tied behind their backs. Over and over they were sent into cities going door to door with death waiting each time they entered. Not being able to distinguish who they were in conflict with, they sometimes took fire without responding to avoid civilian casualties. They weren't functioning as soldiers but as policemen in a foreign land without knowledge of language or customs.

The lack of leadership from Prime Minister al-Maliki created many obstacles. He was so concerned about the resurgence of Sunnis that he created the division between them and the Shiites which he supported. It was our military that convinced Sunni leadership to stop fighting us and work with us to drive out Al Qaeda terrorists and bring peace to their areas. This began in 2006 followed closely thereafter with the "surge".

I accept that this book is accurate in its content. What I do not accept is that we have any business being there or Afghanistan for that matter. If you are interested in learning much more than you have read in newspapers or heard on TV, then I recommend this book to you. I found it at the Public Library.

November 5, 2009

53. *Following the Fort Hood massacre, I react negatively to the response of President Obama and members of his administration and high ranking military officers. The theme of their remarks concerns their fear of backlash against Muslims. They seem not concerned at all that the Major who committed the deaths of so many had given every indication that he was a radical by his speeches and actions. All we want is to expose the failures that led to this tragedy to hopefully prevent a re-occurrence.*

The Islamic Republic of America?

This latest outrage at Fort Hood together with other news items and history compels me to put the following words on paper. Army Major Nidal M. Hasan killed 13 soldiers and wounded 38 others. As the story unfolds it is becoming clear that there had been many instances that should have sounded alarm bells. Soldiers have come forth and stated that they said nothing out of fear of being rebuked for discrimination. The thought of this man counseling soldiers returning from Iraq and Afghanistan is very disturbing. What might he have said to them and what might be the continuing effect of his words? Hasan yelled out "Allahu akbar" as he was killing our soldiers. Checking Google we find that it means "God is the greatest" The God of Islam of course.

President Obama in his eulogy stated that it was the act of a deranged person. "This much we do know—no faith justifies these murderous and craven acts; no just and loving God looks upon them with favor. For what he has done, we know that the killer will be met with justice—in this world, and the next." I don't fault him for this. This was not the time to discuss the larger issue of America and Islam. I am sure in the next few days he will address the American people as this subject will not just disappear. This was not thousands of miles away in a strange different country. This was right here in the heart of America on a base of 50,000 soldiers. If they cannot feel safe there, then is there any place of safety? That is the burning issue.

Six soldiers from Britain were killed recently by an Afghan in their unit. There have been instances in both countries of natives turning on Allied soldiers and killing them. This has happened repeatedly since the first Gulf War as we have tried to train and build local forces so they could provide a safe environment to their people as we start the withdrawal, at least in Iraq.

While the president said nothing, two of his underlings have; Army Chief of Staff General George Casey and Secretary of Homeland Security Janet Napolitano. Gen. Casey is worried about backlash and so is Janet Napolitano the Director of Homeland Security. She has filled top positions with Muslims.

In an interview with John King on CNN's "State of the Union" program the General said, "And frankly, I am worried — not worried, but I'm concerned that this increased speculation could cause a backlash against some of our Muslim soldiers. And I've asked our Army leaders to be on the lookout for that. It would be a shame — as great a tragedy as this was, it would be a shame if our diversity became a casualty as well." He went on to clarify that there were about 3,000 active Guard and reserve Muslim soldiers at the present time. It appeared to others, including myself that the possibility of discrimination was more important to him than the lives lost and the potential danger to our soldiers by some Muslim soldiers that have the same conviction Hasan has. How can this be shoved under the table? The Associated Press reports that while in the United Arab Emirates, DHS secretary Janet Napolitano warned against an anti-Muslim backlash after the attack at Fort Hood last week. "This was a terrible tragedy for all involved," Napolitano told reporters in the United Arab Emirates' capital Abu Dhabi. "Obviously, we object to -- and do not believe -- that anti-Muslim sentiment should emanate from this... This was an individual who does not, obviously, represent the Muslim faith." In other words backlash is her greatest concern. This is the Secretary who just recently placed two Muslims in high positions in her agency; Arif Alikhan, a devout Sunni Muslim to assistant secretary for the Office of Policy Department of Homeland Security. He was instrumental in taking down the LA Police Department's plan to monitor its Muslim community.

Alikhan is affiliated with MPAC, the "Muslim Public Affairs Council". The other is Kareem Shora, who was born in Damascus, Syria. He was appointed by DHS Secretary Napolitano on the Homeland Security Advisory Council (HSAC).

It was Islamic terrorists that destroyed the Twin World Trade Center Towers taking the lives of over 3,000 Americans. For eight years our soldiers have been fighting in two Arab nations against terrorists all of whom are of one sect or another of the Islamic faith. While I will not state that all Muslims are potential terrorists, the fact remains that there are millions worldwide already identified as such.

President Obama has said repeatedly his admiration for Islam in speech after speech and has stated America would never go to war with Islam. The real problem is that we have been at war for many years except it has been one sided. Islamic Fundamentalists are at war with America and our leaders will not accept this as fact. They fall all over themselves to not upset the Muslim followers of Islam. My greatest concern has to do with our current president, who I voted for in the last election. A friend sent me a video of his remarks over the past few years. It was created by Feel the Change media. Click on the following to hear for yourself what he has said and obviously believes about Islam.

http://www.youtube.com/watch_popup?v=tCAffMSWSzY#t=28
After you have done so, ask yourself if this is the person we feel confident in

leading us through these treacherous times. What will happen to the rest of the civilized nations if America falls? Total domination will be the result. If these radicals are allowed to continue being embedded in the highest government positions, sooner or later confusion and conflicting directives will undermine our confidence in government. Check out your history books. Whenever Muslims have attained control they act as a superior race. All who have not converted must live in a subordinate position. I for one will resist this with everything I have. I happen to like the basic freedoms we enjoy in this country while at the same time I am concerned about the direction we are going which I consider to be national suicide. We are doing this on our own, can't blame jihadists.

I just felt compelled to put these thoughts on paper whether they are read or not. At least I am willing to stick my head out. If it gets chopped off so be it.

November 11, 2009

54. I wrote another sarcastic article which the Arizona Daily Star did publish.

Do Your Patriotic Duty
This was published in the Arizona Daily Star

All true patriots gathered early this morning to rush into the Malls, signing their credit cards buying things that they and their family must have to live a happy life. We were instructed to do so following the 9/11 disaster. Let the soldiers put their lives on the line. Our job was to keep the economy moving. This continues today. Thirty years ago, I would have agreed as Americans were producing the things we went to buy, but not today.

This patriotic gesture is on behalf of the Chinese. You see many lost their jobs during the downturn when a few Americans woke up and decided to slow their trip toward becoming bankrupt. So I urge you to disregard your thinking of protecting your family to restoring the Chinese prosperity quickly. It will be a patriotic gesture.

November 27, 2009

55. I use President Obama's theme of his speech to West Point cadets, as the title of this article. He told them his reasons for increasing troop levels in Afghanistan. Within the next year or so graduates of the Academy will be over there giving their young lives, for what? I strongly believe he is wrong.

Our Security is at Stake

The above title was the theme of President Obama's speech delivered last evening to an audience of West Point Cadets, the nation and the world. Once again we are told that is in our best interests to place over 100,000 Americans in harms way, fighting an insurgency that will just not go away. I am convinced that our best days are behind us. We will squander thousands of lives at an additional initial cost of $30 Billion. This of course doesn't include the following year's costs nor the continuing cost of our 140,000+ still remaining in Iraq or the cost for the 71,000 already in Afghanistan. It doesn't matter that our national debt exceeds $12 Trillion nor that our tax and trade policies continue shipping more and more manufacturing jobs to China and elsewhere, nor that the unending give away unemployment fund is nearly consumed while they continue to consider extending for another year. To my way of thinking it might as well be forever since we continue to find ways to live a reasonable life without working for a living. Our government can just continue printing more dollars. So what if the value drops as long as the overseas suckers are willing to keep purchasing our nearly worthless bonds.

It really is easy to scare Americans, at least the Americans of today. It was just six years ago Pres. Bush, VP Cheney and Secretary of State Rice warned us of mushroom clouds and weapons of mass destruction. The Congress and the bulk of Americans bought it then and I believe still do. Half are still convinced that Hussein was behind the attack which has been proven false over and over to no avail. We lost over 3,000 in the 9/11 attack. Since then twice that many Americans have given their lives in the Middle East and perhaps as many as one million Iraqis and Afghans. Perhaps we should not consider them as people in the same class as Americans. That may be your thought but it surely is not mine.

I voted for Obama believing him to be a man of peace. I was wrong. He is no different from any of the other leaders in power since Jimmy Carter. The look on the faces of Defense Secretary Gates, Secretary of State Hillary Clinton and the other over decorated brass showed me that they were proud of our President and that in the end he did just what they wanted. He just dragged it out a little longer on the pretext that he was studying all options.

The comparison with the novel 1984 is eerie in the sameness. In the book we are in continuous war with one or the other great powers. It shifts from time to time. All historical records are erased so no one knows any difference. They only know we must fight the enemy, no matter which one. Being kept in fear makes docile citizens who comply without dissent. Those who try are quickly rounded up and mysteriously disappear. All have implants so the government has no trouble finding those who are viewed as trouble makers.

How close to this we are. We have troops stationed all over the world, 60,000 in Germany, and 35,000 in Korea and a similar number on Japanese territory. In case you don't remember we won WWII in 1945 and signed the armistice with N. Korea in 1953. While it was reasonable to occupy those countries at the time the conflict ended, it is totally unreasonable to remain today. Our excuse is security. With these troops ready and available we can initiate conflicts much easier. These numbers are totally inadequate should we face enemies in the millions as we do in Korea. To me it is all a charade. We continue to follow the dictates of the military/ industrial complex as we were warned about many years ago by President Eisenhower. We cannot win the confidence of the world's people by dropping bombs all over the place. We squander a minimum of a trillion dollars every year in our pursuit of military dominance. In the end we will destroy ourselves. There will be no white knights to come to our rescue. The world will laugh and enjoy seeing us in our misery. It doesn't have to be this way but will come to pass if we do not change. As for Obama he has set his course. Now we wait for our next opportunity to find a savior. I don't think it will be Governor Huckabee after we found out he commuted a 95 year sentence for the shooter in Seattle.

I watched a couple of news shows today just to get a feel. The hosts and their guests are all over the place. Trust me, it is all a sham. In the end when all the rhetoric has been spoken, Obama will get his troops and his Billions. The truth is no one will accept the consequences of pulling out, which brings me to the end. Two years from now, ten years from now or twenty there will still be American boys dying in the desert.

I am too old to do other than write or talk with others about these issues. I will not stop.

December 2, 2009

56. This columnist challenged us to respond which I did cheerfully.

Opinion Article 12/3/09 by Leonard Pitts (Poll as mirror)

Dear Mr. Pitts,

First I want to say that I usually look forward to reading your columns or listening to you on MSNBC. Your insights are normally well done. Where you fail is when you beat the race card thing to death. The last time I wrote was about the cop, the professor and the president. I feel compelled to respond to your latest.

You might be interested to know that I am a white man who voted for Obama. Race was just a side benefit. I liked what he said and after 8 years of the other idiot I wanted a complete change of course. You state that after all Obama is the president, Bush was also the president, I gave him no slack or respect because of the harm he did to America and the world. I never expect total agreement. That is not necessary. What is necessary is that I believe the president, no matter who he might be, makes decisions in the best interest of our future not what is expedient.

The fact that you can count me on the negative side of the poll has nothing whatever to do with his race but has everything to do with the policies he has promoted, those he hasn't but promised during the campaign he would, the old guard he has surrounded himself with which guarantees that no substantive change can possibly take place, his love affair with Islam world wide and placing Muslims in high level government positions, his "don't jump to conclusions about the slaughter at Fort Hood", trying terrorists in court instead of military tribunals, trying to scatter the rest from Guantanamo to US prisons, the multi billion bail out of Wall Street, billions for the ridiculous clunker program, billions for GM and Chrysler (Our reward for this is GM expanding production facilities in China), green jobs for solar collectors, light bulbs and windmills being produced overseas (these were promised for Americans). You get the idea.

If I were black I would overlook many things to provide support to one who had finally reached the pinnacle. What could you expect? For the rest of us who think and care we have had enough. I think we expected too much. Obama's solutions to problems are mostly throwing money without changing the basics that have brought us to where we are today. His latest on the troop increase in Afghanistan is the worst to date. I am including a letter I wrote yesterday for your perusal.

December 3, 2009

57. This letter reluctantly accepts the fact that Congress will give the president the funds asked for to expand the war. I say, so be it, then find the way to pay for it now through increased taxation or cuts in other areas of the budget.

Pay for the War

This is for all of you war hawks and weepy doves. Our Nobel Peace Prize winner president has told you of the dire necessity of increasing troop levels in Afghanistan. So be it. You hawks love the smell of Napalm in the morning and you doves like to look sad and say woe is me. If perpetual war is to be the future for us then I have only one request. Change that. I have only one demand and that is we pay for it. No more adding to the debt for our children's children to pay. This is our war. This is our time. This is our decision. If it is truly needed then we should all be willing to pay for it.

What I demand is the Congress adds a surcharge for those of us paying income tax or creates a national sales tax so that the rest can also contribute. I leave it to the experts to decide how much of an increase is required. I just demand it be large enough to pay every penny of the "surge". Play now and someone else pay later is no longer acceptable. This is not a game. We cannot continue spending money we don't have. The day of reckoning is now.

I know the wars would be over in a minute if your children were to be drafted. Because of the lack of courage or integrity of our elected officials that will never happen. By paying huge bonuses they are able to convince sufficient numbers to sign on or re-up. Therefore the only other way to get your attention is to make you pay for the cost. I am willing to pay my share, are you?

This will be a drag on the economy, no mistake about that, but do we really deserve to buy all these toys and gimmicks while we have boys dying in the desert so far from home. I say no.

I have sent this to my Congressperson and our two Senators which will be promptly tossed in the trash. If in the other hand they received thousands of letters they might get the message. That is all I can ever hope for.

December 7, 2009

58. I cannot accept the logic of bringing suspected terrorists onto American soil, particularly since Guantanamo will still have some of them, meaning that this prison will continue to function.

Transfer of some suspected terrorists to Illinois

The first action of President Obama was his announcement that Guantanamo would be closed. I was glad to hear that. Now 10 months later he advises he will spend millions renovating an unused correctional facility in Thompson, Illinois and transfer most but not all of these prisoners. This means to me that Guantanamo will still be a prison. I fail to see the merit to this decision. I call upon my Congressperson to deny funding so this idea can have a quick death.

Here is my simplistic solution. Put them on a secure plane ride back to their country of origin. Turn them over to authorities and let them decide their fate. This could be release, continued confinement or death as their laws prescribe.

To bring them to the heartland of America is just plain insane.

December 16, 2009

2010

2010

Listing in order by date

1. When you read a book like this you reaffirm how the powerful continue in power. The growth of this industry and the money earned is phenomenal. A must read.

BLACKWATER
THE RISE OF THE WORLD'S MOST
POWERFUL MERCENARY ARMY
By: Jeremy Schill

This book was published in 2007. In my opinion the author did an outstanding job of research. It is almost unbelievable that something this monumental could have been created and expanded as rapidly as it was.

Except for a few items from the book I am rather going to give you my personal conclusions after finishing reading. First, I already knew a great deal about them. I have followed as best I could the story of Blackwater so what I read was more filling in detail rather than discovery.

The idea started innocently enough. The founders decided that there was an ongoing need for a training facility for law enforcement. This was successful.

It was during the Bush/Cheney years that the idea of mercenaries came into full bloom. Blackwater was able to hire the best retired officers and skilled veterans to carry out their missions. At first they were hired to protect American and other officials in Iraq and Afghanistan. Later it grew to where it became nearly indistinguishable between them and our own military. The difference was the pay scale, in some cases well over $1,000 per day. These men returned home with huge nest eggs to support their families. That is those who were able to return home. They were given blanket immunity from prosecution whereas our soldiers were not. Not surprisingly many soldiers refused to re-enlist opting to stay in Iraq and to be financially rewarded for doing so.

Blackwater spawned other companies from around the world to where this has grown to immense proportions. There were well over 100,000 in Iraq alone, very nearly equal to our soldiers in number. My own personal opinion is that the administration, knowing the strain the wars were placing on our regular army and reserves, used this as a way to expand numbers without destroying the standing army. Not only that but all that was needed was appropriations from Congress which could be used as they saw put.

I wonder how many of you know that Blackwater mercenaries were sent to New Orleans. They were there before the federal government and most aid organizations. They claimed to be humanitarians but their purpose was to protect property from looters, etc. President Bush used the Katrina disaster to try to repeal the Posse Comitatus Act (the ban on using U.S. troops in domestic law enforcement), and Blackwater and other security firms initiated a push to install their paramilitaries on U.S. soil.

I have not tried to check on their current situation but I would venture to guess they are still prospering under the new administration. By the way, due to many controversies wherein Iraqis citizens were killed by Blackwater men the company changed its name February 13, 2009 to We.

This book is not a novel. I doubt if many will take the time to read. I do it so I can maintain my anxiety on current events. I'm not ready to settle down and take it easy.

January 3, 2010

2. It is my conclusion that the jobs bill has very little to do with private job creation and in fact mostly continues paying people to stay at home rather than working for a living.

Jobs for Main Street Program

Congress is preparing to pass another multi billion dollar stimulus program in February. One hundred billion of it will not create one single job. It will go for unemployment, health insurance, child tax credit, states Medicare costs, education jobs which are in jeopardy of being eliminated, etc., then another seventy five billion for infrastructure, police officers and summer jobs for disadvantaged children.

All of the above merely helps maintain the status quo but does nothing to create private sector jobs, which is where I would put the funds. I would use the same funds to lower tax for business and industry, particularly industry if possible, regardless of size, but if necessary at least to small business. This would create incentive for employers to increase production or start new businesses.

The Administration and Congress, it appears to me, are throwing funds into the air without a thought of reviving the private sector. A strong private sector will create good paying jobs for people who will contribute to the overall economy by paying taxes. The programs itemized above take away from the government taking us deeper and deeper into debt. It has been proposed to increase the national debt to over 14 trillion in February in part to cover the cost of this new stimulus package and the wars in the Middle East.

The other bold step I would take is to give notice to the Chinese and Indian governments that they must allow their currency to float as all other nations do. There may be other countries that do the same but these two are the giants who have been stealing American jobs. The previous administration and the current one have been too afraid of the consequences fearing these countries selling off American bonds. Should a real financial war begin they would lose as much or more than we would so I do not fear them nor should our government. As long as they are allowed this outrageous benefit American industry cannot possibly compete. Manufacturing that is not labor intensive would return to this country. How great that would be.

I continue to push these ideas as no one else is to my knowledge. I will be sending this to my Congress person and my Senators where it will be placed in the nuisance file.

January 5, 2010

3. I ridicule the thought that American's should buy war bonds to support our current war time endeavors as if this war could conceivably be compared to the Second World War.

New York Times Article

On January 3, 2010 an article from the Times was republished in the Arizona Daily Star. The title was, "War bonds likely won't work today, skeptics say".

It seems that Senator Ben Nelson a Nebraska Democrat introduced war-bond legislation last November similar to what was done in WWII. When he did it he said he hoped to "tap into the same spirit of patriotism and create a sense of participation in the war".

Later in the article were negative comments about saving versus spending since the experts continue to stress that we are a consumer nation and must stay deep in debt to keep the economy moving.

I take issue with both comments.

First, only someone who was not an adult during WWII could suggest that these fake wars with Iraq and Afghanistan could conceivably be compared to WWII. I was alive and old enough to understand the critical situation we faced against the Axis Powers and the consequences should we fail. At the beginning I was a newspaper boy. Except for an occasional 5 cent candy bar all of my earnings went to purchase War Bond Stamps. My proudest moments were when I had enough to buy a $25 Bond. No one told me to do it. I was not alone. There was no question of patriotism, we were all patriots.

I am still a patriot but I have not at the beginning or do I now support the useless blood and treasure being spent in these countries. All we will ever accomplish is to increase hatred for all Americans.

Second, I continue to be astounded at our government leaders beginning with Bush and now Obama in urging us to stay in debt in support of the well being of Chinese workers. The US Chamber of Commerce and the US Association of Manufacturers avidly support moving more and more manufacturing jobs to this new dynamic country while leaving Americans to get by somehow on government giveaways or low paying service jobs.

The reason I took the time to respond is because I am offended that articles like this make their way into print.

January 5, 2010

4. An excellent historical novel that I highly recommend reading.

The Pillars of the Earth
By: Ken Follett

This book was given to me as a Christmas present last month. As many of you know my reading is almost always non fiction. I strive to understand history, important people and current events. My son Andy wanted me to take a break and read a fiction book and I did.

There are 973 pages to read. It is a fascinating book about events taking place in the 1200's. The basic theme has to do with building cathedrals. That may sound boring but take my word, it isn't. Mr. Follett spent years traveling Europe and visiting the many different cathedrals. He researched the different types of construction, and weaves the designs into the story.

We follow the lives of many different personalities. Some are good and some are bad. It doesn't take long before you determine which is which. Tension builds almost on every page. I always try to absorb what I am reading and for that reason limit reading to finite periods of time. This was hard to do as I wanted to learn how each episode ends. Many times the ending was tragic. Other times it was as you would hope it to be. The drama continued to the last page.

Mr. Follett not only researched cathedrals, he also learned what it was like to live 700 years ago including the correct names of household and construction tools. The story takes place mainly in England. We learn about the strength of the church and the division of lands based on customs of the times. The fact that magnificent cathedrals could be built without modern day equipment is incredible. How it was done is explained very well.

It is not construction that is most important; it is the people we get to know and care about, with equal parts of joy and tragedy.

Up to the time of publishing Mr. Follett had 18 other books he had published. This one became one of Oprah's Book Club selections. I am sure it can be found at the Public Library. Mine is available to be loaned, just ask.

January 15, 2010

5. Once again I try to assure that this industry be returned to where interest on short term loans are more reasonable.

Payday Loan Article

I am not always in agreement with your editorials but this one is 100% correct. As you state the voters have spoken loud and clear their revulsion of this bloodsucking industry. As I understand it most states have put them out of business. Let them revert to the 36% which is probably reasonable when default is considered.

Legislators pushing to overturn the electorate's wishes will be sorry as the voters will exact their revenge the next election cycle. They had better keep the bribes as they will have to find other work to do.

You were gracious to publish an article I wrote in 2006. In it I proposed what I felt then and still do to be a reasonable alternative. At the time the issue was about service people. The principle could also be applied to civilians as well. I am attaching that article for whatever it is worth. I hope you keep the heat on until this is over. Thanks.

January 19, 2010

6. *This article is my attempt to interpret the reason for the spectacular election result in Massachusetts.*

Nobody Gets It

On Tuesday January 19, 2010 the voters in Massachusetts voted in a Republican, Scott Brown to fill the remaining two years of the late Ted Kennedy's Senate seat. This was a stunning upset, totally unexpected until near the final weeks of the election process. Kennedy had held that seat for nearly one half century. The Republicans are jubilant. The Democrats are dejected. I listen to the talking heads. They all get it partly right but no one gets it completely right. This article is my attempt to tell them all what it means.

In spite of the long held understanding that Mass. was a liberal State, I noted that nearly 50% are registered Independent. I became one myself a number of years ago mainly to make the point that neither party was acting responsibly. They have both sold out our people on the altar of greed. It is not all their fault as the costs of becoming elected have grown to unbelievable amounts forcing them to beg for corporate or union funds to cover their expenses. On several occasions I have written my thoughts on how to bring sanity back into the process, all to no avail as I do not have the wherewithal to reach those in a position to demand change.

It was the Independent voters that made it possible for Obama to become President. After a year under his leadership we as a group are dissatisfied with the direction he is taking the country. The huge bailouts for those responsible for plunging us into a depression and to this day continue to give out huge bonuses without regard to the harm they did and continue to do, does not sit well with those who are struggling to survive. The 1500 page health bill full of pork, putting the main burden on employers when the opposite is required if we are ever to regain the losses to China and elsewhere, attacking "Cadillac" plans like the ones those of us enjoy as a result of many years of service to our former companies, the forcing of uninsured to buy from the health care providers or face financial penalties, the fact that the costs are applied immediately while the benefits are delayed for four years, and on and on. The plan is a direct giveaway to the health and drug industries. We had expected better than what is being proposed. Then there is the expansion of the "war" in Afghanistan and the inability of the President or anyone else in the Administration to say the word "Muslim" when referring to terrorists when in fact the vast majority professes to be Muslim. Only peace loving Muslims around the world, can bring a stop to the carnage, not so called Christian Americans. As long as we continue to try to dominate Muslim countries like Iraq, Afghanistan and Yemen we will foster more hatred against us.

The tea party types are opposed to the government providing health care. They shout how government cannot do anything right. They are not totally wrong as there is much that is wrong but the blame should not be placed on employees but on the legislation and the burdens under which most federal employees are forced to accept. Nearly all advanced countries have found the way to care for their citizens by the government paying the cost to the providers. Eliminating the health insurance industry would save multiple billions on an annual basis. The Republicans are totally wrong on this. They call it government take over of private industry. They also support the mega banks who continue to gobble up everything in sight getting ever bigger until they are so huge their failure threatens financial stability.

Just today there was an announcement that Kraft is buying Cadbury for $19.5 Billion. This creates the world's largest confectionary company. Whatever happened to prohibiting monopolies? The British employees fear the loss of their jobs and rightly so. It will not be long before their jobs disappear to Asia just as our jobs continue to be lost.

We must strengthen government not weaken it. When the Social Security Commission was severely weakened years ago, millions of cheats found it easy to not pay their share of taxes. Billions are lost each year while those of us who try to do the right thing pay our taxes honestly. The Security and Exchange Commission must be allowed to control excessive speculation by mega banks and Hedge Funds. On the other hand the Department's of Energy and Education are bloated monstrosities that neither lessen our dependence on foreign oil nor improve the education of our children. They do provide high income jobs for thousands of bureaucrats.

My own ongoing concern was clearly shown last evening on Tom Brokaw's television program "Crossing America". From town to town there were boarded up buildings and depression, much of it caused by huge corporations buying up local industries the dismantling and sending to China. Small farmers were shown trying to continue farming as it should be done while the government gives billions to corporate "farmers". Here is my idea. Create a commission to study all factors which are driving good paying jobs overseas and family farmers off their land. Take into consideration the tax burden, incentives provided. (I have read that some factories in China are given free electricity). How can a tire company which has huge electrical costs compete? In some cases they have even provided factories at little or no cost. This distorts Capitalism to where it is unrecognizable. Not allowing their currency to float gives China a 40% advantage right at the start. Every advantage they give must be countered here at home or all is lost. The shipping cost and the real cost of currency should be enough to protect American jobs and would if these other factors weren't so huge. If you have seen pictures of cities in Asia you would see gleaming skyscrapers and prosperity while our cities are decaying structures. It does not have to be this way but we will continue the downward spiral unless those career politicians are removed from office.

If Scott Brown meekly follows the direction of the "so called" leaders of his party then he will deserve to be thrown out of office two years from now. I am discouraged already. Believe it or not we received a phone call this morning from Senator-elect Brown telling us how great John McCain is and that we should be grateful for his leadership in Arizona. This must be another John McCain. The one from Arizona deserted us for two years while he campaigned to be president.

The vast majority of citizens have had it with party politics. We want results and we want it now. I overheard a conversation on a radio talk show. In it they referred to professional politicians. These are the ones we must get rid of, including John McCain. Let them sail into the sunset with their inflated pensions and their gold plated health care. Our only chance to reclaim our government is to get rid of all of the professional types and replace with successful everyday citizens who care and want to restore our nation to its rightful place in the world and then return to whatever their current occupation is. Won't you take the pledge? Won't you vote out all professionals regardless of party? Until Federal term limits are created to limit terms of office to some reasonable number we will be cursed with the same inept leadership we have today. Won't you ignore the big money advertisements saying how inexperienced the candidate is and give them a chance. If they don't produce then vote them out. It should be a simple formula. The reason it isn't is because we are made to fear new people and because of name recognition. Our next opportunity is November 2010. I can't wait to see if voters wake up and take back their country.

January 20, 2010

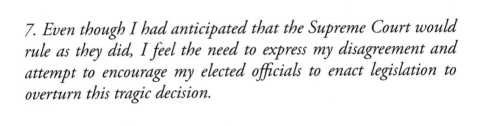

7. Even though I had anticipated that the Supreme Court would rule as they did, I feel the need to express my disagreement and attempt to encourage my elected officials to enact legislation to overturn this tragic decision.

The Supreme Court Decision
January 22, 2010

Yesterday, as expected, the Supreme Court under the direction of Chief Justice Roberts overturned restrictions on Corporations and Unions using their funds for or against candidates running for office. Specifically it agreed that corporations and unions may spend freely to support or oppose candidates for President or Congress, overturning a 20 year old ruling. The decision was five for and four against. It confirmed that the two members appointed by George W. Bush may continue for decades to come, keep promoting his right wing agenda in Washington and every State.

In 1886 there was a case before the Supreme Court between Santa Clara County and the Southern Pacific Railroad Company. In opening comments Chief Justice Morrison Waite stated that the 14th amendment, which protects the rights of individuals applied equally to corporations. This was not however the basis for settling the dispute but his statement has been used as if it had been a decision. From that point forward Corporations have used their wealth to further their causes. Later, another Court granted Labor Unions the same rights.

Administrations and Congress beginning in Teddy Roosevelt's time have passed legislation trying to curb or lesson the impact that the wealth of these entities possessed, with their ability to influence elections far more than individuals or political action groups could. That is all gone now. The flood gates will be opened. The gullibility of most voters convinces me that candidates of their choosing will dominate in the future unless new legislation is passed which meets the High Court's concept of Constitutionality.

Listening to right wing talk show hosts yesterday confirms for me that this ruling will be to the advantage of the Republican Party as they have historically been the party of big business.

As disappointed as I and others like me have been at the feeble efforts of the Democrats in "power", I am saddened that our hope to curb corporate power will come to naught. What this means to me is that the people of America will continue to be manipulated to do their bidding to the detriment of all I care about. This means total domination by the big guys, continuous war somewhere with some country, with our young men dying to further the interests of multi-corporations, degradation of the environment or anything else that limits their ability to increase profit.

I could say more but what's the use.

8. I wrote a second time pointing out that corporations are not necessarily owned by Americans and that this ruling could cause foreigners slanting elections for their countries benefit not our own.

Corporations

I am still incensed by the Supreme Court's decision opening the flood gates to allow them to spend unlimited funds in favor or against people running for the office of President or Congress. This letter is my attempt to explore further the meaning of this. I will start with the definition as found in my 1952 Webster Dictionary. I added the date as definitions may have changed since then. I will leave that research to you.

Corporate – United in a body, as a number of individuals who are empowered to transact business as an individual; formed into a body; united; collectively one.

Corporation - A body corporate, formed and authorized by law to act as a single person; a society having the capacity of transacting business as an individual; the body or bodily frame of a man.

I can see where the idea of granting the same rights to corporations as individuals could be found in the definition, but I insist that is not what is meant. All it means is that when people join together to conduct business, that they then work together as if they were a single person. In no way does it mean that they are an individual entitled to the protections as listed in the Bill of Rights for people.

Further I want to find out the courts definition of a corporation allowed to finance elections. I will be sending this to elected officials and others asking for a response to clarify this ruling to me. The following is a concern. There are many corporations doing business in the United States. Let us assume they are all legal entities. Some of them are owned by Americans, others are owned in total or in part by foreign entities, just for example; Budweiser, Miller, Toyota, Honda. The list goes on and on. We know for instance that the governments of China and other countries have pseudo ownership of their corporations. Are they to be allowed to spend funds to influence our elections? I can remember not so long ago when there was uproar over political contributions given to candidates for President from China. I can envision foreign countries having an opportunity to support candidates who are advocates to the benefit of their countries rather than our own. This would be outrageous. Somewhere, somehow I will get an answer to my concern.

January 23, 2010

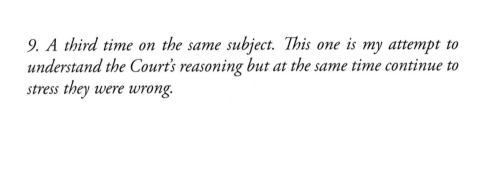

9. *A third time on the same subject. This one is my attempt to understand the Court's reasoning but at the same time continue to stress they were wrong.*

Another look at Corporations

In my previous letter I pointed out the question of foreign ownership. This one is my understanding of what a corporation is. I feel somewhat qualified as I was a member of upper management during the many years I worked for Firestone. I had contact with the top officers and learned how the system worked.

A group of people decide to come together in a common purpose. They put in capital and expertise. They satisfy all legal requirements and then get going. These are people with a common purpose. They think as one, just as the Dictionary described. If they didn't then dissension would cause problems leading to failure. I am talking about the President, Vice President, Chief Financial Officer and Directors of the various segments that make up a company. They are assisted by a Board of Directors who oversee the operation and provide guidance and sometimes prohibit the officers from pursuing a course of action. These people are similarly minded. They come from the outside and possess knowledge helpful to the officers.

With the Supreme Court giving them free license to spend as much as they want for or against candidates for Federal Office, the group mentioned above will make those decisions. My problem with this relates to the employees of the corporation. There could be thousands. Each of these has friends, family and acquaintances. They belong to civic and sports or other types of clubs and go to their place of worship. The people they associate with have an impact on how they feel about issues of national importance.

Now this is the point I wish to make. These thousands, who are the heart and soul of the corporation, have no say in corporate decisions. They are the ones that do the work of producing, designing or in any number of other ways make the corporation a success.

There is another group who have no say and that is the shareholders of the company. They have their own opinions about government. There may be social issues that are of importance to either group.

What I am trying to say is that the corporation might be spending the money created by employees or spending money that could be used to upgrade the company or give to shareholders as dividends.

A corporation is much more than the top officers. The Supreme Court made a dreadful decision. The Congress must find a way to reverse it. I will be following this closely as time progresses. I hope you will as well.

January 23, 2010

10. I really like Mayor Bernaro. He currently is running to become Governor of Michigan. I sure hope he is elected. He is the type I continue to search for, people willing to fight for American jobs.

MAYOR VIRG BERNERO OF LANSING MICHIGAN TEARS INTO FOX NEWS ANCHOR- GREAT!!!

February 24, 2010
http://www.youtube.com/watch?v=a-nLS6FJtSM

I have just listened to your response in defense of working people. It was strong and direct. It is what I have been waiting to hear from elected officials. For whatever reason, there is a bias against factory workers making decent wages. I retired from the Tire Industry and enjoy good health care coverage and a pension which together with social security and the assets I was able to accumulate, allows me to live a decent life.

Why not take a leadership role and get other like minded Mayors to ban together and fight for those employed in factories, both clock and salary. Demand that China allows their currency to float and eliminate the 40% advantage that gives them. Most important our country must go the way of all other civilized nations and provide universal health care to take this unfair weight off of American business and industry. You and I know Americans can compete but not with their hands and feet tied. We need fair trade not free trade.

Please lead us out of this mess. In a few more years all major manufacturing will be gone. Do you really think we can be a super power without and industrial base?

Thanks for listening.

11. This video that I listened to pointed out the failure of give away programs and the dependency that they create. I compare them to FDR's programs of putting people to work.

FDR Democrats vs. Today's Breed

Once again I took a little time before deciding to send this out. It will seriously offend many of you receiving it. The reporter comes down hard on liberals and the promises they continue to offer as solutions to our problems.

I was, and always will be, one who believed that FDR was a great president. He was touted as a liberal. The difference between him and today is that he insisted that men went to work every day to earn a living. He inherited desperate times. Unemployment was more than double what it is today. Since the private sector could or would not provide work, he created programs to pay men for doing something like creating trails and shelters. I have hiked on some of them. Once things started functioning the private sector resumed their normal roll.

The liberals of today expect the government to provide everything to people who do nothing to earn the largess. This video clearly shows the failure of this philosophy. It also comes down hard on unions both automotive and teachers, neither of which were or are responsible enough to make sacrifices for the good of keeping manufacturing jobs or teaching children.

The video is 13 minutes in length. You may not be willing to take that much time. I hope some will.

I will conclude with a statement that the do nothing Republicans have nothing to offer either. They are too busy helping the rich get richer including themselves which is why I want all incumbents thrown out of office.

Thanks Bill, you really struck a nerve with this one.

Jack

February 26, 2010

12. I respond every time an award is given by a judge or jury which results in taxpayers taking a hit.

Pima County Jury awards $40 million in drunken driving case

A 14 year old boy was killed by a female who was intoxicated. This happened 1/12/08. The award was assessed against the city of Tucson, Chuy restaurant and the driver. The cities share was $13 million as the jury felt the road was poorly designed. Evidently a lawyer was able to convince the members of the jury to award as they did. I find fault with it and have the following comments to make.

1-It is not the city that will pay, it is the taxpaying citizens. A city that is deep in debt to where it is taking drastic measures to stay afloat does not have the means to pay a frivolous penalty like this.

2-It is my opinion that the city is not bound by some State mandate to design roads to every persons liking. We could be driving on gravel. An engineer makes a decision and somehow that translates to irresponsibility on the part of the city leaders.

3-The driver in question had driven on this road many times before and even in her inebriated state should have known what the road was like.

4-Perhaps a waiter or bartender recognized that the woman had drunk to much alcohol but again why place such a heavy burden on an eating establishment, one of which is struggling to survive in this down economy.

5-This is for the grieving parents; after paying legal expenses you should take any thing over that and give to the charity of your choice. To rake in millions from the death of a loved one is not morally acceptable. There was no mention in the headline article regarding this. If that was their intent then I apologize for this comment.

February 14, 2010

13. A novel about events occurring in the desert south of Tucson. I found it very interesting. Later I actually met the author. He signed my book.

Crossers
By Philip Caputo

This is a very special novel for people living in Southern Arizona and particularly for hikers, mountain climbers, birders or just plain motor tourists. The reason is that it mentions places that are so familiar to many of us. It centers on the San Rafael Valley south of Patagonia. It includes the Canelo Hills, the Huachuca, Whetstones, Mustangs, Santa Rita's and other mountain ranges. It mentions the Gadston Hotel in Douglas, the Steak Out Restaurant and the cattle shipping yard in Sonoita, Nogales in the USA and Mexico, the Holding Center in Florence where illegal immigrants are processed, Patagonia and south into Mexico. The Rialto Theatre, University Medical Center in Tucson and the Arizona Daily Star are made a part of the places visited and the newspaper read. All are familiar to me and friends from the Southern Arizona Hiking Club (SAHC).

It is a novel, but it is so close to the truth, that it is almost like reading a newspaper account of happenings today. It begins at the turn of the century of 1900 and ends in 2004. It follows the lives of families who settled down into ranching after exploits soldiering in the Mexican War of Independence. We get to know these people as they come to be embroiled into conflict with drug runners and illegal immigrants who use their ranch as the pathway into El Norte as they refer to America.

One of the main characters loses his wife as a victim of the flight from Boston that flew into one of the World Trade Towers. After contemplating suicide he opts instead to seclude himself in the wilds of Arizona living on the ranch owned by his uncle. After a time he comes alive again as he learns the life of a rancher and does find love. We learn much about the cattle industry in the desert country and ride horses into the canyons searching for livestock or hunting.

This is one of those books that stop the present day story by returning to the early 1900's. This is the author's way of tying it all together. The major conflict of the story is a consequence of what happened in earlier days.

The people seem real. You will care what happens to them. There is beauty, love, hatred and greed all mixed together.

If the story took place somewhere else it would still be interesting but when you add in the familiarity of the area, for those of us who have been there so often, it comes alive.

February 2, 2010

14. I found many things in this book that I agreed with. I truly believe there would be as much food grown with greater variety should farms be returned to family farms as they were earlier in this century. One person was extremely upset and let me know he disagreed. He considered this to be Communism. What he doesn't know is that under Stalin farmers were driven off their land and huge State owned farms were created which made me counter that what was happening in America and around the world was basically the same that had been done in Russia 70 years ago.

Soil Not Oil by Vandana Shiva

A book report

This is a small book, only 144 pages, but it is filled with dynamite. She clearly states her beliefs about the direction world leaders are taking on behalf of corporations. This is a theme I have been pushing on a personal basis for some time now. The difference is my thoughts are based on gut feelings; hers are based on incredible technical information that was very hard for me to understand. Perhaps you will do better?

Let me try to explain without resorting to the myriad of terms used by Ms. Shiva. She has particular animosity to the Monsanto and Cargill corporations. If you saw the documentary entitled Food Inc. you would understand her concern. These giants are on a world wide mission to have complete control of food production. With their "patents" they can demand that local farmers only purchase seeds from them. What the effect of this is that variety is sacrificed for increased productivity at an enormous expense for farmers. These patents were granted by our own Supreme Court, the same folks who just recently decided that corporations can spend any amount they wish on Federal elections.

Her premise is that the definition of productivity is all wrong. It is based on reducing the workforce on farms in favor of huge fuel driven machines. She points out the huge cost of transporting over thousands of miles by plane, ship and truck. All of which receive huge subsidies from the governments. The energy used to create the bio fuels, fertilizers and seed are immense. All of this adds to the concentration of CO_2 in the atmosphere which is accelerating global warming. The other tragedy occurring on a daily basis is the destruction of tropical forests to create land to produce bio fuels which in her and my opinion are not energy efficient.

She sees the return to farming worldwide as the solution to problems such as pollution, global warming and unemployment. I agree. In our own country huge giveaways are included in each year's farm program with most going to the mega farms, sometimes just for leaving the ground idle. Her and my program would be just the opposite. Give the greatest assistance to the little guys. The acreage planted would be the same but millions of people could return to life on farms as it was just 30 or 40 years ago. Wouldn't that be better than them migrating to cities searching for employment that doesn't exist and going on the dole? What a man made tragedy and we sit idly by as if everything is OK.

Mrs. Shiva's credentials are impressive. She was a leading physicist before becoming a world-renowned environmentalist. She won a Nobel Peace Prize in 1993. I found this book in the Public Library.

February 14, 2010

15. *Just as I predicted our taxpayer money is going to Chinese factories not American. I feel this is a betrayal of what we had been promised.*

Two articles in today's Star caught my attention.

1 - Four Democratic Senators are pushing legislation to assure that Stimulus funds for alternate energy are spent in America not China. It seems that solar panels and turbines are being produced in China

2 - The second reminded us that in 2014 we will no longer be allowed to purchase incandescent light bulbs. In case you are not aware, all of the fluorescent bulbs being manufactured today are made in China. In addition General Electric just recently stopped producing incandescent bulbs in America. I can only assume they have moved their production to China as well.

I have two questions to ask. Where are our great and wonderful "conservative" Senators? Why aren't they joining forces with the Democrats mentioned in the first item? The second is what right does the Federal Government possess that they can dictate the bulbs every day citizens want to purchase?

March 4, 2010

16. I wrote a letter to the author of Crossers after listening to him at the Arizona Book Fair.

Mr. Philip Caputo,
March 13, 2010

I was privileged to attend your session today at the University of Arizona Book Fair. You autographed my copy of your book, "Crossers" which was very much appreciated. In conversation with my friend Chuck Peters you agreed he could share your e-mail address. I wanted it so that I could send you my review of your novel. In the short time I was near you I stated that your book was more true life than novel which you readily agreed was true. I can just see you on the cattle roundup with branding and neutering and eating the goodies afterwards, and also riding horseback in the canyons that I also know quite well having hiked to the top of every mountain of any consequence in Southern Arizona. South of Patagonia contains the hikes I enjoy the most.

I consider myself to be a writer of sorts, the kind that pours his heart out and nobody cares. What this means is that I have not been recognized and have not had the funds I believe are necessary to get a publication noticed. In my latest book which I expect to finish shortly, I have included a book review of "Crossers". I am adding an attachment of it to this letter so you can see how much I enjoyed reading. When my book is finished I would like to send you a copy. There are some items in it very similar to the thoughts presented by you and the other two authors. Thoughts I have been writing about for seven years now. It all began for me when I acquired my first computer and was able to use Word to compose.

The three of you know what should and could be done to alleviate the illegal immigration and the drug problem. I have no doubt our elected officials understand as well but they are so beholden to big money that they dare not put in reforms; instead they salve our collective rage by building higher fences and hiring more agents. I will keep railing at this as long as I am able to do so, whether it makes a difference or not.

17. I have made it my business to write to Mr. Pitts every time he writes an article with racial overtones.

Response to your article dated 3/14/2010 entitled "A reminder that evil comes in all genders and colors"

Writing to you after reading one of your articles is becoming a habit for me. I only do so when it contains racial content. This one was a real stretch.

You are elated that a potential terrorist was not only white but also a diminutive American female. Most of your article was devoted to hammering other columnists that over the years since 9/11/2001, have called for the common sense profiling of Arabic men who fit the profile of those who died while carrying out their dastardly deed. I could give you a hundred or more examples of other terrorist atrocities over the past decade. I am sure you are well aware, so I won't clutter this note by listing them. As for Colleen LaRose, there was ample evidence for our security forces to stop her from committing the violence she was planning.

Norman Mineta was the Secretary of Transportation under President George Bush at the time of 9/11. He was interviewed on 60 Minutes and stated firmly that profiling would not be allowed. This was quite understandable from his standpoint since his parents of Japanese descent had been incarcerated at the beginning of WWII, unjustly as it turned out. The outrage of Americans to the acts committed on "A date that will live in infamy", was the justification.

What is happening worldwide today is something altogether different. The radical Muslim leadership is committed to converting the entire planet to their beliefs. Only if you bury your head in sand can you ignore this fact. At the time I tried to make sense out of profiling by stating that if the Irish Republican Army was intending to attack us, then we should take special steps to look for white, blue eyed Irishmen. The fact is they aren't but Arabic Muslim men and women are. They will strike us again if they can. Taking precautions of checking country of origin or profiling makes sense to me. No matter how you look at it, LaRose was an aberration.

I do agree with your final comment that evil comes in all guises. No argument here.

March 14,2010

18. I responded to a letter to the editor that convicted Toyota of putting profit ahead of safety. I tried to counter as best I could.

Toyota Letter

There was a letter to the editor this morning that I must reply to. It was from Guy Josserand III. The subject was the recent episode with the Toyota Co. He went too far when he lumped Toyota, Ford and Firestone with Enron. Enron was an out and out scam perpetrated by Ken Lay, a close personal friend of the Second President Bush.

I was a plant manager with Firestone making passenger tires during the 500 problem. This was not greed; it was the direct result of trying to convert too quickly from bias to radial. My company took it on the chin. What is never said is that all US tire manufacturers were having the same problems to varying degrees. The Ford Explorer was tip over prone due to its height. The design was soon changed and no further problems were reported.

As to Toyota, in my opinion they have been crucified by the Media and by Congress. I own one and am completely satisfied with its performance. Toyota led the way into the new world of Hybrid vehicles while G.M. in particular dragged its feet. Toyota Executives earn a third as compared to the Big Three and are scheduled for a 30 % reduction in line with their current fiscal problems. The Democratic Congress enjoys beating up on Toyota executives; I believe to try to prove that they are as irresponsible as the Big Three and to placate the UAW union. Remember Toyota was not bailed out with Billions of tax payer dollars nor will they be. They are aggressively reacting to repair the re-called models. My next purchase will be Toyota and I would venture to guess that other owners feel the same as I do.

March 1, 2010

19. Outrageous law suits filed for alleged drop in value of Toyota vehicles.

American Ghouls

We Americans are a special breed. We are like vultures that descend on dying animals and devour their carcass, not satisfied until the bones are picked clean. I am ashamed to be associated with them. I have always prided myself in being an American but I will not associate myself with what many have become. The following paragraph will explain my wrath.

In today's Arizona Daily Star there was an article from the Associated Press detailing lawsuits in process against the Toyota Corporation. I can accept that persons injured or deaths as a result of sticking accelerator pedals could be justified in filing claims but what appalled me was that to date over 89 class action law suits have been filed to recover loss of value of Toyota vehicles as a result of the mechanical problem being resolved. Kelley Blue Book has lowered the resale value of Toyotas by an average of 3.5%. These law suits could potentially cost the company in the Billions.

I proudly own a Toyota vehicle. Any law firm that contacts me will be rudely dealt with, as I would never be a part of anything as heinous as this. I can only hope there are likeminded others out there that would agree with me.

The law profession being what it is will always try to take advantage of situations as they arise. In addition juries seem to take great delight in granting huge awards. I am not proud of US Senators berating Toyota executives or Federal Judges working overtime to create class action law suits on behalf of all owners. I wonder how it is possible for manufacturing companies to exist in the America we have become.

March 11, 2010

20. More outrageous law suits filed, this time for drop in value of Toyota stock.

Another letter in defense of Toyota

This is my third letter on the subject of law suits against the Toyota Company. It seems the ghouls I referred to before have just gotten started. It was reported on March 22, 2010 that new law suits are being filed against the company. These are to recover losses in stock value due to the recent recalls of vehicles. I wonder what effect these will have on further driving down the value of the company's stock.

Just for kicks I googled the stock history of General Motors. In the late 90's a share of stock was worth in the $80's per share. The latest selling price is $0.75 per share. How about that for losing value. This is even after being bailed out by our government to the tune of billions. I don't suppose closing down the Hummer Division or Saturn or Pontiac had any adverse effect. In fact if you are interested check out the various actions of the company since the 1900's and you will see a continuing process of selling off assets.

In my opinion the mismanagement of this company was outrageous. They refused to enter the new world of fuel efficient vehicles while Toyota led the field. I tried to find out if there were class action law suits in process against the loss in value of General Motors stock. I couldn't find it. Perhaps you will.

To put an end to this letter I would like to come to the defense of all industry. The quality level when compared to a few decades ago is fantastic. The dependability has vastly improved.

Law suits against products produced today our creating havoc with the profitability of many manufacturing companies. The profit margin per unit sold is not large enough to pay out billions. There must be a way to control them or manufacturing will go the way of the Dodo bird.

March 23, 2010

21. I try to take a common sense approach to the subject of Unemployment Benefits.

Welfare and Unemployment Benefits

I have been pondering this subject ever since the Arizona Daily Star placed a two column editorial on March 5, 2010 criticizing Senator Jon Kyl for remarks he made during the debate in the Senate over continuing unemployment benefits for the entire year of 2010. He was quoted as saying "it was a disincentive for people to seek work".

As a reminder to my readers it had been previously been approved for the entire year of 2009. What this means to me is that persons previously in the work force could have a full two years of receiving a weekly check in Arizona of $265/ week. Their only requirement is to keep applying for employment similar to the job they had been doing before being laid off.

I very seldom find myself in agreement with our good Senator but in this case I am, at least partially. The reason for partially is that in the end he did vote to extend, I assume under extreme pressure such as he received from the news media.

I will now show how insensitive I am. I would have voted against it or at the very least modified the process.

I am now going to share comments made by Andy Rooney on 60 Minutes Sunday March 21, 2010. He was also upset. He talked about the need for work crews on construction projects or roads. The only job these out of work people deem suitable for their talents is to be the supervisor. They would never consider manual labor. It is beneath them, what with their educational levels and previous jobs. He added that we need plumbers, electricians and brick layers to rebuild our infrastructure that is crumbling all around us. I thought to myself well done. Millions of listeners heard him; some might even be elected officials.

Let me digress now and discuss welfare. Prior to August 22, 1996 many people had spent their entire lives living on their welfare checks. President Clinton signed the "Welfare Reform Act" on that date. He was working with a Republican Congress who insisted changes be made and they were. From that time forth there were stipulations that set limits on entitlements; required most to engage in job activities which included work experience, community service, job training or vocational education. In addition they must find work within two years or perform community service. It mandated a minimum of 30 hours per week and imposed a lifetime limit. Checking the Internet, even with these changes it is mind boggling the various and sundry rules that I am sure can be bent. Regardless, at least an attempt was made and it has been reasonably successful in getting people back to work.

Now let's return to the subject of Unemployment Benefits. There has to be a way to get these people who are capable back into the work force. The minimum wage in Arizona at the present time is $7.25/hr. That times 40 hours equals $290/week. That would be $25 more than the unemployment check. Of course leaving home and traveling to the job site would be a cost that would deduct from wages earned. I would go so far as to allow deductions that would assure the minimum of $265 is maintained. Most unemployed would be expected to find work paying more than the minimum. My point is that not working for two years is just plain wrong. It is no wonder our nation is on the brink of insolvency. This give away to people in their wage earning years cannot be allowed to continue. It is at this point where I like to remind that FDR's programs got men out of the house. He did not want them to get used to idleness so that when real jobs were available they would step right in. Why can't our elected officials understand this fundamental truth? I would also ask the editor of the Star to reconsider and put forth a proposal of his or her own.

March 23, 2010

22. I just wanted to put my two cents worth after passage of the health care bill.

Health Care Bill Passed

I have waited several weeks before attempting to put words to paper. If you are still with me so far you will have read the articles I wrote attempting to suggest what I thought should be in the bill. I pretty much struck out.

There are high sounding words abounding with praise from the one side and derision from the other side. As for me, I hope that the Supreme Court, upon examination will find that the Federal Government has overstepped its Constitutional authority by demanding that everyone must buy health insurance. This is by far the worst aspect of the legislation. Like everyone else who mentions this I have to state up front that I am not a lawyer but common sense tells me that the founders of our country never had it in their minds that the government should have this much authority over the lives of the people. The power of the Federal Government was intended to be limited in scope and all else the responsibility of State Governments. It has been reported that 18,000 IRS agents will be hired to monitor compliance of citizens and those found guilty were to be fined a hefty sum to get their attention. If we were hiring agents to collect taxes owed by those who deliberately cheat the system, then I would say hooray, but not this.

The unseemly deals cut to purchase votes were smarmy at best and irresponsible at worst. Those involved should suffer defeat at the next opportunity for people to vote. The health insurance industry won out as I had predicted. These millions of forced new customers, most of whom are young and in good health will be a profit boon to the industry. Many of these people are college graduates struggling to find employment in their chosen fields and saddled with debt accumulated to graduate. They will have little to show for their years of dedicated learning and will be forced to put off purchases and improvements in their lives with these costs to contend with.

Depending on the ever changing definition of poverty, those individuals or families will automatically receive free health care thru Medicaid. My question knowing the devastation that can be wrought by illness, why would these people ever strive to rise above the poverty level? The few dollars of additional income would not be worth it if they lost free care. This is just something to think about.

The heavy burden to pay for all this will fall on those who thru skill and effort have reached the upper levels of the middle class. While I am always willing to make sure the very rich pay their fair share, I consider this a disincentive for striving to excel. What do you think?

Another topic not related to health care is the legislation that has already passed the House and is waiting for Senate approval. This is the Cap and Trade Energy bill. Within a year after passage you will not be able to sell your home unless it has been inspected to assure it complies with the ever changing energy and water efficiency standards. I have seen estimates that an average cost could be $6,000. I bet you didn't know about this. You just assumed as I did that the intention was to provide incentive for industry to improve. Once again the Federal Government is taking control over the lives of every day citizens. If this also passes, in my opinion, the light of freedom in America is fading away at an accelerated rate.

March 29, 2010

23. I am astonished that the nations in the United Nations cannot agree on sensible restrictions to assure the survival of fish stocks in the oceans.

1982 UN Committee on the Law of the Sea

I have been reading articles and watching news programs recently which relate to the depletion of sea life in the oceans of our world. According to an article I gleaned from Google, the United Nations has been debating this subject and attempting to resolve at least beginning in 1982. All manner of fish and coral life are disappearing. The coral because of fish nets scrapping the ocean floor. With the technology at their disposal today fishing vessels are extremely efficient and there are increasing numbers putting to sea every year. Many nations led by America have attempted to put some order into the process to little avail. Salmon runs are depleted by the mass fishing of cod which nurtures them during their annual migration. Further with the technology they can be found at sea and harvested long before returning to the streams that spawned them. Tuna is reaching the point of no return and the nations wanting them the most refuse to make even small reductions. These same nations harvest fins from sharks and throw the carcasses back into the ocean and continue to hunt and kill whales for "scientific" purposes while most of the civilized nations accept the need to let them rebuild their numbers. The primary nations involved are Japan, Norway and Iceland.

Recent efforts by the United Nations were thwarted by China, Japan and Russia. What this proves to me again is how useless the United Nations is in resolving issues of critical importance to the world. A few nations can prevent programs from being implemented to curb what some nations consider to be their right, and so populations will continue to be depleted while the U.N continues their useless unproductive debating sessions.

March 29, 2010

24. I just wanted to provide food for thought for any Tea Partiers who might read this article.

Random thoughts about the Tea Party movement

As a self described "Last Angry Man" you would expect that I would rally around this new group of disgruntled citizens. I haven't for a number of reasons. The first is my total disregard of their number one leader, former Governor Sarah Palin. She moves rapidly around the country. Just a week ago she spoke to about 4,000 people at the Tucson Fairgrounds. Her rallying cry was "Do you like your freedom". This was followed by the comment that the new Republican Party wasn't the party of no; it was the party of hell no. Both comments were cheered by the attendees. I totally disagree with every statement she makes. People like her stir up hatred and indirectly incite their listeners to violence as has been noted across the country in the days following passage of the health care bill.

The wrath of this movement is centered on the Democrats and is striving for the defeat of any who voted for the bill. I feel the same way, but what they conveniently choose to forget is that the Republican Party was in power for eight years, during which time nothing of positive value was done for Americans. They can talk about their health care ideas being rejected. Where were those ideas during their eight years in power? They gave us two wars, a senior drug program that was a costly give away to the drug companies and the "No Child Left Behind" program which adds billions to the cost of education without adding to the learning experience. I have proposed many times that canceling this program would allow precious, scarce funds to be spent on education not testing.

There is little chance that a tea partier will ever read any of my writings but if they did this is what I would challenge them to do, vote against any candidate regardless of party who accepts campaign funds from corporations or unions. This may be impossible to do. If that is so then look for any candidate that accepts the fewest dollars. We must wean them off of the bribery gifts they receive today or we will never regain our freedom. Search for populist type candidates who care about the things most Americans care about and not about what the corporations demand.

Just this week there was another article about a major energy company shutting down production of solar panels in our country and moving to China. This would not stand if we had a president who understood that this was wrong. I say that because I have not heard of any comments from the White House that they understand or care. Believe me our former president also did not care. Millions of factory jobs were sent to China on his watch so don't tell me that an overwhelming victory by the Republican Party will be any better.

I strive for the day a third party arises that consists of candidates that do not accept corporate gifts, a party big enough to include all Americans under their umbrella. Then we could begin taking back our country. Until then I urge the tea partiers to not allow them to take your vote for granted that you will be in lock step for any candidate with a Republican label. Feel sorry for those of us who voted in the present administration. All of our hopes and dreams have already gone up in smoke. That in the end is what is most disturbing to us all and that is that rhetoric spoken that we want to hear is not what happens once elected. We must be more vigilant and question all candidates and check their record leading up to their candidacy. This takes time and effort which most would rather not have to do. We don't have any other choice. It is now or never.

March 30, 2010

25. I decided to end these writings with the words of men other than myself. The first are the agonized words of President Lincoln. The outcome of the civil war was still in doubt. He confirms that slavery was the reason for the conflict. He acknowledges that both sides pray to the same God for support. He believes that the sin of slavery must be borne by both North and South and until removed the loss of wealth and life will continue. His last words were a call to put hatred aside and restore the land without rancor or hatred. With his death shortly after this speech was given those words were forgotten.

Abraham Lincoln
Second Inaugural Address
Saturday, March 4, 1865

Fellow-Countrymen:

At this second appearing to take the oath of the Presidential office there is less occasion for an extended address than there was at the first. Then a statement somewhat in detail of a course to be pursued seemed fitting and proper. Now, at the expiration of four years, during which public declarations have been constantly called forth on every point and phase of the great contest which still absorbs the attention and engrosses the energies of the nation, little that is new could be presented. The progress of our arms, upon which all else chiefly depends, is as well known to the public as to myself, and it is, I trust, reasonably satisfactory and encouraging to all. With high hope for the future, no prediction in regard to it is ventured.

On the occasion corresponding to this four years ago all thoughts were anxiously directed to an impending civil war. All dreaded it, all sought to avert it. While the inaugural address was being delivered from this place, devoted altogether to saving the Union without war, urgent agents were in the city seeking to destroy it without war—seeking to dissolve the Union and divide effects by negotiation. Both parties deprecated war, but one of them would make war rather than let the nation survive, and the other would accept war rather than let it perish, and the war came.

One-eighth of the whole population were colored slaves, not distributed generally over the Union, but localized in the southern part of it. These slaves constituted a peculiar and powerful interest. All knew that this interest was somehow the cause of the war. To strengthen, perpetuate, and extend this interest was the object for which the insurgents would rend the Union even by war, while the Government claimed no right to do more than to restrict the territorial enlargement of it. Neither party expected for the war the magnitude or the duration which it has already attained. Neither anticipated that the cause of the conflict might cease with or even before the conflict itself should cease. Each looked for an easier triumph, and a result less fundamental and astounding. Both read the same Bible and pray to the same God, and each invokes His aid against the other. It may seem strange that any men should dare to ask a just

God's assistance in wringing their bread from the sweat of other men's faces, but let us judge not, that we be not judged. The prayers of both could not be answered. That of neither has been answered fully. The Almighty has His own purposes. "Woe unto the world because of offenses; for it must needs be that offenses come, but woe to that man by whom the offense cometh." If we shall suppose that American slavery is one of those offenses which, in the providence of God, must needs come, but which, having continued through His appointed time, He now wills to remove, and that He gives to both North and South this terrible war as the woe due to those by whom the offense came, shall we discern therein any departure from those divine attributes which the believers in a living God always ascribe to Him? Fondly do we hope, fervently do we pray, that this mighty scourge of war may speedily pass away. Yet, if God wills that it continue until all the wealth piled by the bondsman's two hundred and fifty years of unrequited toil shall be sunk, and until every drop of blood drawn with the lash shall be paid by another drawn with the sword, as was said three thousand years ago, so still it must be said "the judgments of the Lord are true and righteous altogether."

With malice toward none, with charity for all, with firmness in the right as God gives us to see the right, let us strive on to finish the work we are in, to bind up the nation's wounds, to care for him who shall have borne the battle and for his widow and his orphan, to do all which may achieve and cherish a just and lasting peace among ourselves and with all nations.

March 31, 2010

26. *This is the second writing I wanted to share with you. They are the words of President Kennedy as spoken during his inaugural address. I have read these words over and over again. They are full of hope and promise for a bright future for America and the World. I had voted against him but listening to his address to the nation erased all concerns I had about his ability to be President. His words inspired us all and hope was rekindled in the hearts of our people. As with Lincoln neither was given the opportunity to completely finish their dreams. Please read carefully and if you have children read to them as well.*

President John F. Kennedy Inaugural Address
January 20, 1961

Vice President Johnson, Mr. Speaker, Mr. Chief Justice, President Eisenhower, Vice President Nixon, President Truman, reverend clergy, fellow citizens, we observe today not a victory of party, but a celebration of freedom—symbolizing an end, as well as a beginning—signifying renewal, as well as change. For I have sworn before you and Almighty God the same solemn oath our forebears prescribed nearly a century and three quarters ago.

The world is very different now. For man holds in his mortal hands the power to abolish all forms of human poverty and all forms of human life. And yet the same revolutionary beliefs for which our forebears fought are still at issue around the globe—the belief that the rights of man come not from the generosity of the state, but from the hand of God.

We dare not forget today that we are the heirs of that first revolution. Let the word go forth from this time and place, to friend and foe alike, that the torch has been passed to a new generation of Americans—born in this century, tempered by war, disciplined by a hard and bitter peace, proud of our ancient heritage—and unwilling to witness or permit the slow undoing of those human rights to which this Nation has always been committed, and to which we are committed today at home and around the world.

Let every nation know, whether it wishes us well or ill, that we shall pay any price, bear any burden, meet any hardship, support any friend, oppose any foe, in order to assure the survival and the success of liberty.

This much we pledge—and more.

To those old allies whose cultural and spiritual origins we share, we pledge the loyalty of faithful friends. United, there is little we cannot do in a host of cooperative ventures. Divided, there is little we can do—for we dare not meet a powerful challenge at odds and split asunder.

To those new States whom we welcome to the ranks of the free, we pledge our word that one form of colonial control shall not have passed away merely to be replaced by a far more iron tyranny. We shall not always expect to find them supporting our view. But we shall always hope to find them strongly supporting their own freedom—and to remember that, in the past, those who foolishly sought power by riding the back of the tiger ended up inside.

To those peoples in the huts and villages across the globe struggling to break the bonds of mass misery, we pledge our best efforts to help them help themselves, for whatever period is required—not because the Communists may be doing it, not because we seek their votes, but because it is right. If a free society cannot help the many who are poor, it cannot save the few who are rich.

To our sister republics south of our border, we offer a special pledge—to convert our good words into good deeds—in a new alliance for progress—to assist free men and free governments in casting off the chains of poverty. But this peaceful revolution of hope cannot become the prey of hostile powers. Let all our neighbors know that we shall join with them to oppose aggression or subversion anywhere in the Americas. And let every other power know that this Hemisphere intends to remain the master of its own house.

To that world assembly of sovereign states, the United Nations, our last best hope in an age where the instruments of war have far outpaced the instruments of peace, we renew our pledge of support—to prevent it from becoming merely a forum for invective—to strengthen its shield of the new and the weak—and to enlarge the area in which its writ may run.

Finally, to those nations who would make themselves our adversary, we offer not a pledge but a request: that both sides begin anew the quest for peace, before the dark powers of destruction unleashed by science engulf all humanity in planned or accidental self-destruction.

We dare not tempt them with weakness. For only when our arms are sufficient beyond doubt can we be certain beyond doubt that they will never be employed.

But neither can two great and powerful groups of nations take comfort from our present course—both sides overburdened by the cost of modern weapons, both rightly alarmed by the steady spread of the deadly atom, yet both racing to alter that uncertain balance of terror that stays the hand of mankind's final war.

So let us begin anew—remembering on both sides that civility is not a sign of weakness, and sincerity is always subject to proof. Let us never negotiate out of fear. But let us never fear to negotiate.

Let both sides explore what problems unite us instead of belaboring those problems which divide us.

Let both sides, for the first time, formulate serious and precise proposals for the inspection and control of arms—and bring the absolute power to destroy other nations under the absolute control of all nations.

Let both sides seek to invoke the wonders of science instead of its terrors. Together let us explore the stars, conquer the deserts, eradicate disease, tap the ocean depths, and encourage the arts and commerce.

Let both sides unite to heed in all corners of the earth the command of

Isaiah—to "undo the heavy burdens ... and to let the oppressed go free."

And if a beachhead of cooperation may push back the jungle of suspicion, let both sides join in creating a new endeavor, not a new balance of power, but a new world of law, where the strong are just and the weak secure and the peace preserved.

All this will not be finished in the first 100 days. Nor will it be finished in the first 1,000 days, nor in the life of this Administration, nor even perhaps in our lifetime on this planet. But let us begin.

In your hands, my fellow citizens, more than in mine, will rest the final success or failure of our course. Since this country was founded, each generation of Americans has been summoned to give testimony to its national loyalty. The graves of young Americans who answered the call to service surround the globe.

Now the trumpet summons us again—not as a call to bear arms, though arms we need; not as a call to battle, though embattled we are—but a call to bear the burden of a long twilight struggle, year in and year out, "rejoicing in hope, patient in tribulation"—a struggle against the common enemies of man: tyranny, poverty, disease, and war itself.

Can we forge against these enemies a grand and global alliance, North and South, East and West, that can assure a more fruitful life for all mankind? Will you join in that historic effort?

In the long history of the world, only a few generations have been granted the role of defending freedom in its hour of maximum danger. I do not shrink from this responsibility—I welcome it. I do not believe that any of us would exchange places with any other people or any other generation. The energy, the faith, the devotion which we bring to this endeavor will light our country and all who serve it—and the glow from that fire can truly light the world.

And so, my fellow Americans: ask not what your country can do for you—ask what you can do for your country.

My fellow citizens of the world: ask not what America will do for you, but what together we can do for the freedom of man.

Finally, whether you are citizens of America or citizens of the world, ask of us the same high standards of strength and sacrifice which we ask of you. With a good conscience our only sure reward, with history the final judge of our deeds, let us go forth to lead the land we love, asking His blessing and His help, but knowing that here on earth God's work must truly be our own.

March 31, 2010

Epilogue

Maybe I am the problem. I should just let go and try to enjoy the declining years left for me on this earth. I could not explain why I continue to read and learn about issues and then write about them, no matter how hard I tried. I realize that my hopes and dreams for our world are quixotic and quaint. I am a dreamer without the ability or means to convince others that I just might be correct in my convictions. All around me I see the seeds being sown which in the end will destroy all civilization as we know it today. There is another course of action we could take. It would be risky but the rewards could be greater than we ever could imagine.

I learned years ago that for every action there is a reaction. A long time ago the New York State Legislature outlawed pay toilets. They were immediately sued as they put the company out of business that produced the hardware. There are major military production facilities in all of our States. Millions earn their livelihoods and support their families. Should we ever decide to cut back it would be unfair to put these people on the street. Our country was able to switch from military to civilian production at the end of WWII. It could be done again if safeguards were put in place to produce here and not keep sending manufacturing jobs to China.

We must put our working age people back on the job instead of handouts while they stay at home.

We must become energy self efficient with a combination of drilling, bio-fuels, solar, wind, nuclear or any combination of the above.

We must withdraw from our occupation of predominantly Muslim countries. Help them as we can but stop trying to dominate them with our military might. Stop selling arms to third world countries, instead aid them in improving the lives of their people particularly those poor nations where children die every day of hunger and thirst without medical care available.

Keep religion out of the equation when deciding who to aid. Religion is a personal conviction but should never be a reason to foster hatred of those of another persuasion.

I am not a pacifist. Should our country be threatened we should put all available assets into play to resolve. Having said this I still believe it is time to return our warriors to bases in America. There can and should be facilities available around the world but not located on the sovereign soil of other countries. The occupation of Japan, Germany, Korea, Iraq and Afghanistan must end as quickly and orderly as possible.

We must return sanity to our political system. Billions of dollars which could be put to more productive uses are squandered every year distorting facts and confusing the electorate. It is common knowledge the amount of time elected officials must spend year round begging for campaign funds, which are given to those who will do favors in return. Limit contributions to voters not organizations. Shorten the primary system and allow voters in all States to vote for candidates as Iowans are privileged to do today.

Bring an end to the chaotic stripping of the resources of the Ocean and stop burning out the rain forests. Work to reduce environmental pollution and attempt to stabilize the atmosphere to the extent humanly possible.

Most importantly as Americans we need to heed the call that President John Kennedy spoke in his inaugural address, "And so, my fellow Americans: ask not what America will do for you-ask what you can do for your country". This was followed by "My fellow citizens of the world ask not what America will do for you, but what together we can do for the freedom of man".

I can think of no better way to end this collection of ideas than his stirring call to service. It's not too late. Won't you answer the call?

I just don't ever learn. A few years ago I became so disgusted that I vowed to never write again, since my efforts were futile. I'm like a man trying to stop smoking or is an alcoholic. Tomorrow I will quit but just one more today.

This book continues following my last one entitled "The Last Angry Man". After finishing I started anew writing to friends and then started my own web site. It is; jackbwalters.blogspot.com, if you are interested. I will continue adding to it as the mood strikes me and I am able.

I decided to put these articles together in book form, hoping that this time I might be able to reach more people who are as concerned as I am about the issues of the day. The way must be found to restore our country to its former greatness which I was privileged to be a part of most of my life.